C000242763

Urban S

Following his acquittal in 2006, Andrew Pritchard worked on *Urban Smuggler* and decided to donate all his royalties to drug-rehabilitation charities. He then returned to his first love – the music industry.

Norman Parker is the author of several true-crime titles, including *Parkhurst Tales* and *The Goldfish Bowl*.

Urban Smuggler

ANDREW PRITCHARD
WITH **NORMAN PARKER**

MAINSTREAM
PUBLISHING

EDINBURGH AND LONDON

In memory of Charles Witter,
gone but not forgotten

Dedicated to my three sons, Giovanni, Stefan and Hayden

This edition, 2011

First published in Great Britain in 2008 by
MAINSTREAM PUBLISHING COMPANY
(EDINBURGH) LTD
7 Albany Street
Edinburgh EH1 3UG

ISBN 9781845964405

This book is a work of non-fiction based on the life, experiences
and recollections of the author. In some cases, names of people, places,
dates, sequences or the detail of events have been changed to protect the
privacy of others. The author has stated to the publishers that, except in
such respects not affecting the substantial accuracy of the work,
the contents of this book are true

The author has made every effort to clear all copyright permissions, but
where this has not been possible and amendments are required,
the publisher will be pleased to make any necessary arrangements
at the earliest opportunity

A catalogue record for this book is available
from the British Library

Typeset in Billboard and Palatino

Printed in Great Britain by
CPI Cox and Wyman, Reading, Berkshire RG1 8EX

Contents

Author's Note		7
Foreword by Donal MacIntyre		9
Prologue		11
One	Made in Hackney	19
Two	Everything Starts with an E	31
Three	Sex, Drugs and Acid House	43
Four	From Genesis to Revelation	81
Five	The Day the Music Died	95
Six	No Man is an Island	107
Seven	A Smuggler is Born	131
Eight	Making a Splash	163
Nine	Close but No Cigar	189
Ten	Armageddon Now	221
Eleven	Trials and Tribulations	249
Twelve	Life Begins at Forty	259
Epilogue		265
Acknowledgements		267

Author's Note

THIS BOOK is based primarily on my first-hand experiences and is a work of non-fiction. However, in order to convey the feelings and actions of others, Norman Parker and I have relied at some points on secondary sources, such as official Customs disclosure documents, detailed observation logs and court transcripts, as well as unofficially released Public Interest Immunity documents generated by the DEA, Interpol, NCIS, Customs and Excise, and other law enforcement agencies. In this way, we have been able to portray accurately events that I was not party to.

Andrew Pritchard

Foreword

IT HAS all the elements of a Hollywood crime movie: gangsters, guns, girls, tons of money and half a ton of cocaine, enough to keep London's clubland snorting for months. And hanging over the entire story is a poisonous cloud of suspicion.

But this story isn't fiction; it's fact. The mean streets aren't in Harlem; they're in Hackney. And the lawmen aren't FBI agents; they're British Customs officers.

This is the story of how one of UK Customs' greatest triumphs turned into one of its biggest disasters and exposed something flawed at the heart of one of the world's most respected crime forces. This is the story of cocaine and coconuts.

The dramatic story reveals Customs officers spying on their colleagues. It exposes dangerous leaks and illicit dissemination of secret documents on a huge scale. The questions that hang over the whole Customs organisation paint a picture of betrayal, incompetence, mismanagement and perhaps corruption in Her Majesty's frontline force against drugs – on a previously unimaginable scale.

In a case which is replete with claim and counter-claim, one fact that is undisputed is that top-secret and incredibly sensitive Customs documents found their way into the hands of the criminal fraternity – indeed, into the country's prisons and, spectacularly, under defendants' cell doors. How this happened remains a mystery but must have involved a chain of events that is startling in its scale.

Many of these documents were marked 'Top Secret', and in select cases revealed the operations of other law enforcement agencies, including the Drug Enforcement Administration (DEA) and Interpol. They included details of covert surveillance and incredibly sensitive policing information involving some of the biggest criminal cartels – details so sensitive they could have cost lives.

The release of these documents has sent alarm bells ringing in the Home Office and in other international police forces, and certainly has more significance than even the extraordinary event that predicated the opening of this Pandora's box.

But this is not just the story of one drugs bust, however sensational. Andrew Pritchard has led an extraordinary life. His story encompasses the reality of mass immigration from the West Indies into deprived post-war London in the 1950s, a time when the capital was crying out for workers for the newly formed NHS and rapidly expanding London Underground. London's East End has always been a magnet for immigrants, from sixteenth-century Huguenots to Polish and Jewish tailors at the time of Jack the Ripper at the end of the nineteenth century. This latest wave of immigration brought with it vibrancy and an explosion of colours and smells, both new and exciting, that would change the fabric of London yet again.

Andrew was known to the police and the underworld from the early 1980s when he was at the centre of the rave scene, which transformed youth culture and drug use in the UK. As a 21 year old, he was running illegal acid-house parties, such as the Genesis events. Later, he went legitimate and staged the 1999 Sunsplash festival in Victoria Park. This attracted 40,000 revellers to hear A-list artists, including Wyclef Jean. He was a magnet for the stars of urban black music, and Mel B of the Spice Girls attended the event as his guest, as did countless other artists from the UK, USA and Caribbean.

From start to finish, Pritchard's tale is, without exaggeration, 'stranger than fiction'.

Donal MacIntyre

Prologue

AS I swam up to consciousness, I instinctively knew that something was wrong. The uneasy feeling in the pit of my stomach was more than just early morning queasiness. As a long-time, experienced smuggler, I recognised some of the signs. The latest consignment was due to arrive today, and there were always butterflies on such occasions. But it was more than that.

I lay there carefully examining the feeling, and, deny it as I might, the underlying rationale inevitably emerged. I had broken virtually all of the golden rules of smuggling taught to me so long ago by my mentor Blackadouch. Thinking about him brought his image, as I had last seen him in Jamaica, clearly to my mind. 'Never introduce A to B,' he had intoned in his deep, calm voice. I hadn't done so directly, but while I was away on holiday my close friend Dean had introduced Bob to Lazarus.

This led directly to the breach of golden rule number two: 'Always know who you can trust.' Yet I knew in my heart that I couldn't really trust either Bob or Lazarus, both of whom I had met only comparatively recently. Already they were trying to take over control of the move, insisting to Dean that they would take care of the consignment.

I had soon put a stop to that. The upshot was that I would be hands-on that night and be there personally to supervise the receipt of the shipment. And therein lay the danger, because of all the perilous parts of the enterprise, this was the most deadly. If the authorities were aware of the move, this was when they would swoop. Which brought me to Blacka's golden rule number three, the three Ts: 'Never trust a telephone or text or tell a woman.'

I had lost count of the number of times I had told all the team about talking loosely on the phone or sending texts. Yet they insisted on calling each other for the slightest reason, rather than waiting for a face-to-face meeting.

As if on cue, I felt Amber stir beside me, and I turned to cuddle her in a protective reflex. I took some comfort in the knowledge that the final part of rule number three hadn't been compromised. Amber knew nothing about the impending events. She might have guessed that something was up – she knew me far too well now to miss the telltale signs of nervousness and a certain shortness in my manner when talking about everyday things – but she took it all in her stride. She never pushed me for details about that side of my life. It spared her the inevitable worry, and, more importantly, it protected her from having guilty knowledge. It could never be said that she was in any way complicit in my smuggling activities.

In some ways, it was a strange and memorable day, one of those that you can look back on and remember long afterwards. We drove down to the south coast in my jeep to pick up a small speedboat I had bought. The jeep and the boat would be put in a container and sent to Tobago for us to use when on holiday.

Even though it was early December, it was one of those bright sunny days that seemed more like early spring. We strolled by the sea, the sunlight bathing us and our surroundings in a golden hue. We held hands and occasionally kissed. I caught myself casting secret glances at Amber as if to reassure myself that she was real. No doubt, dangerous times make people assess what they have, and I knew that I was blessed to have Amber. Our relationship had blossomed to the point that we were both quite comfortable with each other but still madly in love. I resolved that as soon as the business was over we would immediately go to Tobago.

I deliberately drew things out, lingering as long as possible. The drive back was leisurely, as if by taking my time I could delay the impending ordeal. We got back to the grim streets of Stoke Newington at about 7 p.m.

Gavin's arrival an hour later was the final intrusion that broke the spell. Soon I was bustling about the flat in a business-like manner as we discussed the last details of the container's arrival. We knew it had been cleared by Customs, so now it was just a matter of waiting for it to arrive at Spitalfields Market.

I was confident that we were well prepared. Gavin's friend's company was one of the biggest fruit-and-veg businesses in Spitalfields. It hadn't been difficult for Gavin to organise a forklift truck and two drivers to unload the container. Furthermore, a consignment of coconuts was a very normal load. With an absolute minimum of fuss, the first bags of coconuts would be pulled off to reveal the sacks holding our stuff. These would be thrown into the back of two vans, which would leave the market and rendezvous with me in a nearby lay-by. Then all that would be left for me to do would be to follow it to its destination, a safe house a mere 20 minutes' drive away. The scope for failure was minimal. However, I still found myself wishing the time away so that it would be over sooner. I was pleased when Gavin left, saying that he would call me when the container had been unloaded.

I now felt a palpable sense of unease, something I couldn't put my finger on. Yet everything seemed to be running smoothly. There had been no indications that anything unusual was going on. Things were progressing very much like they had for the first shipment, so I pushed these thoughts from my mind. Nevertheless, I did look out of the window, carefully surveying the street.

I closely examined the length and breadth of the road. I had lived in the area all my life, almost 35 years, and knew it like the back of my hand. I couldn't catalogue the ownership of individual cars, but there was nothing that stuck out as being a cause for concern.

Except for one thing. Across the street sat a dark Volkswagen and inside were two men. They seemed to be looking at the door of my house. I examined them more closely. One seemed to be holding a short-wave radio, but there was nothing furtive about them. They seemed to be chatting amiably enough. I thought it could be a mini-cab driver calling his controller. Men sitting in cars was a common enough occurrence in the streets of Stoke Newington. Drug dealing and other nefarious activities were epidemic. A short-wave radio wasn't out of the ordinary, either. The local kids regularly scanned police radio frequencies for advance warning of raids. I turned from the window, confident that I had nothing to worry about.

Gavin's call came at 10.30 p.m. The container had been unloaded and our sacks put on one side. It was time for me to leave.

Amber was in the bedroom, sitting in front of her vanity mirror putting on her make-up. As I cuddled her and pulled her to me, she broke away. 'Mind my make-up,' she said, cautioning me sharply.

Perhaps all the stress had made me uncharacteristically fragile. Rebuffed, I replied, 'Don't be like that. This could be the last time you see me.' It was melodramatic enough to get the desired effect. Turning in her chair, she reached up to kiss me. With a final 'See you later', I was out the door.

My jeep still had the boat attached to it, so I took Amber's Mercedes. I looked carefully for the Volkswagen and its two occupants, but there was no sign of it. I accelerated up the street and headed for Spitalfields.

Even though the hour was late, the traffic was still thick. The streets surrounding the market were clogged with container lorries, so I drove past, did a quick U-turn and parked at the edge of a bus stop. This was where the two vans carrying our stuff would meet me. I settled back in my seat to wait, carefully examining everything around me.

Everything seemed normal enough, although in the hustle and bustle of the outskirts of London's busiest fruit-and-veg market organised chaos was always the order of the day. There was one troubling moment. I had pulled in behind a blue Mercedes with two men sitting in the front seats. They seemed to be in the process of removing the yellow luminous vests they were wearing over their jackets. Also, one of them seemed to be holding some sort of laptop.

It could have been anything. The market was such a hive of activity that there were literally thousands of people going about their daily tasks, even at that late hour. I did briefly consider that they might be some of the Customs staff who were working with us, but they didn't seem to be taking any interest in me, so I ignored them. Instead, I called Gavin. He assured me that the vans with our stuff would be with me very shortly. Once again, I settled back to wait.

Several things then seemed to happen simultaneously. A dark-coloured pick-up truck pulled in sharply behind me and flashed its lights twice. At the same instant, another car pulled up alongside me. However, I only noticed these things peripherally. My full concentration was on the very big guy in a bulky overcoat who was running towards the front of my car screaming like a banshee. In his hands, he was brandishing a long crowbar. His face was contorted, and his guttural scream could be heard clearly over all the other noises of the night.

Then there was an explosive sound like a small bomb going off and my windscreen shattered, showering me with granules of glass. Automatically, I cowered back as the crowbar continued to strike the remnants of the windscreen. I became aware that someone had pulled my driver's door open, and I felt strong hands grip me roughly about the shoulders. I was then pulled from the car.

The violence of the assault had served its purpose. It had been like a nightmare dream sequence. I was frightened, shocked, confused and disorientated all at the same time. I was forced to the ground, blinded by the bright lights trained on me. As the gravel of the road bit into my knees, I cringed from the shot that

I felt would inevitably come, for by now I was convinced that our stuff was being hijacked by some rival firm.

My hands were pulled behind my back, and I felt them being handcuffed. I looked up quickly to see that I was surrounded by about 20 people. With some relief, I noticed that there were no guns in evidence. Any reassurance I got from this was soon dispelled, though.

The voice was clear and measured, but with an underlying tension: 'We're Customs officers. You are under arrest. You are cautioned that anything you say may be taken down and used against you. You will later be charged with the importation of 572 kilos of cocaine.'

It did register, but I was still too shocked and confused to take it all in. Quite bizarrely, I found myself worrying about how I would explain the damage to the car to Amber. Slowly, the message did sink in, though. I had heard it clearly. There could be no doubt. The Customs officer had said something about the importation of cocaine. Obviously, there had been some mistake. Our shipment, like the shipment before it, was counterfeit Cuban cigars. Perhaps they were just trying to frighten me.

I was bundled into a car and driven off at speed. We pulled into a yard at the rear of Customs House in Lower Thames Street, a place I often passed, and I was led inside. I could see my captors clearly now. There were a dozen men and a couple of women, some dressed in Customs uniforms with luminous yellow vests over the jackets. Almost before I knew it, I was inside a cell, and the door was slammed behind me.

My mind was a whirlpool of emotions as contending thoughts fought for primacy. I examined the recent events to try to make some sense of them. The Customs officer had clearly said something about several hundred kilos of cocaine. Mine or not, I was well aware that there were many innocent men in prison. I was also aware that the penalty for importing cocaine in that quantity would be extremely severe. If things went badly, I was looking at spending the rest of my life in prison.

They do say that a near-death experience brings your past life flashing before you. This present situation had all the ingredients of a near-death experience, for it was quite possible that my life as I knew it was now over. As I lay on the hard bed, I found myself regressing through the events that had brought me to that point in my life. It hadn't started out like this at all.

One

Made in Hackney

I DEFINITELY inherited my adventurous spirit from my mother, Winnie. In December 1951, she flew from her native Jamaica to Canada, then took a boat to England. This was just three years after the *Empire Windrush* set sail from Jamaica with West Indian immigrants recruited to work in either the NHS, if they were women, or on London Transport, if they were men. It arrived at Tilbury on 22 June 1948.

Winnie was following in the footsteps of her husband, although the relationship was in its terminal stages. She was leaving behind in Jamaica her daughter Barbara, who would join her just as soon as she was settled.

She came with two of her female friends. The three of them had no family in England and very little money between them. At that time, West Indians tended to settle in Brixton, Notting Hill, Stoke Newington or Stamford Hill. The three friends rented a room in a big house in Stamford Hill, but there was no bed. Periods between shifts in a local factory were spent sleeping in a chair. But Winnie was a spirited woman with a strong work ethic. She worked hard, saved harder and eventually managed to rent a flat. She was even able to send money back to Jamaica for Barbara.

An attractive, light-complexioned woman, she enjoyed dancing. Her one bit of relief from the daily round of factory shifts was to go to the blues parties organised by fellow West Indians at weekends.

My father, Ron, was a white cockney boy with an equally strong work ethic, who grew up in and around Hoxton. People from the area were mostly traders who worked in the several street markets in the district, although some of them were villains. Ron, though, had a business delivering paraffin from house to house. Together with his brother-in-law Tommy, they would load up a small tanker lorry with paraffin and drive the streets of Hoxton selling it. Ron was also something of a builder. He was a good brickie but could do most of the other building trades as well. Sometimes, he moonlighted by doing private building work.

It was the end of a hard week. Ron had done the paraffin round as well as building an extension on a house for a private customer. He had had a friend of his working with him, a black guy called Rodney. Ron liked to get suited and booted at weekends and go out. Rodney invited him to go to a blues party on the Saturday night.

Ron was no extrovert. For much of the party he stood quietly against a wall, just watching and drinking. It was Winnie who had to ask him for a dance. By the end of the party, they were getting on like a house on fire. He asked her to go out with him in the week.

Before long, they were married. They bought the house in Stoke Newington, the same one that I live in today. They paid for Barbara to come over from Jamaica, but times were hard. Their first Christmas was spent without furniture – all the money had gone on the deposit for the house.

When household paraffin heaters had been phased out for safety reasons, Ron started to work for the local council, driving a lorry. He also carried on doing private building work. Through becoming known to the West Indian community, he was getting more and more of this kind of work.

Equally industrious, Winnie had set up two businesses. She became friendly with a guy who owned a clothing factory that made lines for catalogue companies such as Freemans. Clothes were made to a high standard, and anything that didn't pass the stringent tests was sold off to Winnie as 'cabbage'.

Now, other than the odd missed stitch or minor fault, these were perfectly good clothes. They were right up to date, for they had been made for future catalogues, and they were very cheap at about a third of the retail price. Ron converted the basement of the new house into a small boutique, and Winnie sold the cabbage from there.

At this time, the West Indian community in London was very much a unified group that stuck together. Ridley Road Market was virtually the only place where they could buy Jamaican produce such as yams, dasheen, plantain and mangoes. Weekends saw them congregating at the market, buying their food and socialising. Taking full advantage of this, Winnie would cook a big pot of chicken, beef or oxtail soup and give it away for free to customers of her cabbage boutique. Very soon our house became virtually a West Indian cultural centre.

Also at this time, West Indians were finding it very difficult to get bank accounts. This made it almost impossible for them to raise deposits for houses or cars, so Winnie set up a typically Jamaican 'pardner' system. Perhaps 40 West Indians would join together in a club. Each week they would put money in, which would be held by Winnie. They would each take their turn to draw a lump sum out for a deposit or whatever. Each pardner scheme would run for about six months. It was a very reliable system and ran like clockwork. Absolutely no one ever defaulted on a payment.

Needless to say, the pardner scheme was also run from our house. People would drop by, pay in their money, look at the dresses and generally talk about what was going on in the West Indian community.

By then, with money no longer in short supply, Ron and Winnie had started a family. My older sister and I grew up as members of a vast, extended family. Every weekend, our house bustled with scores of uncles, aunties and cousins. There was never a dull moment. My mother and father were now pillars of a growing West Indian community.

Both my sister and I grew up blissfully unaware that my parents' union was one of the first mixed-race marriages and that we were the first generation of mixed-race kids. Within the West Indian community, my father was subjected to absolutely no prejudice whatsoever. He had been fully accepted into the community, and, in fact, many people had come to rely on him. He was a white guy who would intercede on their behalf in sometimes difficult negotiations with the authorities. As a by-product of this, they would all come to him to do their private building work.

The Hoxton community that my father had grown up in was an equally insular and tight-knit group. People were set in their ways and tended to be thoroughly nationalistic and even right wing in their views. This was where Ron met most of the prejudice that he faced, but he hid it well and never brought it home to the family.

My first school was the Princess May, situated at the top of my road. I never had any excuse for being late and always came home for dinner. By then, my parents had rented out the upstairs of our house to a white woman whom I knew as Auntie Lily. She lived there with her mother, an elderly lady whom I came to know as Nan. The latter became a surrogate grandmother to me. She would meet me at the gate every dinnertime when I came home and give me snacks and sweets.

Princess May wasn't a bad place. It was a typically run-down inner-city school with too many kids and too few resources. Located as it was near the racial 'front line', the children were mostly immigrants. There were lots of black kids, and it was convenient for my parents.

Occasionally, we would go back to Jamaica for holidays. One particular trip when I was about seven sticks in my memory. My mother had told me that there was something special that she wanted to do. She took me to the cemetery in St Elizabeth where her father, my grandfather, lay. We entered a family tomb and stood before a large sarcophagus. Holding my hand, my mother chanted and prayed. She asked God to allow the spirit of my grandfather to accompany me through life and to look out for me. I wasn't at all frightened, even though this was undoubtedly my first spiritual awakening. On several occasions in later years, I have been aware of the spirit of an old black man following behind me.

That trip to Jamaica was memorable for another reason. The relatives with whom we were staying had a goat in the yard, a commonplace thing in Jamaica but unusual in the extreme for a kid from Stoke Newington. I adopted Billy the goat as my pet and personal friend. For the duration of the holiday, we were inseparable, following each other around all over the place.

On our final day, I went to look for Billy to say my goodbyes. I searched high and low but couldn't seem to find him. Rounding an outhouse close to the kitchen, I saw the familiar fleecy coat, but there was something wrong. As I drew closer, the reality dawned on me. It was Billy's fleece with the head still attached but the rest of him missing. Our hosts had killed and skinned him for a going-away goat stew for us all. I cried and cried and stoically refused to eat any of the stew.

The trip home was unremarkable, except for the fact that my and my sisters' luggage seemed particularly heavy. We struggled to steer it through Customs. When we arrived home, the reason was soon revealed. White rum was very hard to come by in England at that time. Fellow Jamaicans regularly asked those returning from a holiday to bring them back a bottle of overproof rum. My mum and dad had received many such requests. When our suitcases were opened, they revealed dozens of bottles of white rum. I remember being amused, if not shocked. This, then, was to be my first experience of smuggling.

Back in England, no doubt reflecting our upwardly mobile status, my parents then decided that a church school would be more suitable in grooming me for a staid and sober life. Towards that end, I was sent to St Jude's in nearby King Henry's Walk. I didn't take it personally, but St Jude was the patron saint of hopeless causes. St Jude's was also a Sunday school and was mostly for white kids. All my new-found mates had dads who worked in Chapel Street and Ridley Road markets. They would often help their parents out on the stalls. They were sharp kids, and no doubt some of it rubbed off on me.

I was also getting my own private tuition from my dad. I would regularly accompany him on his building jobs. Now that Indians and Pakistanis had come to know about 'Mr Ron the Builder', his reasonable prices and good work, his business was growing and growing. I managed to learn something about most of the building trades.

At my parents' insistence, I joined the Junos, a group that was very much like the Scouts. We wore a blue uniform and were encouraged to take various courses in subjects such as knot-tying and fire-making to gain proficiency badges. My most memorable experience, though, was a trip to the BBC. I stared in wonder at all the speakers and other electronic equipment. I realise now that seeing all this started me thinking about what I wanted to do in life.

Ron was an ardent third-generation Arsenal supporter, and it was at about this time that my love for the team was born. I would often stand in the back garden on match days, listening to the game on the radio but able to hear the cheers from the old Highbury ground when Arsenal scored. Like all the other kids in the area, I had secret dreams of playing for the club when I grew up. The closest I got was playing in goal for St Jude's. I was Arsenal mad, though, and spent much of my hard-earned pocket money buying Arsenal kit. The rest was spent on buying records.

When the school suggested an outing to a Butlin's holiday camp down on the coast, the risks to us kids seemed minimal. We would be in a virtually closed environment, supervised by Redcoats and accompanied by some of our teachers. They just hadn't taken into consideration our growing street smarts. Although we were all barely 12, we already had ideas beyond our years. A couple of us took a particular shine to some of the young Redcoat girls, who were not much older than us. It seemed quite natural to invite them to our chalet after lights out. A game of spin the bottle seemed an equally natural progression. The only party pooper was my best friend Compton, the only other mixed-race kid. He refused to have anything to do with it and retired for the night to another chalet.

One of our teachers was late in going to bed. Passing our chalet, he noticed the light on and decided to investigate. A chorus of screams met him as he entered. He stood rigid with shock as scantily dressed young girls ran past him and out into the night. It was quite a scandal, but, surprisingly for us, it was all brushed under the carpet. Several of the ringleaders, of which the teachers decided I was one, got caned, but our parents were never told.

My next school was definitely a mistake on my parents' part, although they never really had a choice, as all my friends went there. Sir Phillip Magnus Secondary School at Kings Cross was little more than a breeding ground for criminals. By my second year, I knew all the tricks. Having suffered myself in my first year, it was now my turn to run protection rackets on the games of penny-up-the-wall. I was thoroughly disruptive, too, and terrorised some of the teachers. If throwing water bombs and fireworks had been on the curriculum, no doubt I would have passed with flying colours. As it was, I was regularly caned.

Amongst my contemporaries, the fashion was to be either a skinhead or a mod. I was firmly in the latter camp, complete with Kicker boots, Farah trousers, Fred Perry or Lacoste T-shirts, parka coat and Trilby hat. Our heroes were the groups from 2 Tone records, such as Madness and The Specials. Whilst the skinheads sniffed glue, we smoked weed, and we discovered sex with some of the girls from Star Cross Girls School. There were also regular battles with other schools. The rivalry between my school and Highbury Grove was particularly intense and sometimes vicious.

Arming ourselves with tools from the carpentry class, we would sally out to battle with others similarly armed. The police were frequently called to break up the disturbances.

Any impact this regular breaking down of the social order had on me was massively overshadowed by an event of global significance that occurred in July 1981. Increasingly, the police had been growing unpopular in poorer areas of the country. Under the so-called Sus law, stop-and-search schemes had been introduced, but it was mostly black people who were shaken down for drugs and weapons. Driven by the heavy-handed Special Patrol Group, suspects were often gratuitously beaten up. Pressure had been building up for a while.

Trouble first kicked off in Brixton, then spread as far north as Liverpool. With their position firmly on the front line, it was only a matter of time before the riots reached Stoke Newington and Dalston.

I saw the tension building during the day. The police were guarding the petrol station in the High Street. A phalanx of riot police stood two-deep. Across the street, facing them, were hundreds of people, both black and white.

That night, my mum locked me in the house. I could hear the noise from the riot when it started at the top of the road. All night long, there were the shouts, screams and the sound of breaking glass. Over and above it all was the mournful wail of police sirens.

When I was allowed out the next morning, I was shocked. Whole streets had been devastated. Every shop window in the High Street was broken, and most of the shops had been looted. It made the gang wars between Phillip Magnus and Highbury Grove seem very minor indeed.

By then, my mum and dad had decided that Stoke Newington was perhaps part of the problem for me. They thought I might knuckle down and achieve something at school if I was in a different environment. For this reason, we moved to Chigwell.

Apart from taking me away from all my mates, the move

put me in an all-white school in Edmonton. I didn't like it from the start, and they didn't like me. The white kids wouldn't accept me as one of them, and I became an outcast. This was my first experience of this sort of thing. It was an ideological crossroads for me. Either I could take it lying down or I could rebel. Although both shocked and hurt, I fought back in my own inimitable way by rejecting my rejecters. And it made me embrace my Jamaican heritage more tightly.

I was aware that even in West Indian culture us light-skinned people were referred to as 'redskins' and the younger blacks would call us 'red ants'. There was nothing particularly malicious in it. Generally, black youths believed I was more black than white, and this meant that they could accept me as one of their own. However, some of them also thought that the white blood in me made me weak, so I had to constantly stand up for myself.

The fact that I was rapidly becoming a failure at school didn't go unnoticed by my parents. There were regular initiatives to try to start me on a career: my mum had a part-time job in the Post Office, and she got me onto a British Telecom training course. I took it to improve my knowledge of electronics. At the same time, she bought an off-licence in Hackney Wick, and she expected me to learn the trade. But I had my sights set on a career in music.

I started to bunk off school on a regular basis. My rejection by the Edmonton white kids also brought me closer to Compton. His brother and brother-in-law used to build speakers at his house. They used these speakers to play at parties. Their style of music was called lovers rock, a British form of reggae by artists such as Carroll Thompson and Janet Kay.

I already had a rich musical experience. As a child, I had listened to Mum's records of the original Jamaican beat of Prince Buster and Millie Small, and I became an avid listener of pirate radio stations. On a Sunday afternoon from noon until 6 p.m., Radio Invicta played rap, soul and electro. DBC Radio Rebel, aka the Dread Broadcasting Corporation, based in Ladbroke

Grove, introduced me to the Rankin' Miss P, the sister of Bob Marley's wife, DJ Chucky and DJ Lepke. Capital Radio had David Rodigan, a white DJ. Between them, they played records ranging from roots reggae to lovers rock.

At Compton's, I watched and learned, and before long I was building my own speakers. I also extended my musical education by hanging around record shops. It seemed a natural progression to form my own sound system with two of my friends from Barretts Grove. Mellow Magic played a mix of soul, lovers rock and roots reggae. We began to put on our own gigs at parties, weddings and other West Indian social occasions. We also had flyers printed.

Quite soon, Mellow Magic had a large following. An early venue was a small hall the father of a friend had built, without any planning permission, in his backyard. Here we would sometimes fight it out with other sound systems, such as Apollo Soul Sound, Trends Road Show and True Romancers. Occasionally, we would pay the £60 and hire the hall for our own gig. We'd put a table across the entrance and charge three quid for entry, with girls getting in for free before midnight.

It was just a short step up to playing regular gigs in proper nightclubs, such as Phoebe's and the purely black club The Four Aces. The latter was a very dangerous place and was really a meeting place for the local black criminal fraternity. Violence was commonplace. It was fashionable among some West Indians at the time to wear expensive crocodile shoes. The ultimate disrespect was for someone to tread on your crocs. Savage knife fights would erupt.

The Four Aces was not just a nightclub; it was also a gambling club and black market. Lots of stolen property changed hands there, and you could buy weed openly in the basement.

It was at about this time that I noticed something. Most of my mates were white boys. They would regularly ask me to help them buy some weed. With my contacts in the black community, this was easy for me to organise. I would buy in bulk and take my profit in weed. Then I would bag it up into smaller portions and give it to a friend to sell for me. Not only did it become quite a lucrative sideline, it also helped me to bridge the white–black divide that I was always so conscious of. Now I benefited from both worlds. I remember thinking at the time that it had taken me a while to figure it out, but I had finally mastered a difficult balancing act.

Two

Everything Starts with an E

ALTHOUGH MY heart was still very much in the music business, my parents were trying to get me to make a career out of running the off-licence. I did regularly help out, and it served as a place where my mates could find me.

One evening in July 1988, three of my party mates walked in: Ginger Chris, Freddie and Dino. They came from the nearby Trowbridge Estate, a festering slum that was later demolished. However, these humble beginnings didn't prevent them from having big ideas. Their latest was to stage a pay party at the Oxford House Community Centre in Bethnal Green Road on the coming Saturday night. They asked me to come along with my sound system and promised to pay me £200 for the night. They stressed that they didn't want me to DJ with my rare groove set and that they had their own DJ.

I arrived at the community centre at about 8 p.m. and started to set up my equipment. Apart from a few elderly people playing cards in a side room, I had the place completely to myself. At about 9.30 p.m., two of my mates, Peanuts and Spanner, arrived, and we sat around talking in the deserted centre. I said that if things didn't liven up very quickly, the night could well turn into a flop.

At 10.30 p.m., the DJ arrived. He was a guy I knew called Mervin who worked in a record shop called Paul For Music in Cambridge Heath Road. At that time, few DJs earned enough to give up their day jobs, and their DJ'ing was more of a hobby than a prospective career.

The arrival of the DJ heralded no drastic change to the centre. Only Mervin, Peanuts, Spanner and I were left, as the old people had gone by then. The dance floor of the main room yawned cavernously as Mervin began to play his set, strobe lights flashing all around him. At that point, the security for the night arrived in the shape of Francis, a big black guy who was later murdered at The Frog and Nightgown in the Old Kent Road.

Shortly after 11 p.m., the local pubs started to turn out. We could hear the beery, cheery voices as the drinkers called out their goodbyes to each other. Then suddenly we were mobbed. Seemingly out of nowhere, scores and scores of young people turned up and wanted to get into the centre.

At the front of the crowd were Chris, Freddie and Dino. They immediately set up a table in a doorway and passed people through as quickly as they could, relieving each of five quid in the process. By midnight, the centre was packed with over 400 young people intent on having a good time.

Although I had been surprised at the speed at which the partygoers had materialised, there seemed little else about the night to make it memorable for me. Mervin was playing hard-core acid house, with its distinctive beat generated by the Roland TB 303 drum machine. This was a genre largely unknown to me, and I didn't particularly like it. I settled down for what I expected to be a long and boring night, occasionally chatting with Francis.

However, such was the enthusiasm of the partygoers that I couldn't help but examine them more closely. Most were dressed in the acid-house outfit of denim dungarees, long-sleeved sweatshirts, T-shirts with yellow smiley faces on them and Converse trainers. Some were wearing bandanas and had their hair cut in a 'bobbed' style, falling long at the back.

It wasn't their style of dress that most caught my attention, though; it was their dancing. They were throwing themselves about in a totally uninhibited manner, all the time waving their arms wildly in the air. All over the room, people were meeting and embracing like long-lost friends. From time to time, a chant of 'Aceed, aceed' broke out. Everyone was running with sweat, and some of the fellas had stripped to the waist. They were clearly having a great time, but I couldn't for the life of me see what all the fuss was about. There seemed nothing remarkable about Mervin's set, and the centre as a location for anything was mundane in the extreme.

Chris and the boys only had a licence until 2 a.m., and at the appointed time the music was switched off. I started to dismantle my system as the partygoers, still touching, embracing and clinging to each other, exited into the street, all the while chanting 'Aceed, aceed'.

Twenty minutes later, as I carried my system outside to my car, they were still at it. A car had its stereo system playing loudly, and it had turned into an impromptu street party. Some people danced around the car, whilst others danced on its roof.

I'd like to say that the mood was infectious, but it had all left me largely unmoved. In my trademark smart-casual look, and with my collection of rare groove unplayed, I had felt out of it from the start. As I drove off, I found myself reflecting, 'What the fuck was that all about?'

Now, I was no stranger to drugs and the drugs scene. I had heard of MDMA, or 'E' as it was called, but I had never seen any, nor thought about taking it. I was completely surprised when Ginger Chris told me that the ecstatic party had been driven by the drug. All the partygoers had been totally 'loved up' and E'ing off their faces. Chris was of the opinion that all you had to do was to find any old venue, play acid-house music and the E people would turn up in droves.

Towards that end, he then informed me that they had another party arranged for the coming Saturday night. This would be a much bigger party, in an old warehouse at Curtain Road near Old Street. It would be held on three floors, so my present sound system would be inadequate. I was told to hire in as much extra kit as I thought necessary.

Saturday afternoon saw me setting up at the Curtain Road warehouse. I was shocked at the state of the building. At some time in its life it had obviously been used for making furniture. Piles of sawdust still lay on the floors and covered every surface. Sneezing heavily, I went about my business of setting up the sound system, taking great care as I moved about the place. Not only did it look derelict, but it didn't look particularly safe either.

This time the boys had gone to the trouble of having flyers printed. They called their rave Insomnia. Top billing went to Tony 'Balearic' Wilson, who had become a minor celebrity playing acid house in Ibiza that summer. Completing the line-up was my old friend Lyndon C, who used to hire my sound system when he played at the blues parties. He was an underground DJ who had moved into the house-music scene. On the door was a big fat black guy called Milton, who had done club security all over the East End.

It was another amazing night. Just after the pubs closed, the warehouse was besieged by a small army of people all trying to get in. They passed over their fivers and streamed into the venue. Completely oblivious to the dingy surroundings, they danced manically and chanted.

By the time 800 people had been admitted, the place was beginning to look overcrowded. A decision was made to stop all further entry. Those waiting in the queue didn't take the announcement at all well. There was hissing and booing, and a couple of people threw things. Not to be outdone, a small group seized a ladder from a nearby yard. They put it up against the side of the warehouse, climbed it and attempted to force open some of the windows on the second floor.

This was all part of my learning curve. I was most impressed by the dedication of this crowd. They had stamina, too. We didn't manage to get rid of the last of them until 10 a.m. the next morning. This was one of the first acid-house parties to be held in the East End.

My next gig was at a giant warehouse just off the Mile End Road. The party was scheduled for a Friday night, and the organiser, a guy called Paul Webb, offered to pay me 500 quid to bring my sound system along. I was now earning serious money for supplying my equipment, which started me thinking about how much the organisers were making. I would be watching tricks very closely from then on. I was beginning to think about getting into the business myself.

The warehouse was disused, bordering on the derelict. I arrived early and found that there was no power supply. Paul had already paid the caretaker for use of the building. The caretaker called a friend who said he was an electrician. I don't know where he learned his trade, but he solved the problem by running a cable 500 yards from the caretaker's Portakabin, across a street and into the warehouse.

Once again, a massive crowd turned up just after the pubs closed. Almost 800 people paid to get in. The warehouse was soon jumping to the acid beat. Ecstatic clubbers danced and chanted. Everyone was from either north or east London. Having supplied my equipment for other gigs, I was now known to some of them. Person after person came up and embraced me like I was a long-lost friend. Suddenly, I began to feel a part of the scene.

The next step was for me to go to a gig as a punter. I was obviously building up to taking my first E, even if I hadn't yet admitted it to myself. I was still firmly into being a 'face' on the street. My weight training had built me up into quite a lump, and my aggression lurked just below the surface. Virtually all my friends were into promoting a strong self-image. I wasn't at all sure how my jumping about in a warehouse surrounded by a sea of smiley faces would fit in with this, hence my initial reluctance.

I had been handed a flyer by a guy I knew called Eddie. He and his brother, Bones, were holding a party called Acid Zone in an old slaughterhouse on Backchurch Lane. They didn't need my sound system, as they had already asked Carl Cox, one of the biggest names in DJ'ing today, to bring his equipment. He was driving up from Brighton with his girlfriend Maxine. At that time, the soon-to-be-famous Carl Cox was doing exactly what I was doing, namely just supplying his sound system.

I went to the party and thoroughly enjoyed it. As probably the only person there not on E, I should have stuck out, but the enjoyment was infectious. I boogied about, talking to all and sundry.

One Thursday night, still intent only on soaking up the atmosphere, I went to a small club called The Future. This was next to the well-known gay nightclub called Heaven, later owned by Richard Branson's Virgin Group. About 300 people were dancing to Balearic and acid-house music. Ultraviolet and strobe lighting set off the decor to great effect. This night was one of the seminal influences on the growing club scene, and people still talk about the parties there. Once again, I had a great time.

I was now ready to take my first E, but not on my own. I had rounded up three of my mates who shared my general outlook. Desperate not to look naff or weak in any way, we searched around for a suitable venue.

On Monday nights, there was a big acid-house gig in Spectrum, located inside Heaven. We assured each other that we were just going along to look, even though we had all bought a big yellow 'Cali' E from a dealer we knew for 20 quid each. With our pills hidden in our underpants, we joined the multicoloured, 'hippiefied' queue of ravers outside the venue. Like condemned men walking to the gallows, we entered the club.

Inside, Spectrum was fantastic. The DJ was playing on a raised platform, and a balcony ran all along one side. Lasers probed at the dry ice from the smoke machines. Several hundred enthusiastic clubbers danced and waved their hands in the air. We looked at each other, took a deep breath and took our first E.

I didn't know what to expect. I stood with my mates, privately boogieing to the music, and waited. Suddenly, the DJ played an electric tune. As the first bars of Frankie Knuckles' 'Let the Music Use You' played, I started to come up on my E. Quite involuntarily, I breathed out and flung my arms in the air. I was engulfed in a rising wave of euphoria. I was confident, happy and didn't have a care in the world. I felt all my inhibitions fall away as I was overwhelmed by a feeling of love for my fellow man and woman.

The E was having the same effect on my mates. Normally, we wouldn't even talk to anyone who wasn't from the manor and were likely to attack someone who supported a rival football team. Now we were all at peace with the world and on the same vibe as the acid-house crowd.

Around us, it was like the last days of Rome. Couples were openly having sex, and groups passed around amyl nitrate. We were caught up in the moment and having a great time. Later, people would come to rate Spectrum as one of the most formative influences on the acid-house scene. The finishing touch was the street party outside to the music from a parked car. We mingled with our new-found friends until the police moved us on.

Now that I was a confirmed acid-house fan, I decided to find out more about what I was a part of. The scene had been brought back from Ibiza by a DJ called Alfredo, who played at Amnesia. Then DJ Nicky Holloway, who used to play a rare-groove set called The Special Branch, rented The Astoria in Charing Cross Road and put on an acid-house night called The Trip. Then, in quick succession, the Ibiza DJ Paul Oakenfold and promoter Ian St Paul opened Spectrum in Heaven, where Trevor Fung played regularly. Following that, Danny Rampling opened up a club called The Shoom at Southwark Bridge. The scene might have started off in Ibiza, but it had certainly found a home in London's clubland. The problem for club owners, though, was that they only had a licence until 3 a.m., and in Ibiza people had been used to partying all night long.

To my way of thinking, this definitely offered an opportunity for me to provide somewhere for clubbers to go to after the clubs had turned out. At an unlicensed warehouse party, they could rave on as long as they liked. My role would still be to provide my sound system to other organisers, as well as to lay on the occasional venue. I also decided to try my hand at organising a whole warehouse party myself.

With a couple of friends, I found a venue in an old warehouse near Marshgate Lane, Hackney. I arranged for a couple of DJs who had a collection of acid-house tunes to play. I set up the sound system myself and laid on some lights. At the last moment, I realised that we had no drinks, so I got my mother and sister to open up the off-licence so that I could buy cases of lager and soft drinks to sell at the party.

To promote the event, we went from club to club at closing time, telling people where the venue was. About 300 people turned up, and everyone had a great time. We didn't make a lot of money, but the important thing was that I had staged my first successful acid-house party.

It also gave me the opportunity to sit back and think about what I was embarking on. To a disinterested observer, it might have seemed that my time spent attending raves, culminating in my first E, was purely a hedonistic pursuit. And it might have started out like that, but my whole outlook changed as I witnessed the way people got on whilst taking E. I had watched in amazement as black and white people mixed freely and without the prejudice that passes for harmonious living in normal society. I had observed how toffs and paupers had embraced and chanted 'Aceed' together. Most amazingly, I'd looked on as West Ham's ICF football hooligans partied alongside Arsenal's Gooners. What if MDMA or E was a drug that broke down social and cultural barriers? What if something that had started at our parties could spread to the wider society? It was certainly worth a try. This, then, was my ideology. From then onwards, I was a man on a mission.

By that time, more and more people had heard about the acid-house scene, and it was starting to cross over into mainstream club culture. One night, I was approached to supply my sound system for a massive warehouse party at Waterloo Bridge called London Skat. It was definitely an upmarket event and had been organised by two fashion designers called Mark and Syree. They had made their name in the late 1970s designing puffball and Union Jack skirts, along with Vivienne Westwood, for the punk-rock scene. For this party, they had even managed to arrange sponsorship by leading brands, including Smirnoff.

Although its location was south London, it was clearly a gig for West End people. This cut absolutely no ice with the police, though. They showed up and promptly stopped the party. It had been well advertised, and there were now thousands of people milling about outside. The organisers asked me what they should do. I said that I knew of another warehouse in nearby Bermondsey Street. I would help them to set up the party there, but we would have to share the profits equally between us. With no other options available, they readily agreed.

I rushed over to the Bermondsey warehouse with thousands of people hot on my heels. I quickly set up my equipment as the baying mob outside threatened a riot. Fortunately, the DJs for the night were at the head of the queue. It was quite a line-up. DJ Fabio, who used to play at The Car Wash, came with his large south London following. Tony Wilson also brought his big crowd from both north and east London. Then there was Colin Dale, the radio DJ, with his west London crowd. We let in over 4,000 people and charged them a fiver each. Thus London Skat became London's biggest party yet. It set a precedent that others would try to better.

As much as I wanted to do a party on my own, the problem was finding the right venue. Further, as I didn't have much money to lay out on the organisation, a far safer bet for me was to carry on hiring out my sound system. Even if the gig got cancelled, I still got paid.

By then, more and more people, from all walks of life, were

getting involved in the warehouse-party scene. Jeremy Taylor and his partner Tintin were former public schoolboys who had organised the Gatecrashers Ball for toffs. Now they wanted to get involved in the acid-house scene and were looking for a venue. They thought they had found the ideal place at Queensway. It was a large warehouse that had been used for storing carpets. It was clean and all the facilities were in good working order. I was hired to supply the sound system.

There was another former public schoolboy on the scene called Tony Colston-Hayter, who had already run a few small parties. As a means of getting publicity and promoting the events, he had taken to inviting the media. As the acid-house craze was now a major story, this guaranteed widespread coverage for his parties.

Jeremy Taylor now tried the same trick for his party at Queensway. He invited along the *World in Action* crew, and they came, along with thousands of partygoers. Unfortunately for Jeremy, so did the police, and they promptly stopped the party.

Thousands of people had paid for their tickets in advance. Now, at the very last minute, there was to be no party. The mood of the crowd, milling about outside the warehouse, turned ugly. The police didn't help matters with their heavy-handed approach. Soon, irate partygoers were confronting aggressive policemen. There could only be one outcome. Some things were thrown, and the coppers charged the crowd. Suddenly, a full-scale battle broke out. Standing at the front of the crowd, I was in the thick of it. As I struggled with two officers, the rest of the crowd turned tail and ran for it. For my pains, I got beaten up and taken to the local police station but was later released without charge. At the first signs of trouble, Jeremy had jumped into his cherry-red BMW and roared off into the night.

Jeremy was now in a bit of a cleft stick. He had taken the money for thousands of tickets, many of them sold to friends, and there had been no party. He was now looking to put on another event for all the holders of the unused tickets. He came to me for a venue.

There was a massive old warehouse on the corner of Mare Street. I tried to creep into it to have a look around but was caught by the watchman. He was only a young guy and up for a deal. He agreed to my offer of £500 to turn a blind eye to the party. Jeremy was in business. But only for half an hour. Walking around the warehouse to look for suitable locations for my sound system, I must have triggered a silent alarm. The police duly arrived, and that put an end to Jeremy's second attempt at a party.

The final part of the drama was that Jeremy, desperate now to save face, hired The Hippodrome in Leicester Square. The ticket holders got their party, and Jeremy's reputation was restored, but it had cost him an awful lot of money.

In the face of so much failure all around me, I now decided to make a bold move. I should have known that I was asking for trouble, but the disused Poplar bus garage was such a perfect venue that I just couldn't resist it: it had a large covered open space with first-class facilities. I broke in and set up my equipment. Tony Wilson was doing a soundcheck when the police arrived. They seemed particularly incensed by the fact that we had broken into a bus garage. The upshot was that Tony and I were both arrested for stealing electricity, and we were taken to the police station. The worst part was that they confiscated my sound system!

This was a particularly dark period for me and the acid-house scene in general. The police were starting to come down heavy, and the majority of parties were being stopped. Furthermore, because heavy security was needed to guard the large amounts of cash takings from potential armed robbers, violent people were becoming involved in what had previously been a completely peaceful scene. Realising the profits involved, some of these thugs even began to run their own parties. Seen through my idealistic eyes, the whole theory of peace, love and comradeship was being tarnished.

I still went to acid-house gigs, because I loved the people and the buzz. With my sound system gone, it also allowed me to stay in touch with the scene. I did the rounds of Spectrum, Future, Miami's and Smile at Camden Palace, and I enjoyed it, but I still wanted to be involved in running my own parties.

One night, I was at Camden Palace when they played 'Reaching' by Phase One. It was a catchy tune, but I focused on the words. It was all about keeping on trying to achieve your goals. It was as if the tune was speaking to me.

Three

Sex, Drugs and Acid House

ONE NIGHT, I was at a gig called The Rave at the Cave, which was held in a railway arch near Elephant and Castle. I was surrounded by many of my new-found acid-house friends. One of these was a guy called Wayne. I had met him several times previously at various gigs on the circuit. He was an intelligent, friendly guy who was as evangelical about the scene as I was. We started to talk.

I told him about my experience of both running and working at gigs. I also mentioned that I had just got my sound system back from the police. Wayne had always wanted to run gigs himself. One thing led to another, and we resolved to team up and put on parties.

The name of our gig seemed to be the most important thing about the whole venture. Over the next few days, we proposed and discarded hundreds of ideas. Genesis was one of Wayne's favourite bands. By coincidence, I had been leafing through the Bible, searching for something suitably profound. A line in the Book of Genesis jumped out at me: 'In the beginning, God created the heavens and the earth.' That settled it: Genesis was the name of our gig.

I was broke and Wayne only had £300, so costs had to be kept to a minimum. I had the sound system, some lights and a box of wicked tunes. The drinks would be on a sale-or-return basis. The 3,000 flyers would cost £80. The doorman would be Wayne's stepdad and the bar manager his sister. Wayne and I would be on the door taking the money. It would be one big happy family affair and would cost us about a grand.

If finding a suitable name had been problematic, then the logo to go with it seemed beyond us. It had to represent what our new company was all about, as well as the ideology that drove us. We worked late into the night. The head of Zeus seemed mystical enough, as did an ancient Egyptian background. In view of all the time we had spent on it, it would have to do, and it was printed on our flyer.

The next item on our agenda was to find a suitable warehouse. It would have to be away from residential properties, because local people would be the first to phone the police. Secrecy would be paramount, because if the authorities turned up before we started it would all be over. We kept it just between me and Wayne. Everything was on a need-to-know basis.

We had both found from personal experience that news travels fast on the acid-house scene. If the address got out, people would start turning up at the venue before we were ready to start. This would then alert the police. It also had to be somewhere that people could find easily, and there had to be parking spaces for hundreds of cars.

A strategically placed meeting point would be set up in advance for partygoers to congregate at. It couldn't be too close to the venue, or the police would just drive around the locality and investigate likely buildings. One of our people would watch the meeting point closely and be ready to give out the address of the venue. Experienced clubbers would know that someone close to the organisers would be there and would ask for the address. If you didn't ask, you wouldn't be told. The ones who didn't ask were invariably undercover police. It was as easy as that.

We managed to get the keys to a small warehouse at Aldgate, right next to Tubby Isaac's jellied-eel stall. Early one cold and wet Tuesday morning, we went along to have a look at it. The entrance to the warehouse was on the corner of a busy road, so we had to be careful not to be seen. The East End in general was alive with thieves, and to be seen lurking about in the early hours would surely prompt a call to the police.

We were initially disappointed that the keys we had been given didn't fit the front door, so we crept around the building looking for an entry point. We discovered an open balcony that ran around the front and side of the building and could see stairs leading down from it inside. There were multiple windows along the balcony. If we could open one, we would be inside.

We climbed the wall, up to the balcony, pushed a window open and climbed in. We reckoned that the venue could hold about 400 people with another 50 on the balcony. There was lots of rubbish scattered about but nothing so big that we would have trouble moving it. The final bonus was that we could unlock the main door from the inside, so we didn't have to break into the building at all. We were careful to leave everything as we had found it so as not to arouse suspicion and left in high spirits. We had found Genesis's first venue.

At that time, there were probably no more than a few thousand warehouse-party people in the whole of the country. People involved in the scene knew everybody else, if only by sight. Therefore, news of upcoming parties was largely passed around by word of mouth. The flyers were really to cover ourselves against the licensing laws. Prominently printed on each flyer was 'No invite, no entry' and 'Over 18s only'. Wayne, several of our friends and I went out every night, giving flyers to clubbers coming out of acid-house gigs. It put the name of Genesis out there, and the flyer and the logo got a great response. However, most of those people who actually brought the flyer to the venue were new to the scene.

As 10 December 1988, the date of the gig, drew closer, I started to get nervous. We badly needed this first party to be a success. I briefly ran through all the things that could go wrong. We were in a building we had no right to be in, and the owners could turn up and evict us. The police could find out about the party and stop it. No one might turn up and we would be seriously embarrassed. There were many ways we could fail; we could only hope for some luck.

It was only 5 p.m. when we entered the warehouse, but in the midst of winter it seemed like the dead of night. We were very close to the City, which was always like a ghost town at weekends. There was very little traffic on the roads and even fewer pedestrians on the street.

We had told our van driver with the sound system to park several streets away so as not to attract any attention. After a brief phone call, he pulled up outside, and we quickly carried the equipment in. As I went about setting up the sound system and the lights, Wayne and a few mates set about transforming the refuse-strewn warehouse into a state-of-the-art dance arena. I couldn't help but recall one of my dad's old expressions about not being able to make a silk purse out of a sow's ear. In its present state, our venue was very much a pig of a building.

During the previous week, we had visited various army surplus stores and bought whatever caught our fancy. There were giant snow nets, white-and-green camouflage nets and full-sized parachutes still in their packs. We cleared away the rubbish and draped our props about the ceiling and walls. They radically altered the shape of the building. Two powerful strobe lights were set up, one at each end of the dance area. We had three old oil projectors. Once they were set up to project onto the nets and chutes, our venue looked like some futuristic nightclub.

We set up a bar serving soft drinks in a small room and put a table across the doorway to serve as a counter. We then did a quick soundcheck with the equipment and were ready. All we needed was some customers.

The time to congregate at the meeting point had been set for 10 p.m., and Wayne went to check it out at 9.50 p.m. He called back to say that there was no one there. Long minutes passed, and I was starting to think that it would all be a flop when he called again. Now there were about 15 cars there and nearly 50 clubbers asking where the venue was. Wayne brought them back with him then returned to the meeting point to wait for others. By midnight, we had about 200 people in the venue, and the place was jumping.

The DJs, Tony Wilson and Lyndon C, were late in arriving, so it was left to me to provide the tunes. I varied my set from the normal acid house, playing a kicking party set of Balearic and new beat. It ranged from the likes of The Gypsy Kings, Grand Master Flash and The Cure to Ten City. Together with the lights, the smoke, the strobes and the Es that had been taken, the music brought on an incredible rush, and everyone was waving their arms in the air and partying like mad.

Just when we thought the party had peaked for the night, people started arriving in droves from another gig that had been raided. The police had descended in force on The Rave at the Cave at Elephant and Castle. And they had done so in style, with video cameras, strip-search units, sniffer dogs and the media in tow. The Rave at the Cave's misfortune was our bonus. They swelled our numbers by another couple of hundred.

At 5 a.m., when the party was still in full swing, a fire alarm rang in a neighbouring building. This meant that the police would soon be on the scene. We rounded up all the takings and gave them to Wayne's stepdad, and together with his sister they quietly slipped out of the building.

The police duly arrived and shut off the electricity. I didn't know if this was their first encounter with ravers en masse, but they seemed to be thoroughly bemused by the hordes of bare-chested guys who walked out into the freezing conditions, steam rising from their bodies. They tried to interrogate people who were having serious trouble keeping their lower jaws from wobbling all over the place, then gave it up as a bad job. As for their question of 'Who are the organisers?', that went completely unanswered.

Wayne and I disappeared into the night for a rendezvous with his stepdad and the night's takings. In the event, we made a profit of just over two grand. No great fortune, but, in the circumstances, not a bad start for the fledgling Genesis.

The only downside was that we had left all the equipment behind. We crept back later that day and found that every single bit was still there. We quickly loaded it into our van and drove off. Now we could think about our next gig and another venue. We were out on the road virtually every day, driving about in search of a suitable venue. We toured industrial estates by day and promoted the event by night.

Normally, we would never break into a building before the actual night of a party. A quick look through the window usually sufficed to give us a good idea if it was suitable. Derelict buildings were avoided for safety reasons. If the place was filthy and looked dangerous, the police would never allow the party to go ahead on health-and-safety grounds. The ideal venue was a disused building that was available for leasing. It didn't matter if there was no electricity supply, because by that point we had an electrician on the firm who was an absolute magician. If push came to shove, he would wire us up to a street light, which would give us enough power to run every piece of equipment we needed.

As was the case with virtually everyone who was dragged, drawn or otherwise introduced to our crazy scene, Sparky, our new electrician, came with a story. He was only 5 ft 3 in. tall, with short black hair, a stocky build and an exaggerated cockney accent. However, he was an electrician by trade and really knew his stuff. He had recently been fired from Dynamo Electronics and was now working as a technician in Young's Disco Hire, a shop that hired disco equipment.

Wayne and I had gone into this particular shop one afternoon to hire some strobe lights and sound equipment for a party we were organising that night. From the outset, Sparky was very friendly and helpful, if somewhat talkative. As he checked our equipment, he explained in great detail the specifications and functions of everything. We hadn't exactly asked for a tutorial with an in-depth analysis of schematics, circuits, components and resistors, but we got one nevertheless. All I really needed to know was where the on/off button was located.

Suddenly, Sparky was cut off in full flow by the arrival of a regular and important customer. As he focused on the new client, Wayne and I took the opportunity to wander off and look around the shop. By coincidence rather than design, we were both drawn to a large display cabinet, in the bottom right-hand corner of which stood a smoke machine. We nodded in unison as we contemplated how great the machine would look at the party that night.

As Wayne ran through possible locations for it at the venue, I called across to Sparky to ask if we could examine it. Still engrossed with the other customer, Sparky nodded and waved his permission.

I took the machine from the cabinet and was immediately impressed by the fact that it came with a remote control. As I held the latter in my hands, it seemed only sensible to check the equipment. Sparky invariably checked each piece of equipment leased for hire and return, so I thought that I was just saving him some work.

With Wayne following, I carried the machine into the back of the shop, which was really a garage that had been converted into a stockroom for the larger pieces of equipment. I placed the machine on the floor and connected it to an extension lead. I pressed the on/off button on the remote and a small light turned from red to green. I pressed several other buttons until a small wisp of smoke appeared. A cigarette would have generated more, so I searched for a volume control button to no avail. However, there was one button labelled 'constant', and I pressed and held it down.

Within seconds, the whole back section of the shop was filled with thick, apple-flavoured smoke. Wayne rushed towards some shutters and threw them open. Although a lot of the smoke billowed out into the yard, an awful lot more engulfed the whole shop, so that you could hardly see your hand in front of your face.

Sparky, now in panic mode, but largely invisible to us, shouted 'What the fuck have you done?' at the top of his voice. In the gloom, he managed to locate the smoke machine and wrestled with it to try to stem the flow of smoke. This he succeeded in doing, and after a few minutes the smoke began to clear.

'Please don't fucking touch anything,' shouted Sparky as he returned to the client, who was bemusedly rubbing his eyes. He was preaching to the converted. We would be testing no more machines. Wayne and I were just pleased that he had brought the drama to an end. However, we were blissfully unaware that an entirely new drama was in the process of unfolding.

Opening the shutters had proved an efficient method of clearing the smoke from the shop. Unfortunately for us, though, as it billowed out into the back yard it was sucked in the back door of the next-door pub. Customers who were casually sipping their pints suddenly became aware of this thick cloud of smoke, seemingly with a life of its own, that was rapidly filling the bar. Fear was immediately followed by panic as the customers ran for the doors, some shouting that the kitchen was on fire.

Within minutes, sirens were screaming as several fire engines raced along Kentish Town High Street. As the pub customers crowded together on the pavement rubbing their eyes, teams of firemen with hoses ran past and into the pub. They reappeared a short time later, scratching their collective heads. They had just experienced something that they had never been taught about at training school. Smoke without fire!

I suppose that with normal people this incident would have been considered to be a very poor start. However, with us it was more a case of the coming together of kindred spirits. Sparky immediately became a trusted and valued member of the team.

Apart from any other consideration, it was the end of various dramatic scenarios involving the all-important electricity supply.

No more would we have to hire a generator, or bribe neighbours for the use of their electric sockets, or loop cables, sometimes for hundreds of yards and across roads, to access electricity.

We had regularly experienced overloads, where the party had suddenly gone from flashing lights and blaring music to silence and darkness, while one of the crew searched the hundreds of metres of extension leads for the fuse that had blown, before 'repairing' it with a piece of silver paper.

Now, with Sparky, we had virtually permanent access to a regular three-phase supply to power up the lights, stage cans, sound systems and lasers that would propel us into division one, where Genesis belonged. With Sparky's extensive knowledge of electronics, we were able to instantly 'go in live' and access the live electricity from the disused warehouses. That isn't to say, however, that Sparky didn't have his little idiosyncrasies.

Everyone in the crew had their particular role when it came to setting up the warehouse for one of our events. But before we could start bringing in the equipment and decorating the place, the electricity supply had to be sorted first. Sparky was the main man for this important stage, and he always insisted on two assistants. We wondered why. Not that we were concerned about the cost, he could have had ten assistants if he had so desired. We were more curious about what the other two would be doing. It wasn't long before we found out.

We had watched from a distance as Sparky gave his two assistants a detailed tutorial, including the acting out of the various stages. This was all done by the light of a streetlamp outside the warehouse. Keeping our distance, we then followed the trio inside. We watched as they gathered around the standard grey box that housed the power supply, lit only by the candle that one of them carried. The rest of the building was in total darkness.

Sparky took out two industrial cables similar to those used to jump-start a lorry. Each cable had a thick plastic covering with the stranded copper cables visible at the end. Carefully holding the cables just before the exposed copper, Sparky was intent on tailing in live by hotwiring the two cables directly into the grey box simultaneously.

The emphasis was very much on the 'simultaneously', because if the cables didn't connect at precisely the same time, Sparky would find that he had become the 'earth conductor' of this high-voltage circuit, with all the ensuing ramifications for his health, not to mention his life. That was where the second assistant came in. Standing close by and holding a wooden twelve-inch-by-four-feet scaffold board, should Sparky suddenly become 'live', it was his job to hit him with the board, so knocking him out of the circuit. It wasn't long before this was put into practice.

On this particular night, the three of them were in position, just about to connect to the circuit box. Sparky held the two connectors in his hands, the first assistant held the candle, while the second assistant readied himself with the scaffold board. They were relatively experienced with the procedure now, but Sparky was firmly and professionally in control, barking out the relevant orders.

'Right,' shouted Sparky, 'are you ready, Keith?'

Keith raised the scaffold board to about shoulder height and grunted, 'Yep, mate.'

Sparky began the countdown, calling, '5, 4, 3 . . .'

Unfortunately for everyone concerned, not all the crew were aware of this delicate stage of the proceedings. Two unwitting riggers raced up to the side of the building in a van and jumped out. They ran over to the large metal shutter, at the other side of which stood Sparky nearing the end of his countdown.

'Oi, Oi,' shouted one of the riggers, fortissimo, giving the shutter an almighty bang that echoed throughout the building.

Keith reacted by instinct. Thinking Sparky was in the process of being electrocuted, he gave him a hefty blow with the scaffold board, sending him tumbling to the floor. At the same time, the other assistant dropped the candle, so plunging the building into darkness. A minor panic ensued. It was the work of seconds to re-ignite the candle. It revealed Sparky lying semi-conscious on the floor. The two assistants struggled to bring him round. They smacked his cheeks and even showered his face with Coca-Cola from a nearby bottle, but all to no avail.

Keith pondered the problem. Perhaps it was the Coke bottle that provided the inspiration. Reaching inside his coat pocket, he pulled out a wrap of coke he had been saving for the party. He quickly sprinkled some of it on Sparky's upper lip and blew. Within seconds, Sparky's recovery was complete. He jumped to his feet and carried on working.

We were driving through the back streets of Hackney one evening when we saw flashing disco lights through the windows of a large warehouse. We pulled up at the entrance and went in to investigate. It was big enough to hold about 4,500 people and looked in good working order. It seemed like a perfect venue.

A DJ console had been mounted on scaffolding poles suspended from the ceiling at the far end of the building. Dysfunctional lights on boxes strove to keep up with the acid-house beats that were playing quietly in the background. Around the console lounged about half a dozen young guys.

We approached the group and asked if the warehouse belonged to them. A big-built Rasta guy, who must have been six feet four tall, spoke up, saying that it did. I asked him if it might be possible to hire the building for one night. He dismissed the offer out of hand, saying that he wasn't interested. We left, disappointed that they had found the building before we had.

Ever since our first Genesis gig, a friend of Wayne's called Keith had been asking to join our partnership. As a close friend, Wayne might have been in a difficult position, but I certainly wasn't. I pointed out to Wayne that there were mates of mine who would like to be part of Genesis, but as far as I was concerned the two of us could run it very well on our own.

Keith persisted and asked me if I would reconsider taking him into the partnership if he found a suitable venue, one that held several thousand people. In view of the fact that we presently had no venue, and that the type of venue he was offering to find was virtually non-existent, I agreed, more to keep him quiet than anything else.

Before long, Keith came to us and said that he had found just such a venue. When we asked where it was and he told us it was in Hackney, we didn't believe him. We had searched the length and breadth of Hackney and hadn't found anything even halfway suitable. However, he was so insistent that we went with him to have a look.

You can imagine our surprise when he took us to the same venue we had seen a couple of days previously. However, this time the big Rasta was absent, and Keith introduced us to a guy called Wally, who said he was the owner. We asked about the other group, and he said that he was charging them £300 for one night. I immediately offered him £500 pounds a night for five nights and showed him the two and a half grand. Wally said that the other firm were due to pay a deposit but hadn't shown up with it yet. He added that if he didn't have it by the following day, the venue was ours.

We returned the following evening, and the deposit still hadn't been paid. I pulled out the two and a half grand again, and Wally agreed on the spot. He gave us the keys and a handwritten lease and told us that the building was ours. We couldn't believe our luck. Christmas and New Year were just around the corner, and we now had a first-class venue for our Genesis gigs.

But first we had to clean up the place and decorate it to create a party dreamscape. There were hundreds of used car tyres strewn about the building. At first, we stacked them up at the far end of the space, but then we decided to use them in the decor. We piled them up to form a large bar and constructed a semi-circular wall of them around the DJ console. Wayne's *pièce de résistance* was a tunnel of tyres covered with canopies just inside the entrance, which he lit with ultraviolet light. The effect was amazing.

We also bought more nets and parachutes. The latter were fastened to the ceiling, but we sprayed the nets with paint and hung them from the roof so that they dangled down in front of the DJ. We bought two inflatable props, a skeleton and a multicoloured gorilla, and built cages to put them in. We had a seven foot Christmas tree but no lights, so we stuck bits of coloured card in the branches and hung an ultraviolet light over it. The bits of card looked better than the real thing.

We sprinkled sawdust over the whole of the floor, which not only made a good effect, but also served to cover the pools of oil everywhere. Finally, we fixed our projectors so that they brought the whole thing to life. Only hours earlier, we had walked into a grotty warehouse; now we had our party dreamscape.

We had 5,000 flyers printed, promoting the Genesis Christmas Eve Party, and spent the whole weekend going from club to club. Monday morning saw us back at the warehouse, putting the final touches to the decor. I had just sat down with Wayne and Keith to discuss last-minute plans. Wayne had lit up a joint. Suddenly, the front door was booted open. Thinking it was a police raid, Wayne threw the joint behind the Christmas tree. The three of us jumped to our feet.

Standing in the doorway was the big Rasta who we had met when we first came to the warehouse – the one who had told us he wasn't interested in renting it to us. He was holding a sawn-off shotgun in his massive hands.

'You've nicked my venue, you cunts,' he screamed, clearly out of control.

Wayne reacted first. 'Now hold on a minute, mate,' he said, remarkably calmly. 'Just listen to what we've got to say.'

This seemed to provoke the big guy even more. 'No, you cunts. You fucking listen to me,' he roared at the top of his voice. 'This place is mine. Do you understand?' He walked right up to Wayne and pointed the gun at his head.

I watched with growing respect as Wayne kept his cool. Still talking calmly, he said, 'Look, calm down. You were meant to pay the deposit last week but you never showed up. What did you expect us to do?'

'Where's the owner?' the Rasta demanded, lowering the gun and looking around.

Wayne's reaction was instant. He leapt forward and butted the guy in the face, catching him square on the nose. I wasn't slow off the mark myself. Grabbing a nearby lump of wood, I smashed him in the side of the head with it. The guy fell to the floor, dropping the gun. I jumped in and picked it up. Now it was me pointing it at his head.

'Now you listen to me, you big cunt,' I stuck my face right into his. 'It's your own fucking fault that you lost the warehouse. You didn't pay the deposit. So, if you've got anything to say, you should say it to the owner. We're not fucking idiots. If you want a war, you can fucking have one.'

Suddenly, all the fight went out of him. He nodded a couple of times and muttered, 'You're right, mate. I suppose I'd have done the same thing in your place. It's just that when I was told you were in here, I thought you were taking the piss.'

'No, we weren't taking the piss, mate,' interjected Wayne. 'We're promoters. This is what we do for a living. Put your hands up a minute,' he added.

The big guy now looked concerned, and I was puzzled myself. Surely Wayne wasn't going to rob him. But to back him up, I poked the guy with the gun, and he put his hands in the air. Wayne walked across and searched his pockets. From one of them, he took out four shotgun cartridges. 'Now we're going to give you your gun back, just to show we're not taking the piss,' he said. He unloaded the shotgun and handed it back to the guy. 'If you come back looking for trouble, we'll finish it, OK?'

The guy took the gun and, with a crestfallen look on his face, walked out of the warehouse. The three of us let out a long sigh of relief.

I was impressed with Wayne. He wasn't a fighter, but he had handled the situation brilliantly. 'You surprised me there, mate,'

I said. 'Well done.' I slapped him on the back.

He was shaking his head, the fear now clear on his face. 'Don't worry about that, Andy. I fucking surprised myself,' he replied. 'Fuck knows what I was thinking about. I could have got myself shot.' With that, he burst out laughing. It relieved the tension, and Keith and I both joined in. I reflected that this warehouse-party business could be a dangerous game. I resolved that I would always have some sort of weapon close at hand in future, just in case of trouble.

As part of our new security precautions, we took to barricading the front door when we were in the warehouse. A few days later, there was a loud banging from outside. Iron railing in hand, I went to the door and peered through a crack. Two very well-dressed fellas and an absolutely gorgeous girl were standing there. I recognised one of the guys from the rave scene, so I opened the door.

'Hi,' the one I had recognised said. 'My name's Tony Colston-Hayter. I don't know if you've heard about me, but I run Sunrise.' His voice was cultured and confident.

The incident with the big guy had put us on the defensive and had made us aggressive to boot. 'Yeah, I know you, and I know of Sunrise. What do you want?' I demanded.

He was slightly taken aback but recovered quickly. He stuck out his hand, and I shook it almost by reflex. 'You've got a great place here,' he said, looking around the warehouse. 'We're looking for a venue to stage our Christmas party. I had over 4,000 people at my last party in Greenwich. How about letting us join in with you, and we'll hold one big party?'

Suddenly, there was movement behind us, and two guys we had never seen before walked from the back of the warehouse. Now it was Keith's turn to be aggressive. He jumped up shouting 'What do you cunts think you're doing?'

Tony looked startled. 'It's OK,' he said. 'They're with me.' Waving them forward, he added, 'This is Alf, and this is Terry.' The two guys nodded in greeting.

'Look,' I said, quickly cutting him off. 'I ain't being funny, but we don't need any help.'

He rode the rebuff masterfully and carried on seamlessly. 'It seems that we haven't got off to a very good start,' he apologised. 'I guess I should have phoned first. But we wanted to see the warehouse before we made an offer. This is a great place and very big. You could well have trouble filling it. I can bring 4,000 people. Why don't we all throw in together and cut up the proceeds 50–50?' He smiled engagingly.

'Look,' said Wayne. 'I know that Sunrise have been running some good parties, so I know you can probably deliver what you say. Let us think about your offer. It could be that we will do Christmas ourselves, but we might consider sharing New Year's Eve with you.'

Tony seemed happy with this arrangement. We exchanged phone numbers, and they left. 'What do you think?' Wayne asked.

'Well, whatever we think, we've still got a lot of work to do promoting our Christmas party. So, why don't we get on with that and think about the other at our leisure?' Wayne and Keith readily agreed.

As part of our promotion package, we had a team of three beautiful girls called Amber, Maggie and Leonie. They were very effective. They would appear outside clubs as they turned out and soon a small crowd would gather. The girls would shout out, 'Genesis, this Saturday,' and hand out flyers. They were always mobbed.

The closer we got to the event, the more there seemed yet to be done. There were always last-minute jobs in the warehouse, and you could never do too much promotion. We were continually out and about, reminding people about the gig and maximising the hype. Genesis had taken over our lives. There was no such thing as spare time.

Our Christmas Eve gig would kick off our round of festive parties, so it was important that it be a success. For a meeting point, we chose a well-known spot that anyone could find. The Lea Bridge Ice Rink stood in a prominent position on the Lea Bridge Road. At 10 p.m. on Christmas Eve, we sent someone to man the point, and within 15 minutes over 100 cars had pulled up. They were sent on to the warehouse, and we had an instant queue of about 300 people, all of whom were excited at having found the gig.

With two friends, Tabitha and Tamara, taking the money and four of Keith's mates as security, we declared the party open. As the customers entered the venue, there were looks of amazement. They pointed out the chutes, painted nets and props to each other, but the star turn was the Christmas tree. 'Great lights on the tree,' people shouted out to us. We could only laugh. What lights? They were bits of coloured paper, lit by the ultraviolet light. But you would never have guessed it. The pieces of paper moved in the breeze and changed colour as the light hit them.

By midnight, we had over 600 people dancing wildly and chanting 'Aceed'. The atmosphere was ecstatic. Shouts of 'Merry Christmas everyone' could be heard over the hubbub. Even the police must have been moved by the Christmas spirit. A couple of times, passing patrol cars stopped and asked the doormen if everything was OK, then wished them 'Happy Christmas' as they drove off. This particularly amused Wayne. 'Oi, Wayne,' I shouted across. 'You haven't slipped the Old Bill an E have you?' He fell about laughing.

There was a rumour that undercover police were circulating among the partygoers, but that didn't overly concern me. We specifically made it our policy not to get involved in supplying any drugs. What customers brought was up to them. However, the rumour did concern Wayne – to such an extent that he cautioned several people about taking their drugs too openly. We had one of the very few legal sites in England and didn't want to mess it up.

As he walked around, he suddenly came upon a young guy stretched out on the floor, seemingly unconscious. Wayne splashed some water in his face, and he came round after a few minutes. I was watching all this from a raised section near the DJ console. Wayne asked the young guy his age, and he said he was 15. Wayne then asked him who he was with. The young lad pointed over to a nearby group of older teenagers and said that he was with his brother.

I followed events as Wayne led him over to the group. He asked for the brother and told him that he should not have brought his younger brother and that he should have been watching out for him more closely. I could see it coming a mile off and was already moving, calling to one of the security guys as I ran. The brother promptly punched Wayne in the face, which, to my mind, not only went against the festive spirit of the occasion, but was also a literal slap in the face of everything we were trying to do. I grabbed the ungrateful wretch by the scruff and, together with the security guy, dragged him to the door. I booted him up the backside and sent him on his way with a 'And a Merry fucking Christmas to you too, mate'.

The incident was memorable if only for the fact that it was the first bit of trouble we'd had at one of our gigs. People were normally so loved-up and having a good time that the furthest thing from their minds was rowing with each other.

A total of 900 people attended the gig, and by 10 a.m. on Christmas morning there were still 200 of them singing Christmas carols and introducing themselves to each other. If it was the time of year for good cheer and good will to all men, then they had certainly had that in spades at our gig. I staggered off for Christmas dinner with my family, whilst Wayne partied on.

Later that evening, we returned to the venue to tidy up and prepare for our Boxing Day gig. I suppose we could have paid someone to do the cleaning up, but such was our commitment to what we were doing we even did mundane tasks willingly, almost as part of our mission. I was pinning up some decorations that had come loose when two uniformed policemen walked in. They asked who was in charge, and I pointed to Wayne. We had long ago agreed that he was the one most suited for dealing with the authorities. With his laid-back manner, good speaking voice and polite ways, he could charm the birds off the trees. He was also a top blagger. He could tell a whopper without even blinking an eye and be convincing with it, too.

They said that they wanted to see some kind of document, stating exactly what the terms of the lease were. Wayne always carried the lease we had got from the owner with him. He produced it, saying that we were leasing the premises for private music-business parties. They wrote the details down in their notebooks.

Just before they left, they confided to Wayne that they really weren't bothered about what we were doing. We just seemed to be having a good time without disturbing anyone else. They had far more trouble to deal with from the local pubs each time they turned out. Seemingly satisfied, they left. Grinning broadly and slapping each other on the back, we took this to be the official seal of approval to continue organising dance parties.

By then, Genesis was becoming the talk of London. We were putting on successful parties without them being stopped. Nothing was worse for the average raver than being lost in their own warm, touchy-feely world and then having an aggressive police force eject them out into the cold night. With us, they knew they could party on uninterrupted. Further, with a legal venue, we could print the address on the flyers. People could come straight to the party without hanging about at meeting points. And we went out of our way to conduct ourselves in as professional a manner as possible. We tried to ensure that the venue was both clean and safe. To that end, we even bought fire extinguishers and distributed them about the building. One of the main things that seemed to concern the police were fire and safety regulations. Once they saw that we were taking sensible precautions, they tended to be satisfied.

By 9 p.m. on Boxing Day, a large queue had gathered outside the front door, and we weren't due to open for another hour. We were also having some technical problems with the electricity supply. However, rather than have our customers stand outside in the cold, we let them in. The first hundred got in for free as a seasonal goodwill gesture. They filed into the silent venue, presently lit only by dozens of candles.

Shortly before 10 p.m., our technicians managed to solve the problem, and lights and sound were restored to a roar and applause from the assembled clubbers. As 'Your Love' by Frankie Knuckles played, hands were immediately thrown in the air, and the party mood was on us again.

Almost before we knew it, we had over 2,000 people in the building. Once again, we had only four doormen on duty. But such was the friendly ambience of our parties that they were mostly for show and were hardly ever needed.

Unfortunately, we soon ran out of soft drinks, an absolute essential for thirsty E'ing clubbers. We descended on the local 7–11 and bought up their complete stock.

As further evidence of how Genesis's fame was spreading, we were inundated with celebrities that night. The word had reached them that there was a safe, non-threatening environment where they could have a great time and not be troubled by the paparazzi pack. That night I was introduced to the Pet Shop Boys, Boy George and Milli Vanilli. Lots of West End club owners came along to see what all the fuss was about, or so they said. I remarked to Wayne that what they really meant was that they had come to see where all their customers had gone. Many of them looked decidedly miffed when they saw that they had been deserted for an old warehouse in the back streets of east London.

As the promoters of the successful Genesis brand, we were now on the guest list of all the most sought-after clubs. With the fame came the perks. Beautiful women forced themselves on us just to be part of the scene. Complete strangers shared their drugs with us. After the gig, we would regularly retire to an early morning private party, surrounded by our closest mates and several beautiful women. We were living out a fantasy, almost on a daily basis.

Among the visitors to the Boxing Day party was Tony from Sunrise. He congratulated us on a great night and asked if we had made up our minds about the joint venture for New Year's Eve. We had discussed it at length. We knew we could now pull in over 2,000 people, but the warehouse was a very big building, and there was lots of spare space. It would make sense to unite, and it would immensely strengthen the brand. If we worked together, it was possible that we could capture the whole market and put on the best and biggest events in England. We told Tony that he was on. Our aim was to stage the biggest acid-house party the world had ever seen.

At 8 p.m. on a cold and windy New Year's Eve, reality intruded in the form of an inspector from the local police station. He didn't share our evangelical zeal for promoting large loved-up musical events, and he was looking for an excuse to stop this one. He insisted on looking all over the warehouse to see if he could find any fire risks or anything else that could be viewed as dangerous.

We had made a special effort for that night's gig: we had hired in special lighting and sound equipment; giant stage props were strategically placed about the building; and the security guys all wore black suits with bow ties and communicated with walkie-talkies.

We had also decided to open up a previously unused part of the warehouse, which increased the available area by about a third. We put into this new space three bouncy castles and some fan lights, and hired the Mad Hatters, a local sound system. We connected the area to the main room with a short tunnel.

In another room, we had set up our command centre for the night. Lined up on a long table were ten phones, which would be ringing constantly all night long with people calling to find out if the event was on and how they could get to it.

We had made a last-minute bulk purchase from a local rascal

who had a van full of fire extinguishers, illuminated exit signs and crash barriers. Everything flammable had been removed from the building, and anything marginally problematic had been sprayed with fire-retardant chemicals. Little did the inspector know that the work had only been done that day, but we were determined that the fire regulations would be fully implemented. He couldn't find anything specifically to complain about, but he still wasn't happy about letting the event continue.

I left Wayne and Tony to negotiate with the inspector. He didn't know it at the time, but he certainly had his hands full with two of the most persuasive people you were ever likely to meet. Complete with moody guest lists, they told the inspector that this was a genuine music-business showcase for invited guests only. There would be over 1,000 people from the world's music industry, ranging from major celebrities to managing directors of record companies.

Tony and Wayne explained to the bemused inspector that whilst they could understand his concern about health-and-safety regulations being met, he should also understand that we were completely within our legal rights to hold the event. Furthermore, although we were perfectly willing to discuss these matters in a civilised and courteous manner, we knew our rights. Should our event be compromised in any way, we wouldn't hesitate to pursue the matter through the courts, resulting in massive compensation. The inspector said that he still wasn't satisfied and would bring the local fire inspector in. To that end, he made a call on his radio.

I had been watching and listening to all of this from the relative safety of several feet away. Suddenly, Wayne, still clutching a clipboard with the moody guest list on it, turned and rushed over to me. 'Fuck, fuck, fuck, Andy,' he whispered. 'I've just remembered. All those bin bags full of old plastic cups and bottles are on the rear fire escape. If the fire inspector comes and sees those, we're fucked big-time.'

'Don't worry, mate,' I shouted over my shoulder. 'I'll take care of it.' As I ran back into the building, I rounded up everyone I could find. Bouncers in their new black suits, DJs and sound engineers all ran with me to the rear fire escape, where I threw open the emergency doors. And stopped.

Before us was a knee-deep mess of cans, bottles and plastic cups. We got some bin bags and frantically began throwing the rubbish into them. Each full bag was then thrown over the wall into the yard of the adjoining building. There was nowhere else to put it. Within 30 minutes, we had broken the back of it, but now we were all covered in greasy, sticky slime.

In view of the fact that we were expecting several thousand people and the entry price was ten quid, we knew that there would be a large amount of money on the premises. This would provide a tempting prize for any armed-robbery gang, and the East End was teeming with such firms. For that reason, we had laid on special security precautions. A friend of Wayne's, an ex-marine called Eddie, knew of a team of former soldiers. Some of them had been in the Special Forces for years and had decided to form an agency. Most of them lived on the outskirts of London, and they had false passports and interchangeable identities. They occasionally did security work such as we required.

Eddie had assured us that although they were, in his own words, 'a dangerous bunch of motherfuckers', they were very disciplined, worked well together and were gentle but firm. Regular bouncers usually got between £30 and £50 a night. These military guys weren't cheap at £1,500 for the team of 15, but they had been shot at and had worked behind enemy lines. Some local armed robber shoving a gun in their face wouldn't faze them at all.

Tony had also brought his own security team of six people. They too seemed serious and professional, treating the whole thing like some military operation. But now they were all standing about, wondering if there was going to be a party at all.

Back out on the street, tension was mounting. Precious minutes were ticking away, and our announced opening time was drawing ever closer. Tony, Wayne and the inspector were trying to keep warm in the bitter cold. They were pacing up and down, often circling each other, as if performing some bizarre dance.

Suddenly, a tall thin man of about forty came hurrying up to the three of them. It was the fire inspector, and it didn't look promising. He was from a different generation and didn't look at all pleased. 'What's the problem?' he demanded of no one in particular.

'They're planning some kind of party,' said the inspector, who was almost whining. 'We don't want it, and I'm sure it's not safe.'

The fire inspector gave him a withering look. 'I suppose I'd better take a look, then,' he said. As he walked past us and into the building, he gave me a wink, and I twigged: the reason he wasn't pleased was probably because he'd been called away from his own New Year's Eve celebrations. And the culprit, of course, was the police inspector.

I followed the fire inspector inside and showed him around, pointing out all the precautions we had taken. Only pausing to nod occasionally, he didn't say a single word. Then he headed back to the front door and went up to the police inspector. The latter looked at him expectantly. 'Everything seems fine to me,' the fire inspector said. 'As far as I'm concerned, they can have their party.' Turning on his heel, he walked quickly away. Thoroughly deflated, the inspector walked after him. We were in business. We had our party.

By then, it was nearly 10 p.m., and a crowd of about 500 had gathered outside the venue. When we announced that the party was on and we were open for business, a ragged cheer went up.

Within a couple of hours, there were several thousand people crammed into the warehouse. On the stroke of midnight, thousands of ecstatic party animals sang Joe Smooth's anthem 'Promised Land' and waved their hands in the air. 'Brothers, sisters, one day we will be free, from trouble and violence, people fighting in the street,' we sang together at the top of our voices.

We had booked a really great DJ line-up. One after the other, Trevor Fung, Terry Farley, Tony Wilson, 'Evil' Eddie Richards, Fat Tony, Phil and Ben, and Colin Hudd played wicked sets.

People kept arriving and, of course, no one was leaving, so the areas that were in operation were rapidly becoming full. We decided not to let anyone else in. Suddenly, a call came over the radio to say that there was a massive crowd at the side of the building, intent on breaking in. We had secured the windows as best we could, but it was a very big building, and it would be possible to break into some of the unused areas. Our security team raced to quell the problem.

Perhaps 200 people were trying to force their way in as our security guys arrived. There was a brief melee, and a group of guys started to throw bricks, bottles and anything else they could lay their hands on. Now stretched to the maximum, the security team called for back-up. Within minutes, another ten guys appeared and order was restored, but it had been a close-run thing.

Back inside the building, the party was in full swing. Celebrities mixed with ordinary people, chanting, dancing and embracing each other, everybody thoroughly caught up in the heady atmosphere of the event. The first Genesis–Sunrise joint promotion was a resounding success. We resolved to do further events together.

By 10 a.m. on New Year's Day, we had managed to get all but a few stragglers out of the building. We divided the takings up between Tony and ourselves, and two big bin bags of notes were carried away from the venue to safe houses. All that was left was to divide up the coins. There was about three grand stacked in piles on the big table in our command centre.

We sent most of the security team home and, together with Tony, began to count the coins. All of a sudden, we heard raised voices in the corridor outside. A voice shouted that the area was out of bounds. Another voice called out that they were looking for the promoters. We all grabbed weapons that were lying around the room, and I told Tony to call the security guys on his phone.

The door burst open, and a tall, skinny guy whom we had never seen before ran in. With no hesitation whatsoever, Wayne caned him in the side of his head with a truncheon. The guy fell to the floor, unconscious, but several others ran into the room behind him. Suddenly, we were all struggling with the intruders. The battle raged for what seemed like ages, then they turned tail and fled. Shortly afterwards, our security arrived.

The incident brought home to us just what a target we were for potential robbers. People knew we had a large amount of cash on the premises, much more than they could get from robbing a bank. We realised that securing the takings would be a major priority in future.

The *New Musical Express* voted our event the best New Year's Eve party of 1988. The following week, we held another Genesis–Sunrise party that was our biggest one ever, but there was a nasty surprise in store for us. Three days after the latest party, we were in the venue, working on the decor, when the chief of the local police station showed up. He was very apologetic about it, but the facts were that the guy who had signed the lease for us wasn't the owner of the building – he was just a squatter. Therefore, the lease wasn't valid, and we couldn't use the building any more. We were all shocked, but we had to face the fact that we were now looking for a new venue.

We were back to square one again. Nobody wanted to rent warehouses to acid-house party promoters, and the few clubs that were big enough to hold several thousand people had a licence that only ran until 3 a.m., far too early for the type of event we put on. We put the word out that we would do a deal with anyone who found us a suitable venue, but we also spent long days looking ourselves. We'd go to various estate agents and get a list of all their suitable properties. Then we'd go to look at any that sounded promising, not with a view to trying to rent them, which would have been out of the question, but rather with a view to breaking in.

Wayne and Tony had also been working on perfecting a

convincing-looking moody lease. From the property lists we got from estate agents, we would photocopy an estate agent's letter-heading and logo. Then we would type in words to the effect that the document confirmed that we were renting the said building for a private music-business function on behalf of EMI, Sony or Virgin. It would go on to state the project manager's name and contact details, adding that he worked for the special projects department of the aforementioned company. Then, above where it was typed 'Manager, Estate Agent', we would get someone to forge a signature. With the finished document in his hand, Wayne would then claim that the Local Government (Miscellaneous Provisions) Act of 1982, which dealt with Public Entertainment Licences, kept us within the law.

A group of promoters called Pacha came to us with the location of a warehouse they had found in east London, close to the river. It was a U-shaped building, right on the Thames, with a docking bay at the back for small boats. The promoters had already broken in, and they showed us around. The place was clean, and everything was in good working order, so we struck a deal with them.

With the combined power of the Genesis–Sunrise brand behind us, we also decided to start a membership club. We called our promotion company Young Minds Entertainment and printed what was really our mission statement on a birthday-card type flyer. It read:

> The Genesis chapter began in a small, deserted London street, where three young minds pulled together in the hope of bringing a new light to the world of entertainment, calling this form of entertainment Genesis.
>
> For the support and encouragement from you, the people who made everything possible, we are truly thankful. We offer to you our very own exclusive limited Members Club and promise the struggle will continue.
>
> Summer of Love
> Winter of Joy
> Year of Genesis

At 5 p.m. on a dark Saturday evening, four trucks carrying all our equipment slowed as they approached the warehouse. A main gate swung open, and, without even having to stop, they drove in, closely followed by a van carrying our soft drinks. The gate was quickly shut and locked behind them.

We had barely five hours before we were due to open – not much time to transform a venue of this size, but over 4,000 people would be clamouring to get in at 10 p.m. As our crew started setting up, we found a small room with one entrance high up in the building and declared it our command centre.

The meeting point for this gig was outside our previous warehouse in Leaside Road. We left one of our guys there to control traffic flow. We didn't want big jams building up, because the police would then come and block access to the event. To add to the professionalism of the organisation, we had printed up small foldable signs that read 'GENESIS–SUNRISE MEETING POINT'. We had also made small maps showing exactly where the venue was. As cars stopped, they were handed a copy of the map.

The trick was to get as many people as possible inside the venue before the police arrived. That way you had more bargaining power to compel the police to let the event continue.

It was 9 p.m., and already we had a crowd of over 800 people in the yard in front of the warehouse. Hundreds more were arriving by car and parking in the surrounding streets. Suddenly, one of our security guys came and told us that the police were outside, preventing people from entering. With Wayne in the lead, we ran down to the front gate. There, a police inspector and about 40 policemen were standing in front of the crowd, blocking the entrance to the venue. I took a step backwards as Wayne went into action.

He walked straight up to the inspector and thrust the moody lease into his hands. Then, in a clear, calm voice, he said to the officers, 'This is privately owned land, and I must ask you to take a few steps back, please.' With that, he made small shooing movements with his hand. The officers looked around at each other then shuffled back a few paces.

Wayne turned his full attention to the inspector. 'My name is Claud Ferdinand,' he announced in a voice that was loud enough to be heard by everyone in the immediate vicinity. 'I represent Virgin Records, and this is a private launch party to celebrate a forthcoming album by one of our artists. This is a legal event, and I have the documents to prove it.'

The inspector was closely examining the moody lease. He looked up and asked, 'Can you tell me why I wasn't informed about this event?'

'Inspector,' replied Wayne, 'I'm afraid that really isn't my department. Perhaps you would like to contact my head office.' I knew that Wayne carried around contact details of the head offices of all the major record companies. However, that information wouldn't do an enquiring police officer any good at all at 10 p.m. on a Saturday night.

Suddenly, a fire alarm rang inside the building, closely followed by the ringing of a second alarm. 'Just a minute, inspector,' Wayne called out over his shoulder. 'I'll be right back after I've dealt with this alarm.'

I ran back into the building with Wayne, rounding up people as I went. By then, several more bells were ringing. 'Knock the bells off. Knock the bells off,' I shouted and, grabbing a nearby hammer, ran up to the nearest alarm bell and knocked it from the wall. All over the building, our staff were doing likewise. It took all of 20 minutes, but the final bell at last fell silent.

Wayne and I returned to the front entrance and the inspector. Wayne apologised to him, explaining that he had a large bunch of keys to various parts of the building and that it had taken him a while to find the key to the alarm.

'OK, but how do you intend to control all these people?' the police inspector asked.

'I have a fully trained staff of 45 security men,' Wayne replied. 'They will be able to handle anything that might occur.' The inspector looked impressed. Now smiling, he handed the lease back to Wayne, saying, 'Well, if you do have any problems, please don't hesitate to give me a call.'

As if by magic, Wayne produced a pen, handed the lease back to the inspector and asked him to write his name and contact details on the back of it. We now had a moody lease countersigned by a proper police inspector.

Two hours later, we had over 4,000 people in the building, with another 700 out in the yard. The place was rocking, and everybody was having a good time. I was in our command centre counting the money with Tony and Wayne when a clearly distressed member of our staff ran in. 'Someone's died downstairs. Someone's died downstairs,' he was shouting. Wayne and I were already up out of our seats and running. We followed him down to the main room and over to one corner. A small crowd had gathered around a young guy lying prone on the floor. We pushed through.

Wayne knelt beside the guy and felt for a pulse. 'He's breathing,' he said, slapping the guy several times across the face. The guy spluttered and came round.

'Who are you with?' demanded Wayne. The guy pointed to a group of about ten people standing nearby. 'Come on, you lot,' Wayne said to them. He then took the guy by the arm and led them all over to the door. He gave them back their entrance money and told them to leave.

'Fucking liberty,' he said to me as we returned to the office. 'How dare anyone die at a Genesis event.'

By then, Genesis was famous – or perhaps infamous – throughout the UK entertainment industry. No other promoters would even consider staging an event on the same day as one of ours. From the feedback we were getting from our customers, most of the people who came to our parties had never experienced anything like them before. And once they took part for the first time, they were instantly hooked.

For this unique type of entertainment, London was the centre of the universe. There had been various young people's cults before, but none, we would argue, with the power to change society that our acid-house phenomenon had. There had been the punks, mods, rockers, hippies, skinheads, new romantics, teddy boys and casuals. Between them they had popped pills ranging from Blues, Dexies, Valium and Black Bombers to Mogadon and many others. However, these pills never broke down barriers between people or pulled them together. If anything, they drew people into ever smaller, more insular groups, further fragmenting an already schizophrenic youth culture.

For a while, it did look like LSD could change the world. The hippies preached peace and love, but it had no staying power and soon petered out. Acid aficionados were into tuning in and dropping out; they didn't engage with mainstream youth culture.

However, Ecstasy and acid house united black, white, yellow and brown as one. At every one of our parties, there were people of every race, religion and creed holding hands and giving love and respect to each other. And therein lay the threat to those shadowy people who run our society from behind the scenes. Perhaps we were naive and should have seen it coming, but these people didn't want a united group of young people who might make a unified stand against collective oppression. Fragmented and at each other's throats, young people would never throw off the yoke of their oppression. Youth crime and social disorder – and the fear of it – would enable the powers that be to impose ever more restrictive legislation curbing individual freedom and social justice. For them, the acid-house movement, fuelled by Ecstasy, was a thoroughly subversive movement that threatened their control. With the benefit of hindsight, it made sense that they would stamp it out.

For the time being, though, it was our moment, and we were enjoying every minute of it. As we went into our latest Genesis gig, we thought we had the world at our feet. In conjunction with Sunrise, we decided to call the party Hedonism. We had found a disused, clean warehouse on an industrial estate just off the North Circular Road. It would be easy for people to find, and the mass of cars wouldn't jam such a big road, thus attracting the police.

Early on the Saturday evening, we drove into the industrial estate with our small convoy of equipment vehicles. We had managed to locate all the nightwatchmen's offices the previous week and drove by a circuitous route to avoid them. As the lead vehicle pulled up outside the warehouse gates, I jumped out with a big pair of bolt croppers and cut the padlock securing the chain. Our vehicles drove in quickly, and I shut the gate again, securing it with our own padlock. Then I shinned up the gate to join the rest inside. We were in.

Everyone knew their various roles by heart, and we quickly went about setting up the gig. Right in the middle of the floor of the main room was a large pile of new cardboard boxes. Inside, we found hundreds and hundreds of smart handbags. These would have been worth thousands of pounds, but we were music promoters, not thieves. We found a room high up in the building and stacked them safely out of the way.

The venue was on two floors. Inside a couple of hours, we transformed the place into one of our usual dreamscapes. When we ran out of backdrop, we spray-painted the windows black to stop the early morning light from ruining the ambience. We installed two separate 10K sound systems, one upstairs one downstairs, together with two different lighting rigs and DJ consoles with double decks.

The building's reception area was ideal for the entrance to the party. We turned the warehouse office into our command centre and lined up the phones and walkie-talkies on the table. We were ready to start.

Almost immediately, the phones started to ring. People were asking if the gig was on and how they could get to it. Our meeting point for the night was located about five miles away. Our man on the ground phoned to say that there were already about 2,000 people waiting for directions. We told him to send them on to us.

Within minutes, hundreds of cars were pulling up in the streets around the venue. With the security staff helping, we got people into the venue as quickly as we could. Very soon, we had a crowd numbering several hundred inside. We then got a call from our man at the meeting point that the police were following the convoy of cars. We were then told that they had blocked off the roads to the entrance of the industrial estate and were preventing cars from driving in. The North Circular was now at a complete standstill in both directions.

With Wayne in the lead, I followed him to the entrance to the estate. Four police vans and two police cars were blocking the road. Round them swarmed perhaps 50 policemen. Wayne walked right up to the nearest officer and in a loud voice shouted, 'What on earth do you think you're doing?'

The officer turned round, and Wayne was immediately surrounded by dozens of policemen. 'Are you the person in charge of this?' demanded the officer.

'My name is Michael Mifsud, and I am George Michael's personal manager,' said Wayne confidently, not in the least intimidated by the police show of force. 'I strongly suggest that you remove your vehicles at once, otherwise I shall be forced to phone my lawyer.'

'I'd advise you to calm down, sir,' said the officer, 'otherwise I shall be forced to arrest you.'

'Arrest me, arrest me,' Wayne replied. 'Do you think I'm stupid? I have every right to be on this property and have the written permission of the owner. If you cannot authorise the dispersing of this roadblock, you had better get in touch with someone who can. And let me inform you that every minute you waste in contacting whoever you need to speak to will be added to my account of events and handed to our legal department.' With that, Wayne thrust the moody lease into the officer's hands. As other officers gathered around, he examined it carefully.

Wayne walked a few steps away and got on his radio. He told the crew to send the waiting cars to the back of the estate to park there. Then they could walk to the venue. Meanwhile, other partygoers streamed past on foot.

Wayne walked back to the group of policemen. 'I have just spoken to my superior officer, and he is on the way,' said the policeman who Wayne had first spoken to. Wayne walked back to join me and wait.

Not long afterwards, about half a dozen more police vehicles raced up, and a small army of policemen jumped out. At their head was a flat-capped senior officer. He hurried over as Wayne walked to meet him. 'I have been informed about what you said earlier to my officers, and I can't say that I'm happy with what is going on here,' said the senior officer with absolutely no preliminaries.

'No, no, no,' interjected Wayne. 'Let me inform you, sir, that it is I who am not at all happy with events. I am George Michael's personal manager. This private party is being held to launch a new single, accompanied by a video, which will be in the shops next month. We have erected giant screens inside which will exclusively show the video to senior members of the entertainment industry.'

'Yes, but do you have any proof of your status?'

Wayne took a deep breath as if his exasperation was about to boil over. 'Sir, I really don't have time for this. I am working to a schedule and am now behind. If you choose not to believe me, then that is up to you. Very important people are due to arrive very shortly. There are ten major stars inside right now, including George Michael and Elton John. If you would like to come with me alone, I will take you to them. But I should warn you that George won't be very happy that you are obstructing his guests from arriving.' With that, Wayne showed him a moody guest list with the names of several stars crossed off as if they had already arrived. The officer examined it closely.

'The point is, officer,' Wayne seamlessly continued, 'that I don't doubt that you have a job to do. Nor do I doubt that usually you do it correctly. But in this instance your roadblock is turning our most important guests away. So, could you kindly remove it?'

The officer stood for a moment, obviously thinking hard. Coming to a decision, he said, 'OK, I'm satisfied that this is a private event. In future, if you wish to stage such an event in my area, you must arrange it with my station beforehand. Do we understand one another?'

'Loud and clear,' Wayne said. 'Loud and clear. Now would you kindly remove your roadblock.'

Shouting out orders, the officer got most of his men back into their vehicles, and they drove off. Several were left behind to sort out the traffic chaos. Just as Wayne was about to join me, a policeman came up and asked if Wayne wanted him to direct the traffic to the venue. 'That's very good of you, officer,' said Wayne. 'By the way, is there anyone on our guest list that you would like to meet?' He held out the list for the officer to look at. 'Unfortunately, George and Elton are having a small party inside and don't want to be disturbed. However, how about her?' Wayne pointed to Mandy Smith's name. 'Perhaps I could get her to give you an autograph.'

'That would be very good of you, sir. Thank you,' said the officer, smiling broadly. With that, Wayne came across to join me.

'Amazing. Fucking amazing, mate,' I said, shaking my head in wonder. 'That was a world-class blag. Never seen anything like it. You should stand for parliament, you know.'

Wayne laughed. 'Yeah, for a moment there I thought I was losing it. It could still go wrong, so it's best that I stay here and keep Old Bill sweet. You go back to the party.'

As I returned to the entrance, one of the security guys rushed up. He was one of our ex-military boys and not easily flustered, but I could tell that he was put out.

'Andy,' he began, 'there's a guy just walked into reception

saying that this is his venue because he saw it first. He's got flyers printed with the warehouse address on. I don't know who he is. He just looks like an ordinary guy, wearing a raincoat, with a pit bull on a lead. He's got his hand in his pocket, so I don't know if he's got a gun. He's got some balls, though. To walk up to ten of us like that and demand money.'

'I don't see how one guy can be much of a problem,' I answered.

'I'm not saying we can't handle it,' replied the security guy, 'but our crew know people, and we think he could come back and shoot one of us. Therefore, if we've got to deal with him, we should take him away and serve him up proper.'

Suddenly, the situation seemed very funny. I had just watched Wayne see off a police inspector and scores of police officers. Now our heavy-duty team of ex-mercenaries were worrying about one guy. 'What about the dog?' I asked with a concerned look on my face. 'Look, I'm a bit of an animal lover. I couldn't agree to you harming the dog.'

The security guy looked at me in amazement. He obviously didn't have much of a sense of humour and couldn't see that I was joking. 'Look, here's 500 quid,' I said, handing him the money. 'Ask him if he will accept this as compensation. If so, let that be the end of it.' He walked back inside, and I watched as he gave the guy the money. The bloke and his dog then promptly left.

About an hour later, Wayne returned to the party, wet, frozen and stone-cold sober. Muttering something about 'services above and beyond the call of duty', he plunged into the frantic mass of bodies to get back the party buzz. On cue, the DJ played Frankie Knuckles' 'Tears' and the ravers sang along: 'When the curtain comes down and the circus is through, no one is left here but me, you and all my tears. So many tears, my tears.'

They were still going strong at 10 a.m., but enough was enough. We turned the music off and, after quite a bit of persuasion, managed to get rid of the last of the stragglers. Then I sent all the staff home.

I had arranged for a couple of guys to come and keep an eye on all of the equipment. They were late in arriving, so I sat down to wait for them. By that point, Wayne had changed out of the clothes that had got wet whilst he had been negotiating with the police. Wearing big Timberland boots, a padded jacket and baseball cap, he came and sat next to me.

Suddenly, we heard an engine over-revving. A police van screeched to a halt, closely followed by a police car, and several officers jumped out. Two of them grabbed my arms and told me that I was under arrest. As I was dragged to the van, I saw the same thing happening to Wayne. We had all rehearsed what we would say under such circumstances. When I was asked who I was, I told them I was just a rigger, waiting for a van to arrive to take all the equipment away.

I then asked what I was being arrested for. 'Breaking and entering will do for a start,' said an officer. 'But by the time we get you to the station, we'll have thought up a few more charges.' He carried on, saying that all the equipment was being impounded and that it would only be returned to us if we could produce valid receipts for it.

At the station, we were put in separate cells and left to wait. It was ten hours later that they came for us, and we were taken into the charge room. An officer said that we were being released without charge but that the boss wanted to talk to us first.

'The boss' duly appeared, and it was the very officer who Wayne had conned the night before. 'Don't I know you?' the officer asked Wayne.

'Who me?' he replied, the collar of his jacket turned up and his cap pulled down firmly around his ears. 'I don't fink so, mate. I'm not from around 'ere.' His voice was now pure cockney.

'Well, you and your mate both listen,' continued the senior officer. 'You tell the organisers when you see them next that we are on full alert at this station now, and if they return to any industrial estates on my manor again, they will be met by the riot squad. Do I make myself clear?'

We both assured him that he did and were allowed to go. Thus ended another successful Genesis–Sunrise joint promotion, but it was to be the last one. We were still good friends, but our followings had grown too big. We could both fill large warehouses on our own, so we didn't need each other. In future, we would go our separate ways.

Four

From Genesis to Revelation

OUR FIRST priority was to find a new venue. Further, as the police were becoming wise to our phoney leases and other documents, we had to change our strategy. Keith, Wayne and I decided that in future we would have two suitable venues available. Then, if the police raided one, we could quickly move to the other. We would need to have two lots of equipment to run both sites and two teams to set each up, but that was just a question of logistics. It was worth the double cost just to have an emergency plan in place to reassure us.

Within a week, we had found two potential venues quite close together. The back-up venue could only hold about 2,000 people, was difficult to get to and our customers' cars would cause chaos in the surrounding area. However, our main venue seemed perfect. It stood off an A road and backed onto a river. It was surrounded by a massive yard that could hold over 100 cars. We climbed into the yard and peered through the windows. The building was the size of six football pitches, with a lofty ceiling allowing for a great lighting effects show. It was both spacious and clean, with no large machinery to get in the way.

'Excuse me, can I help you?' The voice surprised us. We turned to see a bearded face peering at us over the top of the wall. Sheepishly, we climbed back out of the yard.

The guy was middle-aged and looked like a 1960s hippie. Long, lank hair complemented a scruffy goatee beard that hung down over a multicoloured bead necklace. In one hand, he held what was clearly recognisable as a joint. It was an encouraging sign.

'Look, I want to be frank with you,' said Wayne in his best voice. 'We organise dance parties, and we're interested in this venue. I wonder if you know who owns it?'

The hippie guy scratched his beard. 'Sorry, I don't think I can help you there,' he replied, 'but there's a watchman in an old caravan just down the road, and he might know.'

We followed him to an ancient, scruffy caravan and a similarly ancient and scruffy watchman emerged. He too confessed that he didn't know who owned it but that it had been empty for over a year and no one had ever gone in or out. This sounded like very good news to us.

'In that case, would our party annoy anyone?' Wayne asked.

'There's only the people on the houseboats live here,' answered the hippie. 'Come on. Let me show you.'

With that, he led us through a narrow passage and onto an equally narrow towpath. There, bobbing at anchorage in the river, were nine houseboats. Beckoning us to follow him, he entered the nearest houseboat.

Inside, it was small but clean and nicely furnished with large scatter cushions all over a polished floor. On a table in the centre of the room was a large 'bong' pipe. He introduced us to his wife, also middle-aged and hippie-looking.

Wayne always carried a variety of drugs with him. He pulled out a block of hash and passed it to the hippie, who by now had introduced himself as Martin. I watched as Wayne, Keith, Martin and his wife all took hits from the bong. Negotiations began.

The upshot was that there were nine houseboat families who would be affected by all the noise and chaos. Wayne arranged that we would give each family £200 to go away for the weekend. We would pay a deposit of £500 immediately and come back with the rest of the money in a couple of days. We had our new venue.

Five thousand flyers were printed, and we decided to record a forty-second radio commercial on one of the pirate radio stations. Wayne read our handwritten script on air like a professional, using 'Pacific State' as a soundtrack. The guy in the recording studio was so impressed that he offered Wayne work reading radio commercials. Now he had a nice little sideline if he ever needed it.

At 5 p.m. on party night, we drove our vans full of equipment to the venue. Once inside, we began setting up. It was then that we realised that we hadn't checked the electricity supply in advance. To our dismay, the circuit box and all the fuses had been smashed to pieces. We sent out an emergency call to our electrician.

Because the building was so perfect for it, we had hired in state-of-the-art lasers. We would be the first to use them at a warehouse party, and the effects would be amazing in such a massive space. However, our electrician arrived and told us that the damage to the fuse box was so bad that he would have to go and get some spare parts from a mate on the other side of London. We told him to be as quick as he could and continued to prepare the venue.

We didn't have a ladder high enough to reach the ceiling, so we fixed our lights, netting and props to the walls. We had just finished our personal version of *The Twilight Zone* when our electrician returned. Within ten minutes, we had power. We plugged the lasers in, and their green and blue beams lanced into the darkness, scrawling weird and wonderful patterns over everything they touched.

Suddenly, Wayne's phone rang. It was the watchman in the scruffy caravan. We had paid him to warn us if the authorities showed up. He was calling to tell us that two police cars were heading our way.

'Listen up, listen up, everybody,' shouted Wayne. 'The police are on their way. Our story is that this is a film shoot for TV. Don't answer any questions. Just send them over to me, and I'll deal with it.' With that, he walked to the front of the building and lifted some shutters. Three policemen were standing there.

They all looked past Wayne at the laser show and gaped. 'What an amazing effect,' said one of the officers, positioning himself so that he could get a better view. 'Who are you? Who's in charge?' he added, almost as an afterthought.

'Hi, I'm Wayne Anthony.' He was in posh mode again. 'I'm from Channel Four Films, and it's my responsibility to manage and maintain this site. My boss is Janet Street-Porter, head of youth programming.'

'Oh, I've heard of her,' said the officer, 'but where's the cameras?'

'The camera and production team will be arriving within the next couple of hours. For the moment, the lighting and sound technicians are setting up,' explained Wayne.

'OK,' responded the officer. 'Our chief will be here very shortly. Just tell him what you've told us, and I'm sure everything will be OK.' They stood looking at the laser show as we continued to work.

About 20 minutes passed, and several cars with flashing blue lights pulled up. Ten more policemen, led by a flat-capped officer, marched into the building. He went straight up to Wayne and demanded, 'Who are you and what are you doing in this building?' Wayne repeated the story he had told the first three officers. 'And do you have any paperwork to that effect?' continued the flat-cap.

'I have a copy of the lease, but the production contracts are at the office,' Wayne replied.

The officer looked thoughtful for a moment. 'Look, would you mind stepping outside with me, please.'

'What's the problem, officer?' Wayne said. 'I really don't have time for this, and you're standing on private property.'

'You're not under arrest, sir,' said the officer firmly, 'but I would like to talk to you in private and not in front of your whole crew.'

Wayne followed him outside as I peered through the window. There were about 400 waiting ravers lined up quietly against the wall of the yard.

'Look, I know what your game is,' said the officer aggressively. 'You're not Wayne Anthony, and you're not from Channel Four.'

'My name is Wayne Anthony, so please don't try those intimidation tactics with me,' Wayne replied, rising to the challenge. 'Now either leave the premises or I will put it in the hands of Channel Four's lawyers.'

'Can anyone here confirm who you are?' demanded the officer.

Wayne looked around him and over at the queue. He must have recognised someone, because he called a young guy over. 'Hey, Crimble, tell this policeman who I am, will you.'

'Look, I don't want to get involved,' said the young guy, a worried look on his face.

'Don't worry about dropping me in it,' Wayne reassured him. 'If someone doesn't identify me to this officer, they're going to stop the party.'

The young guy looked quickly at the officer. 'His name is Wayne, Wayne Anthony, I think. Can I go now?' With that, he hurried away.

'OK, Mr Wayne Anthony, how many people do you expect here tonight?' asked the officer.

'About 800 extras and 100 crew,' replied Wayne.

'Well, you listen to me. I will be returning here at 11 p.m. with a full riot squad, and if I find that there are more than 1,000 people here, or that you have told me any untruths, I will make sure you get a prison sentence.' He and his men then left.

We started the party and got people in as quickly as we could. Soon, there were over 3,000 people partying to the music. The dancing was wild, and chants of 'Aceed, aceed' rang throughout the venue.

Now that everything was running smoothly and the warehouse

was filling up nicely, Wayne and I went up to the office where Keith was counting the money. There was already about 60 grand, counted in bundles and stuffed in plastic bin liners. The office overlooked the yard. Suddenly, ten police vehicles raced up and disgorged about sixty policemen in full riot gear. The flat-cap was in the lead. Blissfully oblivious, 3,000 party animals were going for it inside the venue. For us, though, it looked like it was time to leave.

We grabbed the bin bags of money and ran out of the office. But the police had the place surrounded. There was nowhere to run to. I called our security on the radio and told them to get as close to the police as they could and leave the channel open. I wanted to try to hear what was being said.

The police rushed into the reception area and confronted our security team. 'Where's Wayne Anthony?' shouted the flat-cap. 'I want Wayne Anthony.'

One of our security guys said that Wayne had left the building and would be back shortly. 'Right, turn the music off,' demanded the officer.

'Sorry, mate. That's the sound crew's job,' replied the security guy.

'Well, take me to the DJ console, then,' insisted the officer.

He was led into the heaving mass of bodies and fought his way over to the DJ booth. We watched as he shouted to the DJs and sound technicians to turn the music off. They had already been told what to say. They explained that only Wayne could authorise that and that they would have to wait until he got back. By then, about 50 policemen in riot gear had joined the senior officer around the DJ console. Suddenly, the music went off.

Immediately, the assembled multitude began chanting 'Party, party, party' at the tops of their voices. At the same time, they stamped their feet. The noise was awesome. Looking suitably intimidated by this show of resistance by 3,000 people, the police huddled closer together. This gave me an idea.

I ran to the back of the DJ console and climbed up. Switching the mike back on, I shouted, 'Freedom to party. Genesis 1989.' The place erupted. Thousands of people were jumping up and down, waving their arms in the air. Fearful now of provoking a major riot, the police retreated to the reception area. The flat-cap told our security team that they were holding Wayne Anthony personally responsible for any trouble. With that, they all beat a hasty retreat.

The DJ played 'Musical Freedom' by Adeva, and the party kicked off again. Ecstatic at winning the day, I returned to the office with Wayne and Keith, taking the money with us. We counted another 30 grand of bar takings and added it to the money in the bin liners.

There was a knock at the door, and we all looked up. Our entire ex-military security team entered the room. 'Look,' said the self-appointed leader. 'We want to change the terms of our contract. There's another team in town. We were in the Falklands with them, but they were the top unit in the force, a tough bunch of lads. They've heard about all the money in warehouse parties and have been asking a lot of questions about us. We think they're going to make a move against us. We'll stand our ground but not for a hundred quid a night. Give us 25 per cent of the door takings, and we won't mind risking our lives.'

'Sounds like you're scared of them,' I replied.

'We're not frightened,' replied the spokesman, 'but if we come up against them, it will be a bloody war. For that, we want to be sure that we're earning good money.'

'What if we say no?' Keith asked.

'Then we'll walk out right now, taking 25 per cent of tonight's takings.'

We had a quick whispered discussion among the three of us. The feeling was that if this lot walked out, another heavy mob would come along who might want to take more. We hated having to work with violent people. Their dark aura tarnished the bright and colourful one generated by our partygoers. It also worked directly against the good vibe we were trying to promote in the wider society. But what could we do? If we were going to stay in the business, we would need them.

We told them that we would give them their pay rise but that we still ran the show and their sole responsibility was security. Whatever they had to do, we didn't want to hear about it.

For two days, I had been trying to get hold of both Wayne and Keith, but their phones rang without being answered. I called all their mates, and they hadn't heard from or seen them either. I went to the flat they sometimes shared, and no one came to the door when I knocked. I was becoming seriously worried when at last my phone rang. It was Wayne.

He sounded in a bad way and wouldn't answer my questions. He just said that it was very important that I meet him and Keith in a pub off Stoke Newington High Street. I drove there right away and found them both sitting in a dark corner.

I sat down with them and was about to ask what was going on when I stopped abruptly. They were both in a terrible state. They had heavy bruising around their eyes, their lips were split and there was dried blood in their nostrils. 'What the fuck happened to you?' I asked, shocked. They told me an amazing story.

Two days previously, the door of their flat had been kicked in and several men had run in and seized them as they lay in their beds. They had been kicked, beaten and threatened with knives. The leader of the group had introduced himself as Sergeant Perry. He had said that he knew all about the ex-military guys who were presently doing our security, referring to them as a bunch of tossers. He had also said that he and his crew were now taking over the security role from them and that they wanted 50 per cent of our takings.

Every time Wayne or Keith had tried to speak, the sergeant's comrades had showered them with more kicks and punches. Finally, Wayne had been ordered to give the sergeant a contact number for our security crew and the security code we used. Wayne had given him a number and said that the codeword was 'Acid Teds'.

Using Wayne's phone, the sergeant had rung the number. Someone had obviously answered, because the sergeant said, 'Acid Teds,' laughed loudly and rang off.

A minute later, Wayne's phone had rung, and Sergeant Perry answered it. It must have been our security crew, because Perry called them a bunch of tossers and told them that he and his crew were now taking over.

Keith and Wayne had then been gagged and blindfolded and told that if they made any noise, they would have their throats cut. They had then been carried downstairs and bundled into the back of a van. There had been a 15-minute drive before they had been dragged out into dense woodland. Still gagged and blindfolded, they had then been tied to trees. The sergeant had warned them that he would be in touch and had then left them there.

He must have called our security team and given them directions, because within half an hour they had found and untied them. Wayne said that our security team looked really worried, especially when they saw the sorry state that he and Keith were in. They had confessed that they knew this Sergeant Perry and his crew, saying that most of them were ex-Special Forces and a law unto themselves. They had concluded by saying that they didn't want to go up against them and wouldn't be doing our security any more.

If Keith and Wayne hadn't been sitting in front of me in such a terrible state, I wouldn't have believed them. Their serious injuries spoke for themselves, though. We discussed what we could do. Ever the pragmatist, Keith said that we would still be cutting up about forty grand per gig between the three of us after paying this crew 50 per cent. Then he added ruefully that this time we really would have the strongest door firm in the country.

I suggested that it was perhaps a scam between the two groups of soldiers to increase their share of the take to 50 per cent and to get their mates involved. But even if that was the case, there was very little we could do about it. We all agreed that we didn't have much choice and that unless we wanted our dream to end right then we would have to accept the situation.

A few days later, Perry rang Wayne again. He and Keith then set off for a rendezvous somewhere in the countryside. It was thought best that I should stay in the background for the moment. They were driven to a barn where Sergeant Perry was waiting for them with about 12 others. Several automatic weapons were piled up on a table in front of them. He introduced them to his 'unit' and said that we didn't have any more security worries. They were a professional outfit and a productive crew. Wayne insisted that he didn't want any weapons brought into the parties, and the sergeant agreed. It had been a shotgun marriage, but we were now firmly wedded to our new security team.

Despite all the upheaval, we went ahead with our next party. We found a warehouse that could hold 8,000 people on a big industrial estate in north London. The electricity wasn't connected, so our electrician ran a lead from a lamp post. Our crew started to set the place up as Perry and his men busied about, familiarising themselves with the layout so that they were prepared for any potential security problems. All you could hear on the security channel was 'foxtrot this' and 'foxtrot that', always followed by either 'over' or 'over and out'. They definitely seemed to know what they were doing.

However, we didn't have a good feeling about that particular event and feared that the police would come down on us hard. For that reason, we got our back-up team to fully prepare an alternative venue.

Suddenly, one of our security crew came on the radio, saying that there were about a thousand people at the meeting point but that the police had arrived and had arrested our helpers who were giving out little maps. He asked me what he should do. I told him to send the people along to the venue.

As we were waiting for them to arrive, several police vans screeched to a halt outside the warehouse. About 50 riot police in padded uniforms stormed into the venue. But they were too late for Wayne, Keith and me. We had jumped over the back wall, walked round the front and joined the punters waiting to get in. Meanwhile, the police were telling our workers to pack up everything and go home.

We called our back-up crew and told them to expect us. Then we drove to the other venue as fast as we could, with a couple of hundred punters following us. A crowd quickly gathered in the yard outside the new building, and we rushed inside to start the party as soon as possible. Within 20 minutes, Perry and his crew had arrived with all our kit from the command centre. We set up and were ready to start.

But the riot squad hadn't finished with us. Suddenly, their vans roared up the street and pulled up outside the yard. Scores of riot police jumped out. By that point, we were thoroughly fed up by the turn of events and were tired of being pushed around. We decided to make a stand. I boosted Wayne up on top of a parked car, and he called to the waiting crowd for their attention. 'There's a squad of riot police outside,' he shouted at the top of his voice, 'and the only way we can win is to make them think there are thousands of us in here, so please make as much noise as you can.'

The effect was electric. People jumped on the roofs of their cars, screaming 'Aceed aceed' and waving their arms about. All around them, others did likewise. The din was incredible. You would never have thought that there were only a couple of hundred of them.

A policeman's head appeared over the top of the locked gates. He jumped over and slid back the bolts that held them closed. They swung open to reveal the serried ranks of riot police as they marched through the gates. It was a sight to give anyone pause, and everyone went quiet. There must have been 100 or so policemen. They began to shout some sort of war cry and beat at their shields with their riot sticks as they inched forward.

The noise must have alerted the partygoers who were already inside. Several hundred now poured out into the yard. The police were outnumbered by about five to one. Their cries rang out louder, and there were shouts to 'stand firm'. These were now countered by opposing shouts of 'Aceed, aceed'. The noise was awesome.

Emboldened by their increase in numbers, the partygoers now pushed forwards. To shouts from a flat-cap, who must have been in charge of the riot squad, the police backed up. They continued to back up until they were outside the yard. At that point, someone ran over and shut the gates again.

We later heard that the police then went on to raid The Tunnel Club, a small venue ten minutes away. No doubt they felt that they should have at least one victory that night. We were beyond caring. We partied on until dawn.

Although we had just enjoyed a victory over the police, defeats were also coming thick and fast. We found a big venue that would hold 10,000 people under the flyover near the Westway, but the police were on to us before we could even get set up. Part of the problem was that they were now wise to being fooled, especially by the likes of Wayne. A detailed description of him had been circulated, and for him to put his face up front was to invite his being arrested.

We found an estate agent in north London who we bribed to give us the keys to a large warehouse his company had just leased. On the evening of the gig, we let ourselves in and began to set up. Suddenly, the owner appeared, accompanied by a policeman. He told us that we were on his property and asked us what we were doing. I wasn't in Wayne's class when it came to blagging someone, but I wasn't short of front. 'I'm afraid there must be some kind of mistake,' I began. 'My father is in the process of leasing this property, and me and some of my friends have come along to help clean the place up.'

'Ah,' replied the owner. 'You must be Mr Munroe's son.'

'That's correct,' I said, stepping forward and sticking out my hand. 'Do you know my father?'

'No, I haven't had the pleasure,' continued the owner, 'but we have talked on the phone. The problem is that you have set off the silent alarm.'

I apologised and asked him if he could give me the code to prevent any further false alarms. The owner obliged, and off he walked with the policeman.

That was blag number one out of the way, but the most important blag would be dealing with the police when we started the party. It wasn't long in coming.

Everything was set up and 1,000 people were waiting at the meeting point. Wayne had just told our man to send all the waiting clubbers on to the venue when the police arrived in force. They confronted our security crew, who called for Wayne on the radio.

Reluctantly, Wayne approached the inspector. Before he could open his mouth, the inspector said, 'You're under arrest,' handcuffed him and led him over to a patrol car. The security crew and I surrounded the car, and I told the inspector that he was arresting the only person who had the authority to stop the gig.

'If you're messing me around, I'll arrest everyone in this building,' the inspector threatened. He had called our bluff. We didn't have enough partygoers on site to allow for a confrontation, and if we didn't stop the gig right then, Wayne, and possibly others, would be arrested and taken to the police station. We called off the gig.

Fast on the back of this losing confrontation with the police came another similar shock to the system. Sherry was a pretty young blonde girl who was friends with everyone in our circle. She just loved to party and was forever in our company. She lived in a top-floor flat of a council-estate tower just off the Roman Road, not far from City Airport. Because the flat was centrally located and we were always up there, we asked her to store some of our equipment in the spare bedroom.

On this particular occasion, we were gearing up for a party later that evening. This involved not only testing out the sound system and strobe lights but also getting off our faces on whatever were our individual preferences. As the music boomed and the strobe light bathed the flat in a bright red hue, hash pipes, coke wraps and sundry pills littered every available surface.

Suddenly, there was a thunderous banging at the door. As we turned the music down, we could hear shouts of 'Police, police, open up.' The transition from laid-back to panic-stricken was instantaneous. People raced about the flat throwing hash pipes out of windows and flushing wraps and pills down the toilet. We all crowded into the hallway as Sherry opened the door.

'Turn that fucking red light off,' yelled the first officer as he forced his way into the flat. It seemed that the flashing red strobe had nearly caused a catastrophe at nearby City Airport. A plane had taken it as a warning and had nearly aborted its landing.

Humbly assuring the officer we wouldn't do such a thing again, we showed him out. Then we sat down and collectively rued all the perfectly good drugs we had destroyed.

Five

The Day the Music Died

BY THEN, it wasn't only the police who knew about Wayne's involvement in organising the gigs, as we had already found from the kidnapping incident with the ex-soldiers. The so-called underworld had heard of him, too.

Wayne had just come out of his flat one day when a car pulled up and a tall guy got out. He was known to us from off the manor and was said to be a bit of a nutter. He relished his nickname of 'Razor', and there were apocryphal tales of his slashing people with sharp instruments.

'Step into the car, mate,' said Razor, his right hand menacingly concealed in his pocket. 'There's someone wants to meet you.'

'But I haven't done anything,' pleaded Wayne. It was one thing trying to blag the police – you could only be arrested. It was another thing entirely trying to blag a dangerous psycho – you could get your face slashed.

'Get in the car before I fucking cut you,' growled Razor, bringing the conversation to a premature end.

They drove to a steakhouse in Mile End. Wayne was led inside and down into the basement, which was a large room that served as a gambling club. Hard-faced men sat around several tables playing various games. A swarthy, tough-looking guy in his early 40s came forward to meet Wayne. 'My name's Nick,' he began. 'I'm originally from Cyprus. Here are some of my brothers and relatives.' He waved his hand to indicate the 20 or so men who were standing or sitting around the large room.

His manner was pleasant enough, but the circumstances were menacing in the extreme. 'What have I done?' asked Wayne.

'You haven't done anything, my son,' Nick reassured him, 'but I think you've got a problem that I can sort out for you. I know you run the dance parties. You are using some ex-soldiers from out of town as security. Did they force you into using their team?'

'Look, I don't want to cause any trouble. These guys won't just walk away, and my family and I will be right in the middle,' Wayne said.

'There won't be any trouble,' replied Nick. 'You just call them up and tell them to come here right now.' He pointed to Wayne's phone, and Wayne made the call. He told Perry where he was and what had happened, then sat back to wait.

'Look,' said Nick, 'this bunch of poofs won't be able to protect you properly. I don't care if they are SAS – we're not in the bush now. It's only a matter of time before some London firm moves in on you anyway. You'd do far better to let me look after you.'

Thirty minutes had passed when a guy came up to Nick and informed him that the soldiers were outside. He was told to bring them in. As the team entered, all Nick's people stood up and gathered around behind him. The two groups stood there, confronting each other.

'My name's Nick. These are my brothers Andy, Chris, Luca and some of our friends. Being country boys, I doubt that you've heard of us.' The rhetorical question hung in the air. 'Wayne has told me that you're taking protection money from him and now he wants to change teams.'

'Why don't we ask him about that?' said Perry.

Turning to one of his brothers, Nick said, 'Andy, get me a bottle of milk.' The guy walked to the bar, got a bottle of milk from a fridge and handed it to Nick, who turned to face Perry. 'Don't you give me orders, soldier boy,' he said, threateningly. 'You're only a bunch of fucking pussies. Here, have a drink on me.' With that, he smashed the bottle to the floor.

Everyone in the room stiffened. Hands tightened on concealed weapons. The tension was palpable. 'Pah,' shouted Nick. 'Get out of here you fucking bumpkins and don't let me see you again. Don't worry about Wayne. We'll drop him home.'

'I think it's best that we take Wayne with us,' said Perry.

Nick grabbed a pint glass from a table and threw it at Perry. He ducked, and it smashed against the wall. 'Now fuck off before we give it to you,' Nick raged.

Perry and his team backed towards the door. 'Give us a call when you get home,' he shouted to Wayne, and then they were gone.

One of Nick's guys dropped Wayne at his flat, and we never heard from him again. It was just another violent and bizarre episode in what was fast becoming a bizarre and violent business. We tried to put it behind us as best we could.

However, not only were the stakes constantly being raised on the security front, the police were also resorting to increasingly confrontational tactics. They had formed the Pay Party Unit specially to deal with us. There was also a media campaign, advertising the message 'Shop a Promoter'. They were talking about us as if we were public enemy number one. Informers were encouraged and rewards were offered. And now their paramilitary Special Patrol Group would descend on us at the first sign of a party.

Barely had we set up one Saturday evening than two Special Patrol Group vans arrived and disgorged their teams of riot police. We had to beat a hasty and undignified retreat as they ran through the venue looking for the organisers. As they spread out through the surrounding buildings, we crawled through bushes until we came to a narrow river.

It was freezing cold, but the police were closing in on us. We were faced with the prospect of arrest and a night in the cells. With no other option, Wayne and I slipped into the icy waters and waded across. Dripping wet and shivering with cold, we made our getaway. Wayne, though, developed pneumonia and had to spend a week in hospital.

It wasn't just the cold bath that concentrated our minds, though. The prospect of continuing failures ruining Genesis's good name loomed large in front of us. Then there was the cost. We were spending, on average, about £25,000 to stage each gig. We were determined that we would pull out all the stops to ensure that our next party went ahead no matter what.

We found a large venue in north London that could easily hold about 5,000 people. We broke in and checked the place out. It was clean and tidy, and the electricity worked just fine. We printed our flyers and announced the party for the coming Saturday.

On the night of the party, we set up without a hitch and were ready to open. We told our man to send the 1,000 or so people who had turned up at the meeting point along to the venue. Our strategy would be to get as many people as possible inside in order to deter the police from violently confronting us. We had about 2,000 people inside with another 1,000 in a queue when the riot squad arrived.

Once again, several Special Patrol Group vans screeched to a halt outside the venue. I remarked to Wayne that they never seemed to arrive anywhere in a normal fashion. Wayne said that it must be part of their training. Whatever the case, the flat-cap in charge, backed up by his cohort of 100 or so stick-wielding riot police, demanded to see whoever was in charge, adding that this was an illegal event and that he was stopping it.

The big doors to the warehouse were open just far enough to get our table across the space and to allow the customers to file in in twos. I ran to the doors and pulled them wide open. Two thousand loved-up clubbers turned to face fewer than one hundred policemen who had anything but love in their hearts at that precise moment.

Seizing the moment, Wayne jumped up on the table and, addressing the clubbers, called for attention. 'Listen up everyone,' he shouted over the hubbub. 'The police are going to try to stop this party. It's a legal venue, and it's up to us. We're the only ones who can stop this from happening.'

'Oi, you, get down from there or you're nicked,' yelled the flat-cap and made to come forward. To the chants of 'Aceed, aceed' from the crowd, Wayne suddenly did a swallow dive into the outstretched arms of the first ranks of the clubbers, and they passed him over their heads to safety. The crowd roared in unison and clapped thunderously.

The temperature outside was sub-zero, and it had started to snow. It wasn't warm by the open doorway of the warehouse, but at least all the bodies so close together generated a degree of heat. Outside, exposed to the elements, the police were literally shivering. As his men silently confronted the clubbers, the flat-cap realised that he was in a no-win situation. He backed his men up, then they got into their vans and drove off.

Apart from the upsurge in police activity, dark clouds were gathering on the wider legal front. A bill had been proposed in parliament to completely outlaw events without a valid entertainment licence. Graham Bright was the MP leading the campaign. He went on record as saying, 'I have not found anyone who is opposed to what I am trying to do, such has been the impact of news stories relating to illegal acid-house parties.' Not one MP opposed the bill.

The promoters of the various acid-house events met regularly on the circuit. We often discussed what we could do to raise the consciousness of the general public and show them that we were not the menace that we were being made out to be. We decided to mount our own campaign.

We got together with Anton of World Dance, Tony of Sunrise, Jarvis of Biology and Jeremy of Energy and formed an organisation called the Association of Dance Party Promoters. We circulated the word amongst clubbers, other illegal party promoters, pirate radio stations, recording companies, DJs, magazines, club owners and others sympathetic to our cause. And we went about promoting the event in the same way as we went about promoting our gigs. A record for the campaign was made called 'Freedom to Dance'.

We also set up a rally for 27 January 1990, the venue for which was a byword for democratic movements: Trafalgar Square. A sister rally was scheduled to be held in Manchester at the same time. Under the new legislation, there were tight guidelines regarding the playing of music, but it was intended to be a rally not a party. There would only be speakers, not singers or musicians.

All the leading lights met up at Biology's offices, and we drove to Trafalgar Square in convoy. We arrived at 1 p.m., and the rally was scheduled to start at 2 p.m. We joined about 1,000 people already waiting in the rain. Gathered around them were several hundred police in riot gear. The media had put in a strong appearance, too. There were several TV crews and dozens of photographers.

By 2 p.m., there were in the region of 8,000 young people in attendance, and we decided it was time to begin the proceedings. We climbed onto the first level of Nelson's Column, which put us above the heads of the crowd. A small amplifier was rushed through the crowd, but the police saw it coming. There was a brief melee as they wrested it from the carrier and retreated to their lines.

One after the other, Tony, Jarvis, Anton and a couple of DJs made impromptu speeches to the crowd, who shouted and clapped enthusiastically. The talk was all of civil rights and our entitlement to party.

At one point, a guy appeared with a music centre, put it on one of the raised levels and blasted out house music. That lasted for approximately two minutes, as the riot squad rushed in and seized it. At the same time, there was a movement in the crowd. I saw a group of about 30 young guys running towards the riot policemen who had seized the music centre. From the looks on their faces, I could tell that they had serious violence on their minds. This was completely against the ethos of everything we were fighting for. Ours was a peaceful, live-and-let-live creed. A serious riot in Trafalgar Square would damage our cause irreparably. I jumped down and intercepted the group. A few words of explanation sufficed. They returned to where they had come from.

The crowd sang, chanted and waved makeshift banners. The TV crews zoomed in for close-ups, and the photographers snapped away as if they were possessed. By then, a couple of hours had passed, and we felt that we had made our point. Furthermore, there was a party scheduled for that night, and everyone wanted to go home and get ready. Our rally broke up peacefully.

The following morning, I made a point of buying all the newspapers. I also watched every news programme that I could. In the middle pages of one newspaper there was a small article saying that 500 people had attended the rally. I knew from personal experience that there had been perhaps 8,000 present. I could only reflect that the system controlled the media, which only reported the news that supported the status quo.

If we had thought that our security problems had now sorted themselves out, we were to be disappointed. It seemed that we were such a choice and juicy bone that every dog in the neighbourhood wanted to fight over us. We were approached by a guy who was linked to the ICF. He said that there were some people who wanted to speak to us. I knew many of the ICF, and, in fact, a couple of them were mates of mine. I told my friend Curtis, who was linked to the firm, about the approach, and he agreed to come with me to the meeting.

Of the 20 or so people who were waiting for us, I must have known about half of them. There were some glum looks when I walked in with Curtis. Grudgingly, it was accepted that we should be left alone.

That wasn't the end of the matter, though. Curtis came back a couple of days later and said that the boys didn't have a problem with our doing parties, but what did get right up their noses was that we were employing a bunch of outsiders to do the security. As we were operating right on their manor, it was quite a considerable affront to them. The upshot was that they wanted to meet with us again, together with our security team. If we didn't go, they would turn up at our events and cause trouble.

I walked into the meeting place with our security team right behind me. Curtis was waiting with about 20 guys, many of whom I again knew. The ICF was well represented among them. As I entered, they all stood up. 'I know how this looks, but I don't want any trouble,' I called out. 'You told me to bring these guys, so I've brought them.'

'It's OK, Andy,' said Curtis. 'It's not you we've got the hump with. It's this country bumpkin wankers brigade.' With that, they all pulled out a variety of weapons.

'Just a minute, just a minute,' cried Perry. 'There's no need for this.'

'No?' queried Curtis. 'If you think that we're going to let you fucking farmers waltz into our manor and take money out of our pockets, then you'd better think again. Now either you walk back out that door or we'll do you, and you'll have to fucking crawl out. So what's it going to be?'

'Look,' said Perry. 'None of us have been making any money. Nearly all of the recent parties have been stopped. We've had enough anyway. We've actually lost money over the last month. This will do for us.'

'Good,' replied Curtis. 'Now fuck off, you bunch of pricks. And if we ever see you around here again, we'll do you on sight.' To the accompaniment of cheering and jeering, Perry and his team backed out of the meeting, and we never saw them again.

We sat down and negotiated the new deal. The new crew would get 25 per cent of the takings. I just hoped that they would be strong enough to withstand any further challenges.

Shortly afterwards, members of the ICF proper came to us and said that they had a venue in Canning Town that would hold 3,500 people. We agreed to do a Genesis gig with them, sharing the profits equally between us. The venue was excellent, and we set up with no problems. The ICF were providing their own security, but I felt that we needed some kind of counterbalance. I didn't want Genesis being taken over by anyone. I talked to Curtis, and he brought along a few members of our new team. Many of them were ICF anyway, but in this instance their main loyalty would be to Curtis. The rest, as they say, is history!

The event went off smoothly, everyone enjoyed themselves and we divided up the money. Curtis and the team went away well pleased with how things had gone. We didn't know it at the time, but they now had the taste for this kind of work. They started to call themselves G-Force, and within a few weeks the word got around that they were the door team to have. Soon they were doing the doors at Dungeons, Echoes and even clubs out in Essex, among other places. To the police, it must have looked like this new firm was taking over all the doors in London. It was now no longer about illegal parties; the focus was firmly on dealing in class A drugs and protection rackets. Unfortunately for us, G-Force were seen as the Genesis security team. Therefore, as far as the police were concerned, it was Genesis that was taking over London. This put a price on my, Keith and Wayne's heads.

Absolutely fed up with most of our events being stopped, we now chanced upon a legal venue in Essex. We were put on probation by the owners, who would only agree to let us have the place for an all-day event on a bank holiday weekend. The premises weren't ideal, and we would have problems blacking out the windows to stop the light coming in. However, we felt that this was a valuable opportunity to stage a legal event in legitimate premises.

One of the conditions of hiring the hall was that we also had to hire the venue's twenty-strong security team at a cost of two grand. Nevertheless, we felt that we should have a couple of members of our own security team present, just to be on the safe side. Their job would be to protect us and mind the cash in the security room.

With time before the event short, we rushed to get the flyers out. We took some consolation from the fact that we could print the address of the venue on them. We went about distributing them outside various clubs. I didn't expect an enormous crowd, so we promised that we would let in for free anyone who had a ticket to one of our previous events that had been stopped.

Under no pressure at all, we leisurely set up the equipment on the day of the party. The DJs arrived, we did a soundcheck and declared the venue open. People began to arrive in dribs and drabs, and the venue slowly filled up as the day progressed. However, I could detect a distinct feeling of negativity in the air. Its source was immediately apparent. The venue's own security team were all over 35. In their penguin suits, and with fat guts and fleshy jowls much in evidence, they stood out like the dicks they were. And they all growled aggressively at our customers. Some even walked about pushing them out of their way. For people as sensitive as an E'd up acid-house crowd, this was like a cold shower. I wanted to say something about it, but was on my best behaviour, because we wanted the venue for future events.

However, tensions did rise throughout the day. One of the venue's security guys had taken an instant dislike to Wayne and twice tried to punch him in the face. I fetched the head of their security team. His lack of interest clearly showed where his sympathy lay. I concluded that I couldn't expect a lot of help from him in the event of trouble.

A couple of hours passed, and I was sitting in the command centre with Wayne and Keith. We were counting the takings and bundles of money were on the table. Our three-strong personal security team were sitting about on chairs. Suddenly, the door burst open, and Winston, one of our friends, ran in. Out of breath and clearly afraid, he told us that the venue's entire security team were heading our way, armed to the teeth.

I ran to the door and looked out. Advancing towards us across the main room was a long line of security guys carrying baseball bats, bottles of ammonia, clubs and knives. All the dancers had retreated to the relative safety of the sides of the room, leaving the field clear for battle to commence. By that point, we had also armed ourselves, intent on protecting our lives as much as the money.

All of a sudden, the music dropped in volume and a booming voice came over the microphone and echoed around the room: 'We're the ICF. Kill those fucking cunts.' Wayne, Keith and I stayed to guard our money, as some of east London's finest screamed and ran towards the venue's security team. The latter soon found that standing about looking tough and waving weapons about really didn't cut much ice with our guys. They were used to actual hand-to-hand combat. Weapons were torn from the hands of the enemy and turned upon them. Screams and shouts of fear rang out as the erstwhile bullies realised that they had more than met their match.

Surprisingly, some of the clubbers joined in. One young lad, though, had wandered into the fray quite oblivious to what was going on. He stood there lost and disorientated. Taking this as his cue, one of the venue's security guys walked up behind him and smashed him in the side of the head with a set of brass knuckledusters. The lad went down like a sack and lay there unmoving.

Instantly, a cry went up. Everyone went running towards the security guy. He turned tail and ran towards one of the exits. Someone tripped him as he ran, and he fell heavily. Then the crowd were upon him. He disappeared beneath a mass of flailing arms and legs.

For me, this was the last in a very long line of last straws. My dream of a peaceful movement that would spread throughout society lay in ashes. I was in a very violent business, surrounded by extremely violent people, and the law was firmly set against us. As far as I was concerned, it was the end of the line.

Carrying the money with us, Wayne, Keith and I headed out of a side door and made our way through the car park. As we were leaving, we could see the police arriving in force. They were trying to secure the doors and keep everybody inside. Not surprisingly, this was a fate that most people wanted to avoid. They dodged among cars and ran off into the surrounding streets.

The following day, we heard that someone had died at the venue. The police were treating it as murder, and I could only conclude that the security guy with the brass knuckledusters was the victim. It was nothing to do with me, Wayne or Keith. We had been in the office guarding the money and had seen nothing. However, the police still wanted us to tell them who had been there, something we wished to avoid at all costs. For a few weeks, I stayed with friends, avoiding all my usual haunts.

I guessed that the police would soon figure out that I wasn't involved in the murder and would remove me from their priority list. With Wayne and Keith, I set up a company called London Dance Tickets, selling tickets for World Dance, Biology, Energy and others. We worked from a Portakabin on the front of a used-car lot in Bow Church Lane. But as ill luck would have it, a fellow worker had become a suspect in another unrelated murder. He disappeared, and the police came to the Portakabin looking for him. It was time for an extended holiday abroad until the heat wore off. I packed my bag and left.

Six

No Man is an Island

AFTER THE lunacy of the warehouse-party business, life on the run was relaxing by comparison. There was the initially fraught trip to Paris on a false passport, but only a freak occurrence could have led to my arrest once I was past Customs. I was confident that the police weren't looking for me as a suspect in the death of the bouncer. No doubt they just wanted me as a material witness. That would have meant my having to name those who had been present or risk facing a conspiracy charge. Quite clearly, either prospect was daunting, so I was content to keep my head down for a while and lead a quiet life.

I booked into the Hotel California at £200 a night and settled back to enjoy the luxury. My days were spent exploring the sights of Paris, much the same as any other English tourist. After a couple of weeks, I did begin to get bored, but I reminded myself of the alternative: arrest and interview by the English police.

After being constantly surrounded by people in the warehouse-party business, life as a lone tourist inevitably led to a growing sense of isolation. A couple of weeks passed, and I decided to ask an old girlfriend to join me. Michelle and I had remained friends after we had parted, and we still met occasionally. She was pleased to hear from me and readily agreed to join me for an extended holiday abroad. Well aware of my chequered past, she wasn't at all put out by my request that she bring my real passport out to me.

Paris had now lost virtually all of its novelty for me and was still a bit close to home and all the troubles that awaited me there. America seemed a much more welcome prospect. We flew to Miami, travelled on to Fort Lauderdale and spent the next four months exploring Florida.

But I was restless. Michelle was a good companion, but the early romance of our relationship was long gone. I regularly phoned friends in England and was told that much of the hue and cry had died down. The police hadn't been to my family address, and it wasn't thought that there was a warrant out for my arrest. It was time to move on.

Michelle's leaving was something less than a tender parting. I put her on her plane shortly before I took my own flight to Jamaica. I was returning to the home of my ancestors. Despite being of mixed race and so light-skinned I could easily pass as white, I had always embraced my West Indian heritage. I was confident that Jamaica would be the ideal place for the next period in my life.

Kingston was hot, chaotic and dangerous. I stayed with relatives, well-to-do, professional people who lived in the exclusive Jack's Hill and moved in elite circles. I didn't want to embarrass them in any way, so I kept them in ignorance of my present predicament as well as my criminal history.

For this reason, I took advantage of an offer to use a cousin's luxury flat on Jamaica's west coast. It was located at a place called The Point on the outskirts of a town called Negril. Negril was very much a holiday resort for tourists and had a trendy, hippie vibe. Many of the street traders had a sideline dealing in weed and coke. Needless to say, with my East End streetwise outlook, I soon befriended most of them. Days were spent in their company, talking and drinking. As a measure of just how laid-back the place was, I often drank with some of the local police. I didn't know it at the time, but this would soon stand me in good stead.

As luck would have it, my apartment was sandwiched between

two hotels: Sandals and Hedonism. The former catered exclusively for couples, but the latter was famous for attracting swingers out for a no-holds-barred good time. Much of its clientele was American glamour models on location for *Playboy* and *Penthouse* photo shoots. It might have been made for me.

I soon became close friends with Sean, the hotel's events organiser. He and I regularly partied together. He confided that he had slept with over 2,000 women in his time at Hedonism. I resolved to try to break his record.

Sean allowed me to enter the hotel through a side gate next to my apartment. Once inside, it was accepted that I was a regular guest. As everything was provided in the holiday package, this meant that I could take advantage of free meals, and I had the run of all the hotel's facilities. It also meant that I had the run of its bars and discos.

Immediately, my life was one continuous round of drinking, clubbing, partying and making love to a succession of beautiful young women who were staying at the hotel. They regularly arrived by the coach load. Many of them would want to buy small quantities of weed and coke from the local street traders who were already my friends. The girls would often ask me to help them to get a good deal. This, together with my streetwise charm, proved to be a deadly combination. I was the life and soul of every party and never lacked for a beautiful bedroom companion. But my success had perhaps made me complacent. There were clear warning signs that trouble was brewing, but I ignored them.

One night, I was in the hotel disco when I spotted a stunning new girl. Inga was a German student with shoulder-length blonde hair and a figure to die for. She was also fluent in English. I introduced myself, and we were soon deep in conversation. It was lust at first sight.

A complicating factor was that her holiday had been paid for by her companion, a shifty-looking German who was a senior manager at the company where Inga worked. Quite obviously, he had paid for the holiday with the ulterior motive of sleeping with

Inga. Equally clearly, my appearance on the scene had thrown a large spanner in the works.

Within hours, we were both largely oblivious to him. He floated in and out of the picture, but, as anyone could see, Inga and I were very much caught up in a holiday romance. Soon we were inseparable. Inga then revealed that her parents were very wealthy German manufacturers. She wanted to tell them that she intended to move to Jamaica and live with me.

Up until that point, I had been very much on my best behaviour. Life in the bars and discos of Negril was very laid-back and unthreatening. There was absolutely no call for me to indulge my hair-trigger temper and occasional violent outbursts. Or so I thought.

By then, Inga's former companion had been fully relegated to the margins of our lives. We still saw him about the hotel occasionally and sometimes spoke briefly. It seemed that he had accepted the situation with as much good grace as he could muster, and we did our best not to flaunt our relationship in front of him.

One evening, Inga and I were dancing in the disco. The music and the atmosphere combined to lower our inhibitions. Soon we were smooching sexily on the dance floor. Suddenly, Inga's former companion was next to us. Clearly irate, he grabbed Inga by her long blonde hair, dragged her from my arms and proceeded to pull her across the room.

For someone in laid-back mode, I reacted surprisingly quickly. Running after them, I grabbed the guy by the throat and propelled him through the disco doors. As he flailed at me with both hands, I responded to a stinging blow on my nose by head-butting him in the face. He fell to the floor, blood pouring from his mouth.

Almost immediately, the disco security staff were on the scene. One burly guy pulled out a baton and made as if to hit me with it. I managed to deflect the blow, tore the baton from his hand and coshed him to the floor with it. By then, the place was in an uproar. I beat a hasty retreat out of the hotel, through the side door and into my apartment.

The following day, it was clear that I had caused quite a commotion. Hedonism is a prestigious hotel with an international reputation. It was supposed to be a haven where its privileged guests could party safely. Now the clear light of day revealed an unfortunate guest who had been assaulted in the hotel disco, said assault resulting in the loss of several teeth and copious amounts of blood. Quite clearly, the search for the culprit would be a priority.

An immediate problem was that no one of my description was registered as a guest. However, I had been seen about the place with such regularity that the staff all knew me. It was inevitable that the police would find me. Fortunately, one of the investigating officers was an erstwhile drinking companion. He promised that he would play down the incident as much as possible. The upshot was that the hotel paid for extensive dental work for the guy and agreed a generous compensation package, and I returned to Kingston, after a hasty goodbye to Inga.

Kingston's social circuit was wild but decidedly less drug-raddled and violent than the one I had left behind in England. People let their hair down and enjoyed themselves, but there was a clear line beyond which respectable people did not go. In my present state of development, I was quite loud, confrontational and sometimes violent. I had to constantly remind myself that one of my 'normal' outbursts wouldn't be viewed as normal at all in Kingston. This did serve to slow me down a bit.

I still had some money from my acid-house ventures, but that wouldn't last for ever. I realised that I would have to find some way to earn a living. I wasn't long in finding a move. Through a friend, I met an import broker. He introduced me to his friend who worked for the Jamaican Customs, assessing the tax to be paid on imported cars. Used English cars imported into Jamaica were subject to a massive import duty. For cars between 2,000 cc and 3,000 cc, the tax was 100 per cent of the value of the car. For those above 3,000 cc, the tax was 260 per cent of the value!

The assessor initially agreed to help me by assessing the cars by the American guidebook rather than the English one. This served to reduce the duty by about two-thirds. However, the other moves were all of my own invention. I bought late-model BMWs and Mercedes in England. I would then turn the mileage clock forward from say 20,000 miles to 100,000 miles. At the same time, I would put four very worn tyres on the car. This was enough to virtually halve its book price. So, together with the two-thirds reduction I would get from the assessor, this meant that I would have to pay a much reduced amount of tax.

Once I had the car in Kingston, I would put the clock back to its original mileage and replace the worn tyres with four new ones. I would always buy the cars to order, so there was no time lost searching about for buyers. With the minimal tax I was now paying, I could make a very decent mark-up on each car, normally amounting to about £10,000. It was more than enough to fund my lifestyle in Kingston, where the cost of living was significantly lower than in England.

Now that I had overcome my money worries, I threw myself with renewed vigour into a life of clubbing and parties. Through my cousins, I was introduced to a beautiful girl called Tiffany, who was friends with another beautiful girl called Mishka. There was instant chemistry between us. Even from very early on, it was clear that we would be partners.

Delightfully well-mannered with no airs and graces, the more I got to know her the more intrigued I became. Her father was a very powerful man in Jamaican politics. Her brothers were junior MPs. In Jamaica, where political clout is all-important, I consoled myself that should my problem in England raise its ugly head at any time, the people I was moving with would certainly be able to help me.

Through Mishka, I met Paul, a young Jamaican guy who was about my own age. Like me, he was an enthusiastic party animal. We immediately hit it off and became best friends. His background was even more intriguing than Mishka's. His father had been one of the original 'Gang of Five' who had been expelled from the Jamaica Labour Party in a blaze of publicity that had shaken Jamaican politics to the core. He had represented the extremely violent Kingston constituency of St Andrews for many years. On expulsion from the Jamaica Labour Party, he had immediately joined the ruling People's National Party and promptly won the Cassava Peace constituency for the party, the first Jamaican politician ever to do such a thing. As a direct result, his reputation in Jamaica was legendary. I was now moving in very privileged circles indeed, especially for someone who was on the run from England.

My social life with Mishka and Paul was one long round of clubbing and partying. Although Mishka and I had grown closer, there was an underlying acceptance that there was no long-term future in our relationship. The most apparent evidence of this was that we didn't get a place together. Then she fell pregnant. We were both mature enough to accept that this didn't really change anything about the way we felt for each other. I would be there for her and, of course, help her to support our child. Or at least that was my plan, but, as the saying goes, 'The road to Hell is paved with good intentions'.

One night, I was out with Paul at a prestigious nightclub called Godfathers. Kingston's beautiful people were very much in evidence. Stone Love, my favourite band, were playing in the background. Suddenly, through the throng, I saw the most amazing woman. Her angel's face was framed by an immaculately trimmed Afro. She was tall, with the body of an athlete, but she moved with the grace of a catwalk model. Her eyes sparkled with a mischievous glint.

I'm not that easily impressed, but this woman stopped me in my tracks. I wasn't exactly standing there with my mouth wide open in wonder, but I was taken aback. However, I recovered quickly enough to run and get Paul.

We found the woman easily, and Paul smiled broadly. 'You can pick 'em, Andy,' he said, laughing. 'That's Erica Aquart. She was Miss Jamaica in 1990 and runner-up in the Miss World competition the same year. She's only just come back to Jamaica.'

This information only served to make it more of a challenge to me. I had to get to know her. Switching on the charm, I walked over and asked her if she wanted a drink.

Perhaps I wasn't as confident as I thought I was. Maybe I had been intimidated by her beauty and there was a certain hesitation in my manner. 'You look like you need one yourself,' she replied as quick as a flash. Then, shaking her head as she laughed, she walked off.

As first encounters went, I'd had better ones, but I had made her laugh, so it wasn't a complete rebuff. Paul was laughing himself as I returned to our table. Seconds later, the smile disappeared from his face as Erica joined us with a beautiful friend.

We relaxed in each other's company and began to enjoy ourselves. I became aware that there were lots of looks in her direction, as she was the most beautiful woman in the club. If she realised this, she handled it very well, and all our attention was on each other anyway.

At a break in the music, she and her friend announced that they had to visit the bathroom. They stood up and walked off. Almost immediately, two other women appeared and sat down in their seats. Remonstrate with them as I might, there was no moving them, and they ordered drinks. I didn't know what to do. I could hardly physically drag two women out of their seats. I was still mulling the problem over when Erica returned.

She had no such inhibitions. I explained what had happened, and Erica told the two girls, in no uncertain terms, to move. One jumped up confrontationally and thrust her face into Erica's. Chairs fell over as the two women tussled. The security staff separated them, and Erica, now raging, took a kick at the girl. She let out a sharp cry as she missed the girl and kicked the leg of the table. Limping now and obviously in pain, we helped her outside, and she went off with her friend. It was a rather inglorious end to what had started out as a memorable evening.

It was all very much unfinished business for me, though. Fortunately, I had her telephone number. I was determined that the next venue for our continuing romance would be entirely more private. Paul's father had a 180-acre banana plantation in the wilds of the island, somewhere near St Thomas. There was a substantial villa and a beautiful freshwater lake. As a romantic setting, it was ideal.

'How would you like to be kidnapped,' I asked Erica when I called. She sounded pleased to hear from me and obviously didn't blame me in any way for the incident at the nightclub. I told her to pack a bag and that I would pick her up the following morning.

I had hired an open jeep for the trip, and as I pulled up outside her apartment she ran out and jumped in beside me. Up close in broad daylight and wearing her street clothes, she seemed even more beautiful than when I had first seen her.

The Jamaica that the tourists see is far from being the real Jamaica. Manicured lawns and concrete paths can't begin to compare with the island's natural beauty. The interior has a kind of mystical charm that is almost mesmerising. We drove towards St Thomas and were soon enchanted by our surroundings. We stopped briefly at roadside stalls to sample fresh coconut, pineapple and other exotic fruits. We arrived at the plantation late in the afternoon. Other than some house staff, we were the only people in residence.

Hand in hand, we wandered down to the lake, which was an improbably deep shade of blue. The water was crystal clear, and we could see right to the bottom. Myriad multicoloured fish swam lazily in circles. We settled in sun loungers and felt a wave of tranquillity settle over us. Leaving nothing to chance, I had brought my portable music centre. I put on the tape of Shabba Ranks' latest album. As if on cue, the track 'Mr Lover Man' played, and we made love for the first time.

It was apparent right from the very start that this was going to be a full-on and intense relationship for both of us. In the idyllic setting of the banana plantation, our romance grew until it knew no boundaries. Two partial strangers had set out on the trip; a couple who were very much in love returned.

I bought a flat in Stony Hill, a nice part of Kingston, and Erica moved in with me. Neither of us had a full-time job. I was still bringing in used cars from England, and Erica had modelling or promotional assignments no more than two days a week. Long days spent in each other's company further cemented our relationship, and we were married in 1992.

Needless to say, Mishka wasn't too pleased about the developments, especially as she was by then several months pregnant. I hadn't seen her at all in recent months, as I had been far too engrossed in building my new life with Erica. Now, though, common decency dictated that I give her some support.

In the circumstances, Erica was very understanding. With her blessing, I visited Mishka a couple of times a week. I also gave her some money and arranged for her to be paid a fixed sum each month.

Perhaps the episode with Mishka had made Erica broody, because she now announced that she too wanted a baby. I could hardly have said no, but I was fully in favour anyway. Within two months, Erica was carrying our child.

High summer was approaching, and Kingston was too hot, dusty, frantic and downright dangerous for a woman in the latter stages of a pregnancy. Further, I had decided that although dodging the duty on the imported cars wasn't the most serious of crimes, it was a crime nevertheless. A conviction for me could possibly compromise Erica's career. It was time to change my line of business. As befits a man with a new wife and young child, there would be no more fighting or otherwise loutish behaviour. I was seriously intent on changing my ways.

I sold the Kingston flat and moved to Ocho Rios on Jamaica's north coast. This was one of Jamaica's busiest tourist areas. I realised that it would be best if my new occupation was centred around catering to the tourist industry. With this in mind, I sold the last of my imported used cars.

We moved into a beautiful villa in the St Mary's Country Club, a residential complex whose hundred or so small buildings made it seem more like a small village. My fellow residents were all returning residents, expats and middle- and upper-class Jamaicans for whom St Mary's was a second home. There were extensive leisure facilities, and the complex had its own security staff, some of whom manned a gate at the entrance.

With the money I had from my used-car business, I bought six small Daihatsu cars and set up a hire-car business specifically for tourists. At the same time, I started to import new and second-hand mopeds from England with a view to hiring these out as well.

Before long, I was an upstanding, respectable member of the local community. The residential complex had a governing board comprising 12 of the residents. Trying hard to channel my excess energy, I allowed myself to be elected as chairman. Erica duly had our son, Stephan, and the whole complex turned out to celebrate his christening. I couldn't help but reflect that this was the most stable period of my life to date, and I was blissfully happy. However, as so often in my life, there was a cloud just over the horizon.

I had asked a former friend in England to source the mopeds for me. I didn't want to be forever flying backwards and forwards looking for prospective purchases. At first, this worked very well, and within a couple of months I had a small fleet of several mopeds. One day, though, I went to the docks to pick up the latest shipment. I was asked to wait in an outer office, and suddenly a Customs officer walked in accompanied by two policemen. It seemed that my former friend in England had attempted to increase his profit margins by obtaining stolen mopeds and then shipping them out to me. This latest shipment contained four stolen bikes.

I honestly hadn't known, and there was no evidence to prove that I knew they were stolen or had a hand in their theft. Red with embarrassment, I received a caution followed by a stern lecture. I returned to St Mary's, fervently hoping that the incident wouldn't come to the attention of my fellow residents. A moped thief was hardly a fit person to be chairman of their committee.

Another facet of my life that I was still trying to come to terms with was that storm clouds seemed to come along in twos and threes and sometimes travelled in packs. The second cloud wasn't long in looming.

Among the residents of St Mary's was a Canadian guy of about 50 called Ralph. Rumour had it that Ralph had won a substantial settlement in a Canadian court case and had retired to Jamaica, buying a villa in the complex. He was a morose individual who was both an alcoholic and an inveterate chain-smoker. He arrived on his own but soon moved a local maid in with him and prevailed on her to sleep with him. Any fledgling hopes of romance the maid might have had were soon dispelled by Ralph's towering rages, which he invariably took out on her, as she was the person most in his company. He regularly cursed and otherwise verbally abused her, often in public. He treated her like a slave, and it was plain to see that her life was a misery.

Despite all this, there was a degree of insularity among the residents, especially with regard to people's private lives. Everyone maintained a public face of respectability and refused to interfere in other people's private affairs. Ralph's dysfunctional relationship with his maid might have been the source of secret gossip, but outwardly it didn't affect his standing in the community.

There was more to Ralph though than just the abuse of his maid. I soon discovered that he was quietly hated and reviled by virtually all the other residents. He would regularly drive about the complex, often inebriated, and verbally abuse any fellow residents he might see. He especially seemed to hate middle-class, professional Jamaicans and had ongoing feuds with several of them. Desperately trying to avoid any confrontation, they responded by just trying to ignore him. This, in fact, seemed to inflame him the more.

At first, Ralph tried to befriend me. However, in respectable mode or not, I realised that being physically close to Ralph and his tantrums could easily trigger one of my outbursts. I maintained my distance, although I was always polite and friendly when we met. Initially, this sufficed to spare me from Ralph's ire.

I hadn't made a study of it, but in my observation of Ralph about the complex I had come to the conclusion that his problem was that he was lonely and had too much spare time on his hands. If we could find something for him to do, perhaps he could channel his spite into something positive. I suggested that we appoint him general manager of the complex, a position I had just invented.

At first, it worked out very well. Suddenly, Ralph was a man on a mission. He raced about in his pick-up truck, removing unsightly piles of rubbish, pruning bushes and otherwise attending to the fabric of the complex. His masterstroke was to paint all the kerb stones white. At the next board meeting, the general opinion was that the appointment had been an unqualified success, and I was congratulated for my idea.

However, there was one older resident of the complex who Ralph particularly had it in for. He was a retired solicitor with something of a courtly, fawning manner. The more abusive Ralph was towards him, the more submissive he became. This only served to enrage Ralph even more. It all culminated in him confronting the gentleman at his front door and roundly abusing him. Perhaps it was the realisation that taking Ralph's abuse wasn't the best idea and that he now had no other strategy, but the old gentleman responded by having a mild heart attack. He was rushed to hospital in an ambulance.

This served to focus the minds of all the rest of the residents wonderfully. Whereas previously Ralph's abuse had been viewed as something you could ignore, now it had been revealed as something that was positively life-threatening. An emergency meeting of the board was called. It was unanimously decided that this latest outrage couldn't be ignored. It was further decided that Ralph should be sacked from the post of general manager. As chairman, it was left for me to tell him.

I had spent the day on the beach at Ocho Rios. Erica and I took turns to swim, as Stephan played in the sand. It was an idyllic interlude that had become commonplace in my new life as a respectable member of society. I drove back to the complex without a care in the world.

I saw it as I manoeuvred to enter my drive. There was something, as yet indiscernible, on my front lawn. Since being at St Mary's, I had embraced gardening. I found it both interesting and calming. I had spent many a happy hour pottering around among the bushes and plants. I often reflected on what my former associates from the acid-house days would think. I guessed that there weren't many keen gardeners among the boys of the ICF.

Curious rather than angry, I parked the car and examined the pile of rubbish, for that is what it was, in the middle of the lawn. As I prodded at it with the toe of my shoe, it revealed household refuse, fish heads, broken glass and the corpse of a dead cat. A yellow rose was sticking out the top of the pile, the only visible bloom of the rose bush I had lavished so many hours of care and attention on.

By then, Erica had joined me, holding Stephan by the hand. As the stench of rotting rubbish wafted over us, Stephan stared intently at the dead cat, until Erica pulled him away and hurried into the villa, clearly upset.

Ralph! The name sprang into my consciousness like a bright light coming on in a dungeon. Quite strangely, I felt uncharacteristically calm, courtesy no doubt of the idyllic day at the beach with my family and my present respectable status. But underneath I was aware of an almost insane rage that seethed at the margins of my mind.

Leisurely, I strolled over to the gatehouse and asked the lone guard if he had seen who had dumped the rubbish. Reluctantly at first, he admitted that he had seen Ralph drive his pick-up truck onto my lawn, elevate the back and dump the rubbish. In my most reasonable manner, I requested that the next time Ralph drove to the gatehouse to be let out of the complex, the guard should delay in raising the barrier in order to keep Ralph there. I returned to the villa to wait. It didn't take long.

The angry honking of a car horn, accompanied by impatient shouts, alerted me to the fact that Ralph was now at the gate. I walked slowly out of the villa and saw the familiar pick-up idling at the barrier. In my hand, I was carrying a wooden pick-axe handle that I had just removed from one of my gardening tools. I couldn't help but reflect that this was just what the boys of the ICF would have used it for.

As I walked to the front of the pick-up, I could clearly see Ralph's face through the windscreen. In one smooth movement, I swung the pick-axe handle in a tight arc and smashed it. Although covered with glass and obviously shocked, Ralph recovered quickly. Throwing the truck into gear, he accelerated forward and tried to run me over. But I was too quick for him.

I stepped to the side of the truck and put the driver's window through. Throwing the pick-axe handle to the ground, I pulled the door open and dragged a struggling Ralph from the truck. Still quite calmly – it was almost as if I was watching someone else in action – I proceeded to give Ralph a sound beating. Mostly I gave him open-handed slaps to the face, but I also administered a few hefty kicks to Ralph's fleshy buttocks. As I strolled back to the villa, with the retrieved pick-axe handle in my hand, Ralph lay in an untidy heap, whimpering like a child.

The effect on the rest of the residents was electric. If I had thought that I would now be a social outcast, I couldn't have been more wrong. Resident after resident came hurrying to the villa, some carrying flowers for Erica, to thank me for doing something that they had all longed to. Their visits were accompanied by almost unbelievable stories of Ralph's reign of terror, from shooting out windows with an air pistol and digging up prize plants to shouting abuse in front of young children, causing them to cry. The general opinion was that it was a miracle that someone hadn't done something to Ralph before.

Had I been in the mood for celebration, it would have ended abruptly two days later. Two police officers came to the villa and told me that Ralph had decided to press charges. They acknowledged that they had received over two hundred and eighty complaints about him in under two years but that they would have to be seen to be doing something about his complaint.

The following week, I had to go before the local magistrates' court. No doubt imitating the English model, the wheels of Jamaican justice turned exceedingly slowly. First, the case was delayed for six weeks. When I returned to the court, it was delayed again for four weeks, followed by another four-week delay. Despite the fact that I had a pile of statements and testimonials from the residents, it was a serious charge and hung over us like a cloud.

I can't say with any certainty that it was because of the incident with Ralph, but there had been a shift in my relationship with Erica. The change was subtle at first, but it mutated into us bickering, finally culminating in outright rows. Erica had always been a thoroughly respectable person, living in a middle-class Jamaican society with clearly defined rules of behaviour. To have her husband, the chairman of the local residents' committee, arrested for malicious wounding might have been a bit too much for her.

Then there was the fact that she had seen another side to me when I had morphed into the thug who had attacked Ralph. Whatever the reason, it was enough to ruin our relationship. After a final blazing row, she left for Miami to stay with relatives, taking Stephan with her.

Thoroughly disenchanted with 'straight' living, I returned to

Kingston, intent on going back to England and living by my wits again. Emotionally wounded, I recuperated among my friends and relatives while I made my plans. By then, of course, Mishka had given birth to our son Giovanni, and I tried to see as much of him as I could before I left.

On the eve of my departure, several of my female friends and relatives came to me and asked me to go with them. Puzzled, I complied. Following their directions, I drove out of Kingston, along roads bordered by dense bush, finally coming to a river. We parked on the bank and everyone got out.

I was told to strip to my briefs, then watched as they took oranges and limes from a bag and proceeded to cut them in half. They then rubbed the cut oranges and limes all over the upper part of my body. Taking me by the hands, we all waded into the river. As they chanted, they splashed clear water over me, washing the orange and lime juice into the river, symbolically giving something back to nature.

Back on the bank, a candle was lit. Using a mobile phone, they called one of our relatives in England and a candle was lit there at the same time. Both would be kept burning until I had arrived safely. At the same time, they prayed to our ancestors to protect me on my journey to England and to bless me in my next ventures.

My return to Stoke Newington was uneventful. Within days, I was back in the madness that passes for life among those who aspire to live by their wits in the big city. However, I put all concrete plans on hold, preparatory to my returning to Jamaica and seeing the case through to its conclusion.

I duly returned to Ocho Rios intent on getting it over with. My solicitor had advised me that although the charge was malicious wounding, I would probably get away with a fine. With that advice in mind, I entered a guilty plea.

As I stood before the magistrate, it became abundantly clear that he and the solicitor had been reading from fundamentally different law books. Saying that this was a very serious charge indeed, he remanded me in custody for sentencing. I remember reflecting on a period spent on remand in an English jail that hadn't been too much of an ordeal at all. Unfortunately for me, I had no knowledge of Jamaican jails.

The police jeep took me to Annotto Bay Prison. From a distance, surrounded as it was by dense vegetation, it looked almost picturesque. Up close and personal, it was a very different story indeed. The flaking and eroded stonework and rusting wire attested to a place that had been around for quite a while.

The large double gates swung open as the jeep approached, and with an absolute minimum of fuss we were waved through. We parked outside a small building attached to the main building and went inside. The prison guards seemed uninterested to the point of boredom. No doubt, they had done this business of receiving prisoners thousands of times before. The few valuables I had and a small amount of money were taken from me. I walked out of the office with what I stood up in: T-shirt, slacks and expensive new trainers. I walked along a corridor, one of the guards unlocked a door and I was ushered inside.

At first, I thought it was some kind of waiting room, because it was densely crowded with standing men. As I pushed into the crowd and looked around me, the reality became immediately apparent. This was the cell I would spend all my time on remand in.

I examined my surroundings more closely. Four walls enclosed a space that was about twelve feet square, and a dozen men were crammed into this tiny area. Most of them were standing up, simply because there would not have been enough room for all of them to lie down at the same time. However, two men were lying down. Their 'beds' were sheets of newspaper spread on the floor. I noticed several more sheets similarly placed and realised that there were no proper beds. If you wanted to lie down, you would have to do so on a sheet of newspaper.

As I was digesting this information and trying to come to terms with it, I became aware of two things simultaneously. The cell was stiflingly hot, and the stench of sweat, urine and excrement was almost overwhelming. That was when I remembered a newspaper report I had read several weeks previously. It concerned some other Jamaican jail and detailed how, on a stiflingly hot day, the guards had crammed so many men into a cell designed for just nine that three of the men had suffocated!

I attempted to get close to the small barred window in the far wall, but this was clearly a prime position. Densely packed bodies blocked my progress, and I stood in the throng, frustrated, trying to breathe deeply, as if by so doing I could somehow draw fresh air into the cell.

Suddenly, there was a minor commotion by the cell door, and it opened to reveal two guards carrying large steaming trays. Plastic bowls and plates were handed out, and the guards ladled the contents of the trays onto them. One of the other prisoners had already told me that it was fish and rice for dinner. What he had forgotten to mention, though, was that a more accurate description would have included the fact that it was in fact fish heads and rice, and wet and lumpy rice at that!

I was hungry but not that hungry. I passed on the meal as eager hands quickly took the food from me. With everyone now intent on the act of eating, I decided that it might be a good time to use the toilet. I banged on the door and waited for the guards to open it.

A small room opposite served as both toilet and shower room. The stench of excrement was particularly strong there. The reason for this was immediately apparent. The sole toilet was completely encrusted with faeces. To sit down would have been an act of sheer recklessness and disregard for one's health. Passing a motion had to be accomplished by half-squatting and trying to direct your shit into the toilet bowl. From the evidence before my eyes, this was a feat quite beyond the capabilities of many of my fellow prisoners.

As I finished, I looked at the shower facilities. Any notion I had cherished of having long cool showers to relieve the oppressive heat of the cell instantly vanished. The shower was in fact a small pipe high up in the wall from which dripped a weak stream of discoloured water.

Back in the cell, my mind was working furiously. If you were searching for hell on earth, this cell would certainly suffice. I pondered the lasting effects on my health should I receive a custodial sentence and be returned here. I resolved to move heaven and earth to avoid such a fate.

As if the situation wasn't intolerable enough, I soon found that prisoners weren't only at risk from the appalling facilities. Other prisoners could also be a menace. Before entering the cell, I had been required to remove my footwear. My spanking new white trainers were placed in a line with the scuffed and dirty footwear of the other prisoners. You can imagine my surprise when I found my trainers were missing when we were let out for exercise.

I was determined not to miss the opportunity to escape the confines of the cell, so I padded out into the exercise yard in stocking feet, gingerly placing them to avoid sharp stones. I found a corner of the yard and sat down, intent on enjoying the fresh air.

More prisoners were let out until there were about 60 men in the yard. The vast majority were unremarkable, shuffling around in their crumpled clothes. Except for one guy. He was heavily built, several years older than me and outweighed me by a couple of stone. Beetling brows overshadowed dead-fish eyes. As he shuffled around the yard in his dishevelled attire, there was one striking anomaly. On his feet, he was wearing a pristine pair of new white trainers. My fucking trainers!

Discretion being the better part of valour in an environment that I was already discovering to be inimical to my health, I decided to find out something about him. From a guy who I had been talking to in the cell, I learned that he was a convicted murderer. No one knew who he had killed, but it was common knowledge that he was doing a life sentence. This didn't overly concern me. I was no stranger to violence myself; in fact, when push came to shove, it was a language that I was remarkably fluent in. The trainer thief was only flesh and blood, like any other man. If I put my mind to it and made my plans carefully, I was sure I could get my revenge. In my present state of mind, there was one thing that was crystal clear to me: there was no way that I was going to let him get away with this!

Due to his obnoxious character and the fact that he had been terrorising the jail for years, he was universally hated by his fellow prisoners. They weren't at all reluctant to give me information about him. I quickly found out that he took a shower at a certain time every day and that there was nothing personal in his robbing me. He would have done it to anyone and probably didn't know or care that they were my trainers. This latter fact was important information. It meant that he would be neither alarmed nor suspicious if I got close to him. I further learned that the guards treated violence amongst the inmates as a very minor transgression. In some cases, they even encouraged gladiatorial contests to help them pass the time.

I deliberately allowed two days to pass to lull him into the belief that he had got away with his latest theft. Late in the afternoon of the third day, I saw the telltale signs: the guy, with his towel in his hand, heading in the direction of the shower room. I waited five minutes until I was sure he would be naked and under the shower, then I asked the guard to let me out to use the toilet.

Years spent taking liberties without fear of sanction had no doubt made him complacent. He stood erect with his eyes tightly closed against the water that was falling on his face, quietly humming an indiscernible tune.

My head-butt caught him flush on the chin. With a deep grunt of pain, he slumped to the floor unconscious, banging his head heavily against the wall as he fell. But I was far from finished with him. This was a dangerous guy who had been getting away with things for many years. I didn't want to risk his recovering quickly and coming after me with a weapon.

The discerning observer would have noticed that throughout this brief encounter I was barefoot. There was no strategic significance to this whatsoever. It wasn't some battle tactic to ensure deftness of foot on a wet and slippery floor. My barefoot state was entirely to do with the fact that I had found a much better use for my socks. Putting my hand in my pocket, I pulled them out, wrapped one inside the other. Ugly bulges attested to the presence of several sizeable rocks that I had taken from the yard and stuffed inside. It might have been makeshift, but it was still a formidable cosh.

Bending over the prone form of the trainer thief, I swung the improvised weapon with considerable force. First, I targeted his knees and ankles, closely followed by his elbows. Just for good measure, I aimed several hefty blows at the area of his kidneys. There was one thing that I was sure of: a career in either ballet or boxing was now clearly out of the question for Annotto Bay's horizontal ex-champion. Furthermore, there was a better than evens chance that he would be pissing blood for weeks!

As I nonchalantly left the shower room, I bent to pick up my trainers, which my former tormentor had so kindly left by the door. He was beyond caring.

Just as I had expected, the guards took no interest at all in the incident. The only thing that changed was that I was now treated with greater respect by my fellow prisoners. I took no satisfaction in this. I hadn't done it for them; I had done it for me. I would never have been able to look at myself again in the mirror if I had bottled it and let it go.

That problem solved, I now focused all my attention on the far greater problem of my continued incarceration. Should the magistrate so decide, I would have several more years of the hell on earth that was Annotto Bay Prison. It was time to bring my situation to the attention of my influential relatives in Kingston.

The next time I appeared in front of the magistrate, there was a major difference in his attitude. The permanent scowl was gone from his face, and he had changed his mind about the seriousness of the offence. I wasn't at all surprised when he announced that there would be a stiff fine. As I walked from the dock a free man, I briefly wondered about the size of the bribe.

As far as I was concerned, that was the end of the matter between me and Ralph. However, there was a sequel of sorts. Several months later, I heard that he had been found dead, poisoned. His house maid was the obvious suspect, and she was held for questioning for several days. Jamaican police are considerably less anal than their English counterparts, though. There was no clear evidence against her, an absolute army of other suspects with cause to hate Ralph and a general feeling that he had got what he deserved. The maid was released without charge. It came as no surprise that no one knew of any relatives who might wish to inherit Ralph's estate, so the maid got everything!

There was little of the conquering hero about my return to England. I had lost my wife and child, my business, and most of my money, and I had nearly lost my freedom. I would miss the beauty and spirituality of Jamaica, which only served to emphasise the grimness of my native Stoke Newington. My only consolation was that with a bit of luck I wouldn't have to suffer it for too long. With that in mind, I set about renewing all my old contacts like a man on a mission.

Seven

A Smuggler is Born

I RESOLVED to find a move that would allow me to return to Jamaica as soon as possible. With my extensive contacts in England and the Caribbean, the obvious move was a smuggling one. Good weed grew on trees in Jamaica, but in England it could fetch a lot of money. I had absolutely no reservations about dealing in it. Tobacco and alcohol were infinitely more harmful to people's health, yet no one said anything about the vast profits that both industries made.

My first task would be to find a method to receive a shipment into England, and I found it right on my own doorstep. Spitalfields was the largest fruit-and-veg market in England, supplying 80 per cent of London's needs. Because the goods were perishable, there was always high-speed clearance of shipments. Further, it had a small army of workers, many of whom were known to me personally. It was made to order for my next move. Confident that I now had the English end of the move sewn up, I returned to Jamaica.

If I was looking for advice on how to smuggle, I reasoned that I could do worse than to ask my old family friend Bible. He was long retired from smuggling, but he agreed to tell me about his operations as long as I didn't tell him the details of any specific consignments. I spent several enjoyable and informative days drinking with him and listening to his stories.

In many ways, he was very wise. Despite all his vast experience, he cautioned that the smuggling game was constantly changing. Many of the methods he had used were now out of date, often rendered inoperable by new technology in the hands of the Customs. He recommended that I speak to his good friend Blackadouch for an up-to-date assessment.

Blacka was a legend, both in Kingston and in Jamaica as a whole. Now in his early 50s, he had cut a broad swathe through Kingston's underworld as a young man. He was born in Jonestown and had risen to control the area known as the 'Jungle'. It was officially the constituency of Omar Davies, the minister of finance for the People's National Party under Prime Minister Patterson, but everyone knew that Blacka was the don and that the real power lay with him.

Blacka was a man more loved than feared. A natural negotiator and diplomat, he regularly interceded in disagreements between powerful and dangerous people. Such was the respect he was held in, Blacka invariably brought the dispute to a mutually beneficial conclusion. If the situation demanded it, though, he could employ more direct methods.

On one occasion, he had been called upon to negotiate a truce between two warring posses. There had been several murders, and it was rapidly escalating into small-scale civil war. Blacka arranged for the two opposing dons to join him for a meeting. They settled down to negotiate.

Very soon, feelings were running high between the two dons. Voices were raised and insults exchanged. When Blacka forcefully called for order, one of the dons made him the target of his anger. He asked Blacka who he thought he was and told him that he should watch out.

Blacka always carried a 9-mm Beretta loaded with hollow-point shells in his waistband. Without saying a word or even changing his expression, he pulled out his gun and in one smooth movement shot the offending don through both knees. The don was crippled for life and the problem resolved.

Despite having this capacity for unrestrained violence, Blacka did have a thoroughly good side to his nature. He was especially revered by many of Kingston's street sellers. He would regularly put himself out and bulk-buy cheap goods for the street sellers to sell from their makeshift stalls. He would only accept the cost price of the goods in return.

Nevertheless, he had accumulated great wealth over the years, and he owned several houses. There was one particularly luxurious house in the exclusive Cherry Gardens that he rented out to a government minister. Rumour had it that Blacka didn't believe in banks and kept all his money at home, hidden in a fireproof mattress. It went without saying that no one had ever tried to relieve him of this cash.

Bible arranged for me to meet with Blacka in a bar in West Kingston. I arrived early, but he was already waiting for me. As we ordered our drinks, I quickly tried to weigh him up. He was of short stature but quite stocky. Smartly dressed in a light-coloured linen shirt and matching trousers, he chain-smoked Craven A cigarettes. He had a round, pleasant face and smiled a lot, revealing perfect white teeth.

I found myself relaxing in his company. I had obviously come well-recommended by Bible. However, I must have felt a need to impress him, as I started to tell him about some of the Yardies I knew back in England. Blacka fixed me with a quizzical look, and there was an amused sparkle in his eyes. When he spoke, his voice was very deep, and he had a thick Jamaican accent. 'The very first thing I must do is tell you something of Jamaica's history, especially about your so-called Yardies,' he said. I settled back, listening intently.

According to Blacka, the term 'Yardie' was a serious misnomer. It was actually an English word used to identify recent Jamaican immigrants to the UK. In view of the fact that the absolute vast majority of Jamaican immigrants were honest, hard-working and law-abiding citizens, to use the term 'Yardie' to refer to criminals or gang members was a particularly offensive slur on ordinary Jamaicans everywhere.

Blacka went on to say that the correct terms to refer to Jamaican gangsters were 'Rudies' or 'Rude Boys'. These originated in West Kingston in the late 1950s. The unemployed youth, living in dire poverty, reacted against a system that had never done anything for them. They had their own inimical style of dress and music, one heavily influenced by American street culture. Both impoverished and humiliated, they wanted to be seen to make a stand. They lived in revolt against the sinful 'Babylon' system that enslaved them, preferring to die in the attempt to better themselves. They formed themselves into gangs or posses, and were both fearless and phenomenally violent. Kingston often witnessed battles bordering on small-scale civil wars. In some areas, anarchy was the order of the day.

As was the case in so many other parts of the British Empire, when the colonial power finally gave up its claims to Jamaica and granted it independence in the early 1960s, it left no stable political system in its place. Neither the Jamaica Labour Party under Alexander Bustamante nor the People's National Party under Norman Manley could comfortably fill the void. This situation continued under their successors, Edward Seaga and Michael Manley. There was little difference in their ideologies or policies, and there have been allegations of the use of force and intimidation to win votes by corrupt factions in both their governments. It is widely acknowledged that such corrupt factions exist in Jamaican political parties, recruiting the various posses to their causes and, especially at election times, relying on them to coerce their constituents into voting for one side or the other.

Many bloody battles were fought in the ghettoes until one posse triumphed by force of arms. Many innocent citizens were killed in the crossfire. The rest were terrorised and subjugated. These constituencies came to be known as 'garrison constituencies'. Supporters of the triumphant ruling party were rewarded with jobs, housing, public services and other benefits. Supporters of the losing party got nothing.

This system proliferated and, in time, came to be institutionalised, with the posse leaders or dons becoming the de facto partners of the politicians. In effect, the posses had become private political armies. The way it worked was that the elected politician channelled money, benefits and other largesse to the ghetto don. He would pass some of this on to his immediate posse and some of the ruling party's supporters. Thus the don became the unelected community leader. Not only would he provide those services that it was the duty of the state to provide, the final irony was that he would also administer the local law.

The situation was further complicated by another factor. Marijuana, otherwise known as ganja, was widely grown on the island. Despite various initiatives by the ruling parties to curb both its growth and its use, sometimes dispensing long prison terms, the trade continued to flourish. Then the ganja farmers discovered a vast and growing new market a relatively short distance away in the United States. Very soon, they had a multimillion-dollar industry on their hands.

This wealth brought with it security problems, so the farmers employed the Rudies to protect them. There was plenty of money to pay them for their services, and weapons could easily be bought on the American market. Before long, the posses outgunned the Jamaica Constabulary Force, or police, and the Jamaica Defence Force, or army.

Back in the wider world, Russia and America were caught in the death grip of the cold war. The contending ideologies fought for primacy everywhere. No country seemed too small to be strategically significant. Now it came to be Jamaica's turn.

Seaga's Jamaica Labour Party leaned towards America, whilst Manley's People's National Party had close ties with Cuba. This latter fact particularly incensed the Americans. The CIA was ordered to train and equip the posses supporting the Jamaica Labour Party. Not to be outdone, Manley turned to the Cuban equivalent, the Dirección General de Inteligencia.

In spite of their sophisticated weaponry and their fearlessness in battle, the Rudies were still an undisciplined and relatively inept fighting force. Courtesy of the CIA and DGI, they now learned combat and espionage techniques. Election times degenerated into fully fledged street battles. But far worse, a dangerous monster had been created, one that would later use these recently learned skills in pursuit of purely criminal goals.

In the election year of 1980, Seaga won a particularly bloody victory, with 1,100 people killed, 125 of them in a single month. He came under strong international pressure to act. Many Rudies were encouraged to go abroad. With a combination of threats and bribes – and maybe even official connivance in the shape of false papers – the Rudies headed for greener, less fraught pastures.

In reality, their choices were extremely limited. In order to continue in a life of crime and terrorising their fellow countrymen, they would have to go to countries where there were already well-established Afro-Caribbean communities. The United States was the obvious first choice. It says as much for America's institutionalised racism as it does for the Rudies' chameleon-like abilities that they slipped in largely unnoticed.

Their handiwork soon became apparent, if only to the black inhabitants of the ghettoes. The Rudies targeted and began to take over the local drugs trade. The professionalism and organisational flair taught to them by the CIA and DGI, coupled with a capacity for extreme violence, gave them an edge. Local black criminals were gunned down, sometimes with automatic weapons, in public places and in broad daylight.

Soon, every major American city had posses made up of members from all the leading Jamaican gangs. Often there was no link to the parent posses, further evidence of the Rudies' self-serving nature. And there was no need for them to import drugs, for the American ghettoes were already awash with them. The Rudies just stepped in and took what they wanted.

The authorities either missed this happening or were indifferent to it, even though it could hardly be argued that the Rudies weren't a significant threat. However, as late as 1987, one federal agency did make some kind of estimate of the number of Rudies operating in America. They calculated that there were approximately 70 posses in the USA, comprising between 20,000 and 40,000 members. In 1980, the Rudies had murdered almost 250 people in New York City alone.

Meanwhile, back home in Jamaica, the international demand for cocaine was changing the face of drug dealing. Following government-inspired campaigns to reduce marijuana production, including extensive crop eradication, the posses quickly switched to cocaine. Jamaica soon became the major shipment point for the Colombian cartels. Seeing an opportunity, Nigerian producers also flooded the country with heroin. The posses shipped both narcotics onwards to the USA.

Before long, the Jamaican posses were fabulously wealthy and extremely heavily armed, with everything from bazookas to rocket launchers. This further served to tip the political set-up on its head. Whereas formerly it had been the elected politicians who had channelled largesse to the posse, now, with the economy in decline and the state struggling to meet its commitments, it was the posse who was the provider. The balance of power had shifted, and the politicians were now firmly in the pocket of the dons.

The corruption went all the way to the top. Government ministers had leading posse members as their business partners. Funerals of powerful dons became semi-official state affairs. When Jim Brown, the notorious gangster and mass murderer, was burnt to death in his prison cell, Edward Seaga was reported as being a mourner at his massive funeral. The opposition People's National Party wasn't immune from this either. Michael Manley was at the head of the procession at the funeral of People's National Party gangster Winston Blake.

Blacka stopped abruptly and looked down at his watch. It caused me to look at mine too. Over an hour had passed since he had started talking. I had sat through it all quite mesmerised. It was a fascinating subject that I was deeply interested in, and Blacka was very articulate.

'The reason I've told you all this is so that you can realise exactly what you are up against,' Blacka continued. 'If you are going to be involved in crime in Jamaica, you have to know how corrupt the system is, how you can use that to your advantage and how you can avoid antagonising powerful people. And with regard to the so-called Yardies back in England, you should now know that the majority of them can't be trusted.'

It was a good note to end on. Blacka then said that he had an important meeting and would have to leave. We made arrangements to meet the following day. After he left, I sat there for ages, mulling over what I had just learned.

The following day, I met Blacka at the bar again. I had brought a bag containing some clean clothes, as he had told me that we would be gone for several days. As I waited for him, I sat in the shade of the bar as close to the fan as possible. Even after all this time, I still hadn't got used to the intense heat.

About 20 minutes passed, and I heard the beeping of a car horn. As I looked up, Blacka waved at me from behind the wheel of a large silver jeep. I ran outside, threw my bag in the back and climbed into the seat next to Blacka, who immediately drove off.

Blacka was cheerful and welcomed me, but there was no reference to our conversation of the day before. I guessed that Blacka had assumed that I had taken it all in. Clearly, he wasn't a man to waste words.

We chatted amiably as we headed out of Kingston. Blacka didn't say where we were going, and I didn't presume to ask. I accepted that he would tell me anything he thought I needed to know, when he thought I should know it. Reacting in this way was more important than most straight people would realise. I knew that Blacka was still feeling me out and weighing me up. If I was found to be loose with my mouth and forever asking questions, it would be a serious mark against me.

As the roads changed from tarmac to rough earth, so the surrounding countryside also changed from riotous, unrestrained greenery to coarse brush and red earth. The colours were both quite beautiful and unearthly, almost as if we had ventured into some alien landscape.

We turned off a wide road onto a smaller dirt track, which seemed to herald the beginning of a valley. In the middle distance, green-clad peaks towered on both sides. Suddenly, Blacka said that we were now in the St Elizabeth parish and quite close to the ganja factory. As if on cue, we rounded a sharp bend and there, right across the road, was a Jamaica Constabulary Force patrol car.

My heart missed a beat, and I physically jumped in my seat. Blacka didn't turn a hair. Slowing only slightly, he vigorously pumped at the horn. Two police officers appeared as if by magic, lighted cigarettes in their hands. Clearly, they had been sitting in the shade of a tree, smoking. One jumped into the patrol car and reversed quickly out of the way. Blacka waved casually at them with one hand as they eagerly waved at him with both.

'Remember what I told you yesterday?' said Blacka, turning towards me slightly. 'In Jamaica, everything and everyone can be bought. It's just a matter of knowing the price.'

Approaching another sharp bend, Blacka slowed visibly and once again pumped at the horn. Driving slowly now, we rounded the bend. At the side of the road was what looked like a sand-bagged fortification. Bags filled with red earth had been piled on top of each other, leaving slits higher up that were obviously gun ports.

Two men with long dreadlocked hair lounged against one side of the fortification. Beside them, propped against the bags, were two automatic weapons. From my limited knowledge of weaponry, I guessed that they were M16s. I noticed spare clips of ammo attached to the men's belts.

Blacka stopped the jeep and climbed out. He strolled over to the two dreads, and they embraced warmly. They chatted animatedly for several minutes. At one stage, I saw Blacka turn and point at me, and the men nodded. My presence wasn't required, though, so he clearly didn't intend to introduce me. He returned to the jeep, and we drove off.

Ten minutes or so passed, and we emerged from the narrow

track into a broad clearing. The brush had been stripped away, revealing the stark red earth. Several wooden hut-like buildings stood in a semicircle. In the middle of the clearing, a couple of dozen people were gathered, both men and women. They were standing and sitting under a large blue tarpaulin that had been stretched tight between several trees. Another blue tarpaulin was stretched across the ground underneath the first.

Blacka climbed out of the jeep and beckoned for me to follow. We halted before we reached the tarpaulins, and he pointed out beyond the huts. Stretching as far as the eye could see were fields and fields of green crops. I didn't need Blacka to tell me that it was the ganja.

Blacka began to explain the production process to me, but up close it was all self-explanatory anyway. Several men, sweating profusely, carried armfuls of the ganja plants and deposited them on the tarpaulin. Other men separated the sticks from the seeds and the buds.

Six women sat on chairs in a circle around a large table with a gigantic mound of buds on it. As they cut at the buds with small sharp knives, Blacka told me that they were 'manicuring the weed'. From time to time, they would scoop up the finished buds and put them into large bags, like those from supermarkets. Then, sometimes in pairs, they would struggle to lift the bags onto a weighing machine.

A short distance away, out in the sunshine unprotected by the tarpaulin, a group of men were gathered around some kind of machine. It was a strange contraption that looked even more bizarre up close. Parts of it were clearly sections of rail track. Joined on to these was what looked like an enormous car jack. The buds were tipped from their bags into the space bordered by the rails. The jack was then turned, compacting the buds between the rails. The finished product was a solid block of weed. Blacka explained that it was pressed and shaped according to the weight of the buds.

The solid block was placed onto the ground next to the

press. Eager hands picked it up and passed it through a small machine that shrink-wrapped it with polythene film. Another guy wrapped the block in brown packaging tape with amazing speed. The finished package was then placed on a pile with the rest of the blocks. It was quite an efficient production process, and I was duly impressed.

It was readily apparent that Blacka was on intimate terms with all the workers. He sat with the women for a while, asking how they were and enquiring after their families. All the men greeted him like an old friend. It was good man management; the personal touch ensured their loyalty.

Suddenly, raised voices could be heard. I turned in the direction of the sound. To the side of the circular area was a large weighing machine. The three men gathered around it were arguing heatedly. Blacka stood and shouted across to them. They immediately fell silent.

Blacka strolled over to me. 'See the guy standing next to the big sacks. He's the farmer, and the sacks contain his ganja plants.' Blacka pointed in his direction. 'Ganja farming is a hard life, and the farmers are always struggling for money. They always argue over something, whether it's the weight of the sacks or the price to be paid. The fat old guy is doing the weighing, and the taller guy with the pistol in his belt is security. If things start to get out of hand, it's his job to sort it out.'

Sure enough, the guy with the gun was waving his finger at the farmer, who by then had dropped his head. He stuck out his hand and the guy doing the weighing thrust a bundle of notes into it. Muttering to himself, the farmer headed back to his truck and drove off.

Hardly had the truck disappeared than there was a cacophony of noise. I turned in the direction it was coming from and saw an enormously fat guy standing close to the huts, hammering away at a large metal pot with an equally large ladle. 'Are you hungry?' enquired Blacka. 'That's the cook, and the noise signals that it's time for dinner.'

There were some benches and tables set out between two of the huts. On one table sat a gigantic black stew pot, columns of steam issuing from around its ill-fitting lid. Workers were taking their places at the tables, and it now was clear that there were about 20 in total. When I asked if the guards with the M16s would be joining us, Blacka said that their food would be sent down to them later. For everyone to be in the same place at once would make the farm vulnerable to a sneak attack.

The cook ladled me a big bowl of stew, and I sat down next to Blacka to eat it. It was thick with large pieces of chicken and various kinds of vegetable. It made for a substantial meal and was delicious.

'I'm beginning to enjoy this life,' I said to Blacka.

'Just as well,' he replied, 'because you'll be seeing a lot of it. Most of our work is carried out here. As you can see, I get on well with the workers, but if you're not on top of them – that is, constantly about the place – it can very quickly turn bad. Either the weed isn't prepared well enough or it isn't packed properly. Whichever, substandard weed arrives at the other end and has to be sold cheaply. The transport is both costly and difficult to arrange, so you might as well send only top-quality weed through.'

The combination of the heavy meal and the oppressive heat served to make me sleepy. Blacka nudged me awake with a dig from his elbow. 'I need to tell you about the three golden rules of smuggling,' he said. All the rest of the workers had disappeared by then, and we had the table to ourselves. Blacka leaned back in his chair and put his hands behind his head, letting out a deep sigh. 'Smuggling is a very serious business,' he began. 'There are literally hundreds of ways you can lose your money, your freedom and your life. But if you stick to these three rules, you will considerably lessen the chances of any of those three things happening.' He paused, staring at my face to see if I was concentrating or nodding off again. When he saw that I was sitting upright, listening to his every word, he continued. 'Rule number one is never introduce A to B. That is, never allow the people with the product to meet the people who will eventually buy it. If you do, it's a sure way to get cut out of the deal. They'll figure out that they don't need you.

'Rule number two is that you must know who you can trust. I don't mean trust to stick with you when you have a fight or all those other things that mates down the pub do for each other. I mean, can you trust him not to run off with a million pounds of your money? Or if he's facing 20 years in jail, will he take the fall and not land you in it? That's what I mean by trust. There are many men who are now penniless or sitting in jail doing very long sentences because they thought they could trust someone.'

Blacka could see that I was thinking deeply about this point, so he paused again. In truth, I was running through all the people I knew and putting them through Blacka's test. 'I can think of two people,' I said finally.

Blacka nodded and smiled. 'Then you can think of one more than most can,' he replied. 'Which brings me to rule number three. This is the three Ts: telephone, text and tell-a-woman. The Americans have a gigantic agency with billion-dollar funding called the National Security Agency. All it does, 24 hours a day, 365 days a year, and it's been doing it for the past 30 years, is trawl through billions of phone calls and text messages. Their computers search for key words. One of these key words will trigger their system, which will bring your phone call or text to their attention. Then, once they're on to you, it's all over. So, never, ever, ever say anything compromising on a phone or in a text. Otherwise you'll end up seeing it again when they present the evidence against you in court.'

Once more, he paused to let this sink in. I was deep in thought, recalling the multitude of times that I had been indiscreet on the phone. I made a secret resolution to radically change my ways. Blacka gave me a knowing look that said that he knew that I had to change.

'Last but not least,' he said with some finality, 'the ladies. Now

I know that you think you're one hell of a ladies' man, and there's nothing wrong with that, but keep it in its place. Bedroom talk has been the downfall of many a clever man. Things change, relationships change, people fall in and out of love, and some women can be very devious. Why give someone something they can destroy you with when there's no need for them to know in the first place?'

I recognised it for the rhetorical question it was and knew that Blacka wasn't expecting an answer. Once again, I was deep in thought. Face after female face flashed through my mind as I recalled secrets I had shared or times when they had known too much. Blacka's three golden rules had brought it all very much into perspective for me. As things stood right then, I didn't have much prospect of becoming a successful smuggler. I could only hope that from that moment on I would change.

Late afternoon brought the next phase of my smuggling education. I had seen how the ganja was harvested, prepared and pressed into blocks. The next step was to move it from the farm up to Kingston, preparatory to the final move to the docks.

If I had been expecting some sophisticated plan involving bribery and subterfuge, I would have been disappointed. Blacka explained that there was no need to bribe everybody. The Jamaican police were, by nature, very lazy. Unless the matter was very serious or they had a vested interest in the outcome, they were content to sit in their patrol cars and do the absolute minimum.

The finished blocks were carefully placed in the bottom of a large flat-bed truck. (There were literally thousands of these trucks hauling farm produce all over Jamaica.) Then sugar cane was piled on top of the ganja until the truck was filled. It was strenuous work filling the truck. By the time they were finished, the farm workers were dripping with sweat. To unload it again would have been even more strenuous, as the sugar cane tended to clump together in tangled bundles. It would be a very inquisitive policeman indeed who would go to the trouble of off-loading everything in order to properly search the truck.

The truck set off, with Blacka and me following at a discreet distance in the jeep. On the long drive up to Kingston, we must have passed dozens of policemen in patrol cars. Not one of them took so much as a second look at us. Once in Kingston, there was even less chance of being stopped. We drove into a particularly poor neighbourhood and stopped outside a dilapidated dwelling that stood in a row of similarly tumbledown houses.

An alley led to a small yard at the back. With the help of a guy who obviously lived there, the truck driver and his mate quickly unloaded the sugar cane and carried the blocks of ganja into the house. A hanging tapestry concealed a hidden room, and the blocks were placed inside. Blacka explained that they would remain there until it was time to move them to the docks.

'Tomorrow,' said Blacka, 'I'll show you how we get it into the containers. Have a good night's sleep, and I'll pick you up in the morning. I'll be introducing you to several people, so it's best to be dressed quite smart. As in most areas of life, appearances are very important.'

The following morning, Blacka picked me up dressed in one of his usual immaculate linen suits. Not to be outdone, I was suitably attired myself. Looking like two businessmen about to go to the office, we climbed into the jeep and set off.

Kingston docks were a hive of activity. Lorries and vans of every description, carrying every commodity under the sun, waited in long queues or jostled for position in the approach roads. Blacka drove blithely past them all.

He got out at the gate and spoke a few words to the uniformed guard. Turning, he pointed at me, and the guard gave me a long, careful look, as if committing my face to memory. Then the barrier across the road was lifted, and we drove through.

'All the people you will meet this morning are paid off by me,' Blacka explained. 'It's probably the major overhead of the smuggling business. The ganja itself costs next to nothing by comparison. But without paid assistance, we wouldn't be able to get it past Customs.'

We drove into an area where there were hundreds upon hundreds of large containers, painted in various colours and stacked one upon another. Large forklift trucks scurried around them, sometimes stopping to lift a particular container from its stack and move it to another part of the enormous yard.

Blacka pulled a large envelope from within his jacket and handed it to me. 'I want you to give this to the next guy we talk to,' he said. 'It's the best way for people to get to know and remember you.'

I followed as Blacka walked over to a short guy standing next to a new yellow forklift. Blacka shook his hand and introduced me as his new business partner. The guy shook my hand vigorously and said that he was very pleased to meet me. He smiled broadly as I handed him the envelope.

He drove the forklift to a nearby stack of containers, lifted off the top one and placed it on the ground. A lorry that had been parked a short distance away suddenly drove up and parked next to the container. The driver jumped out and swung the back doors open to reveal sacks of produce stacked on wooden pallets.

Taking my arm, Blacka led me closer to the container. He pointed to an embossed metal strip that was fastened around what seemed to be the door lock. 'That's the Customs seal,' said Blacka. 'If that were to be broken or otherwise tampered with, the Customs would thoroughly search the whole container. But watch closely and you will see what we do to get around that.'

The forklift was manoeuvring quite carefully now. The driver had raised the forklift blades until they were level with the container's upper door hinges. Gingerly, he slid the blades underneath the hinges. With a high-pitched whine, he began to raise the blades. Slowly, with a squeal of tortured metal, the doors lifted upwards and off their hinges. They hung from the blades of the forklift, swinging gently, the Customs seal still intact around the lock.

Another forklift appeared in front of the now open container. It began to remove the first row of produce stacked on pallets and placed them next to the lorry. Then several pallets were lifted from the lorry and put in the newly created space in the container. The forklift holding the doors moved in and carefully put them back on their hinges. Finally, the other forklift put the pallets taken from the container into the lorry and it drove off. The whole operation had taken no more than 20 minutes.

'Smooth, eh?' said Blacka, chortling. 'The pallets from the lorry contain our ganja. The ones we removed were our normal produce. We'll put it in another container. The Customs will look at the seal of this one and see that it is unbroken. It will pass through untouched and go to our people at the other end. This particular method is called "piggybacking". We've just piggybacked our illegal load onto the back of a legal one.'

I was duly impressed. It all seemed so simple. But the secret of the success was, of course, the bribing of key staff. Without that, nothing would have happened. There were more surprises in store, though.

Telling me that this wasn't the only way to bypass Customs, Blacka drove out of the docks. A five-minute journey took us to the gates of a produce shipping company. Once again, the guard on the gate knew Blacka, and we were waved through. Containers identical to the ones we had seen at the docks were piled up in the yard. Several forklifts moved them around.

We walked inside a low building and into a small office. The manager, a small, wiry man, rushed over and embraced Blacka, who, once again, introduced me as his business partner. As the manager busied himself supplying us with cool drinks from a fridge, Blacka passed me another envelope, saying that he would tell me who to give it to when the time came.

Blacka chatted amiably with the manager as we sipped our drinks. About 20 minutes had passed when there was a knock on the office door. It opened and a tall man dressed in the full uniform of a Jamaican Customs officer walked in. I was getting used to surprises when in Blacka's company, so there was no shock or fear on my behalf. Curious, I stood and shook the man's hand as

Blacka introduced me. At Blacka's nod, I took the envelope from inside my jacket and handed it to the Customs officer. Without so much as acknowledging it, he put it in his inside pocket.

With the Customs officer in the lead, we all filed out of the office and into the yard. We waited by a closed container while the Customs guy collected a small bag from a nearby car. As he joined us, he opened the bag and took out a small hand-held machine. He punched some information into its keypad and, with a whirring sound, an embossed metal strip appeared. Without so much as looking inside the container, the Customs guy looped the metal strip around the door lock. He stepped back to reveal an official Customs seal now securing the doors.

On the drive back to my apartment, Blacka told me that I had now seen the complete process of ganja smuggling from production to shipping. Once again, he emphasised the importance of bribery – 'keeping everybody happy', he called it – and, of course, the supreme importance of sticking to his three golden rules.

One morning, Blacka asked me to meet him very early. We had to travel to the ganja plantation to check that the workers were on schedule, as we had a very important shipment that was due to leave. A long-established Jamaican bakery would be sending a huge order of Jamaican buns over to England to meet the expected Easter demand. There would also be a container of large, circular drums of Jamaican tinned cheese leaving the same week. It was very important that the weed was meticulously cleaned of the sticks and seeds, as we had been receiving lots of complaints from our people in England. But more importantly, we had to get our dimensions precise, as the weed had to be pressed into the same shapes as both the tins of cheese, which were circular, and the buns, which were the size and shape of a standard loaf of bread. The latter were each to be placed in individual white-and-green boxes then shrink-wrapped. These were professionally prepared products that had a high chance of getting through Customs undiscovered, so it was worth the extra effort.

Around 5 a.m., Blacka turned up at the country club where I was staying. He was in his '85 red Ford pick-up. He owned better vehicles, but this one had made many runs to the plantation and could deal with the Jamaican country roads, which were riddled with potholes. Although it was early, the sun was already very bright and blazing hot, and there was a long drive ahead of us. We had to cut across from the north coast, where I lived, to get to the Alligator Pond region of St Elizabeth, which was on the other side of the island.

As we pulled out of the gates of the country club and headed down the winding, treacherous road of Prospect Hill, the scenery was breathtaking. On either side lay miles of lush green trees ranging from mahogany to pimento. The early-morning brightness and the clarity of the air made everything stand out in stark relief. Once again, I couldn't help but be affected by the natural beauty of the Jamaican countryside.

As we arrived at the T-junction at the bottom of the hill, Blacka called out to me in his broad Jamaican accent, 'Ya yam breakfast yet?'

Although firmly in Jamaican mode now, at times my diction lapsed into broad cockney. 'Nah, mate, I'm starvin' like Marvin,' came my reply.

Blacka fixed me with one of his quizzical stares, the beginnings of a smile playing around his mouth. A couple of times in the past, there had been a slight communication problem between us, his 'Awha dat?' sounded confused. So, speaking slowly and clearly, with the beginnings of a smile on my own face, I said in my best approximation of the Queen's English, 'No I haven't eaten yet. Is there somewhere we can get a fry-up? Eggs, beans, chips and a cup of tea?'

Chuckling audibly now, Blacka drove across the junction and onto a gated dirt track that led down to a place known as Reggae Beach.

At the end of the track, there was a beautiful white sandy beach. We got out of the pick-up and headed towards two brightly coloured wooden shacks, one of which served as a bar, the other as a restaurant. But these were not our destination. With wonderful breakfast smells tormenting my nose, we walked past them, across the beach and towards the shoreline.

The shoreline was a hive of activity. Just offshore could be seen several small fishing boats, the crews working hard to land their catch. A fisherman in the closest boat was making dramatic hand gestures towards a score or so of other workers who were waist deep in the water, equidistant between the boat and the shore. They were struggling to stay on their feet, while at the same time pulling in unison at a partially submerged rope. Further along the beach, a similar scenario was playing itself out.

As both groups of men pulled at ropes, all the time shouting encouragement and cursing, a gigantic fishing net started to emerge. It soon became clear that what I had at first thought to be two separate groups working to land two separate nets, now turned out to be one large group trying to land one enormous net.

This was my first experience of fishing Jamaican style, and the whole process was unlike anything I had seen before. The workers stood in a line, one behind the other, and pulled with all their might. Then the guy at the back would run to the front and pull again at the net. This process was repeated over and over again as the guys at the back constantly ran to take up the slack, pulling the net ever closer to the beach. Once it was in very shallow waters, a number of the locals ran to help, including several young boys. It seemed that everyone in the vicinity pitched in to land the catch.

Another ten minutes or so passed and I began to see an amazing array of colourful fish of various sizes and types. Red snappers fought for space alongside bright blue-and-yellow yellow-tail. Strange-looking goatfish, with beard-like barbells under their chins, thrashed against hook-nosed blue parrot fish.

In between, there were many other types of fish, the names of which I didn't know. All were dragged in close to the beach where many helping hands seized them and threw them by type into various piles on the sand. Blacka later told me that the locals who helped were rewarded with a few fish each, the only way they could put food on the table for their families.

Suddenly, Blacka shouted and waved at a fisherman in the boat nearest the shore. The guy waved back, jumped overboard and waded towards us. As he and Blacka embraced, I was introduced to Quincy, a long-time friend of Blacka and one of the most experienced fishermen on the island. He was renowned for always having the best catch.

Quincy called to one of his workers, who hurried over with a large, blue and white cooler box. Quincy removed the lid to reveal slabs of ice covering freshly caught fish, some of which were still moving.

Blacka pointed to two large red snappers. Quincy took them out of the box and passed them to the worker, who began to de-scale the fish with an ingenious device that was a masterpiece of simple improvisation. A foot-long piece of broomstick had numerous metal beer-bottle caps nailed to two thirds of its length, the sharp edges outwards. Holding the stick by the end clear of bottle tops, the worker quickly rubbed the device backwards and forwards over each fish, so removing all the scales. Then, taking a small knife out of his waistband, he gutted the fish from head to tail.

Meanwhile, a small Rastafarian boy who had appeared as if by magic, was busy chopping and dicing a variety of vegetables, spices and seasonings, including scallions, onions, tomatoes, callaloo and Scotch bonnet peppers.

With the insides of both fish now removed, the worker took handfuls of the chopped seasoning and stuffed each snapper with it. Laying each fish on a sheet of aluminium baking foil, he dropped in a large knob of butter before expertly wrapping both fish. He then handed both packages to Blacka and pointed towards a nearby grill. Almost rubbing my hands in anticipation, I walked across towards it.

Blacka shook his head. 'Me ave no time fe dat. We ave to hit de road,' he intoned. My mouth gaped in amazement as he walked over to the pick-up. Opening the door, he reached for the release catch for the bonnet. For one second I thought he was just checking the engine for the rest of what was turning into an extremely long journey. You can imagine my surprise when he stooped over the open bonnet and placed each fish on the engine flange, where the exhaust manifold meets the engine. Then, without ever once offering a word of explanation, he slammed the bonnet shut, started the engine, and we both drove away from the beach.

Needless to say, I was absolutely dying to ask him what was going on, but with the radio blaring and a smile of sheer satisfaction showing on Blacka's face, I decided against it. I had already been wondering how, in the absence of the cool box, we would keep the fish fresh until we arrived at our destination. Puzzle at it as I might, Blacka's actions defied a logical explanation. I sat there nursing both my curiosity and my hunger.

From Ocho Rios we went through Runaway Bay, past Discovery Bay and on to Montego Bay, known to locals as Mo' Bay. We stopped at Flankers, under a big almond tree shaped like an umbrella. In the terminal stages of hunger pangs, I looked around for a restaurant as I explained to Blacka that I was now very hungry indeed.

'Cool na, man,' he replied. 'I go feed yuh.' So saying, he got out of the pick-up, releasing the bonnet as he did so. Standing in front of the engine, he reached in and pulled out the two packages wrapped in aluminium foil. They must have been piping hot. 'Blood claart, tha hot,' cursed Blacka, shaking his hand.

As Blacka opened the foil, an immense amount of steam poured out. When it cleared, the fish looked cooked to perfection. Handing me some paper towels. he passed me the fish package, which I then placed on the towel. Plastic forks appeared from the glove compartment, and I settled back to enjoy the meal.

There was one last ritual to be observed, though. A street vendor (known as a higler) with his cart was parked nearby, and Blacka bought two ice-cold Dragon Stouts. Snapping the tops, he passed me one. The fish was cooked to perfection and delicious. Washed down with the cold beer it made for a culinary experience as close to ecstasy as could be imagined. I reflected that the day had definitely been one of new and surprising experiences. We finished the meal and hit the road for the next leg of the journey.

I was immediately in love with this new life of mine. Most weekdays, I was down at the ganja farm near St Elizabeth. Sometimes Blacka joined me, but my role as his business partner was clearly a working one. It was up to me to make sure that the workforce got on with things when he wasn't there. I soon lapsed into an easy familiarity with everyone, regularly joining in with the work. Soon, there was no part of the process that I couldn't do. At the same time, I listened to all that was told me and learned as much as I could.

However, I did feel confident enough to apply some of my big-city smarts to this rural Jamaican operation. Blacka had complained that the police had recently taken to flying over the countryside in light planes and helicopters, looking for ganja plantations. Several had been discovered in this way. From a friend, I got some army camouflage netting and draped it over all the buildings and work areas of the farm. I also bought a supply of smokeless fuel so that the smoke from the cooking fires wouldn't be noticed.

I also started to experiment with containers. A friend of Blacka's had a car scrapyard just outside St Elizabeth. I arranged for several empty containers to be delivered to the yard and set about dismantling some of them with a blow torch and angle grinder.

My first invention was the 'sardine tin'. I built a false bottom into a container and welded the floor back in place. But not before packing the newly created space with ganja. In England, the boys would peel the floor back, just like opening a sardine tin, to get at the ganja. As I pointed out to Blacka, it did away with the necessity of having to pay off the Customs, thus increasing our profit margins.

If Blacka was impressed, he didn't show it. 'And what if the Customs do somehow find the compartment?' Blacka asked. 'When our friends in England cut it open, the Customs will swoop and everyone will be taken.'

I hadn't thought of that. I had only been thinking of success. Blacka, with all his experience, was no stranger to failure. However, it wasn't just negative thinking on his part, because he had a solution. He told me how to pile up dust from the produce just inside the container doors, arranged in a certain way. If Customs did open the container, they wouldn't take any notice of the pile of dust. Once they started to remove the pallets, it would disturb the dust pile. Our helpers in England would be looking out for this. They would then merely unload the container and not strip back the false floor.

Not to be outdone, I also added my own city-smart touch. From a friend who was something of a whizz-kid with electronics, I obtained some sophisticated listening devices. I then planted several in the false bottom of the container. The receiver was given to one of our people in England. We knew which docks the container was being delivered to. It was then just a matter of sitting in a car outside the docks with the receiver and listening to any traffic. Dead silence would mean the container hadn't been touched. Drilling, banging and voices would mean that it had been examined. And if the container was compromised, our people would just unload the main compartment and leave the stuff in the false floor.

Blacka listened to all this but still insisted that we use the pile of dust trick too. It was just as well, because the listening devices refused to work on several occasions.

In the event, we got away with it seven times. On the eighth occasion, the Customs were heard drilling the bottom of the container, so that was the end of the sardine-tin trick. However, I already had another up my sleeve. It was now time for me to reveal to the world the 'dead end' trick.

Many of the containers I was working with were 40 feet long. I was sure that no one would miss the odd foot. Using steel sheet identical to that of the interior of the container, I built a false wall at the back. Behind this, there was now a space a foot wide, ten feet high and ten feet broad. A considerable amount of ganja could be crammed into this space. We had several successes with this before the Customs found us out. Such were our profit margins, though, that it hardly mattered if the occasional shipment fell.

Now that my new smuggler's life was ticking over quite nicely and I was earning lots of money, I started to focus more closely on my social life. I had several casual Jamaican girlfriends, but there was nothing serious.

Veronica was a girl I used to go out with back in England. A friend told me that she had asked after me, so I contacted her and invited her over to Jamaica. She was a sensible girl who never asked probing questions.

Suddenly, my life was complete again. Veronica and I would spend weekdays down on the farm, and at weekends we would return to Kingston to party. She obviously knew that we were producing ganja, but that was all she knew. I never took her to meet those involved in the shipping process, thus abiding by Blacka's third rule. As far as Veronica was concerned, we were producing ganja for the domestic Jamaican market.

Even though things were running smoothly, Blacka still continued with my smuggling education. It revealed to me just how much there was to the game and prevented me from becoming complacent.

One day, Blacka took me aside and explained that the containers weren't the best or only way to smuggle contraband. Sometimes it was easier and more economical to send smaller shipments. One method was by suitcase on an international flight. However, I immediately questioned the profitability of moving such a comparatively small amount. Blacka responded by laying it out for me. You could get 26 kilos of weed in a suitcase. At £50 per pound for top-quality weed, this represented a layout of about £2,600. It would cost another £2,000 to pay a Jamaican baggage handler to put the case on the flight and another £3,000 for a courier to carry it through Customs at the other end. Thus, the total cost of the shipment amounted to £7,600. In England, top-class weed was fetching about £5,000 a kilo. So our 26 kilos were worth £130,000, a clear profit of over 120 grand. Hardly small beer by any standard.

As simple as the financial side was, the actual operation was quite ingenious. Our courier would board the flight in Jamaica and check in his case. At the same time, our paid baggage handler would place an absolutely identical case containing the weed amongst the baggage. Absolutely identical, that is, except for a pronounced scratch on the top. Both cases would have combination locks.

On arrival in England, our courier would wait by the baggage carousel, pick up the case with the scratch on it and go through Customs. In the event of his being stopped and asked to open the case, he would punch in the code for his original case. Of course, the case wouldn't unlock. The Customs officer would then force the case open and find the weed.

Our courier would vehemently deny that the one containing the weed was his case, saying that the real one contained his holiday clothes. He would insist that his case must still be on the carousel. A Customs officer would go to look and, of course, find the identical case. The courier would then punch in the correct code, opening the case to reveal his dirty laundry. Then he would proceed on his way, with the Customs officer's apologies ringing in his ears.

We got several shipments through by this method and were then fortunate enough to find a friendly Customs officer who worked at a major London airport. We still operated the scheme in the same way but with a built-in safeguard. Our Customs officer would be waiting in the arrivals hall, looking out for our courier. As the latter approached the Customs area, our Customs guy would walk to meet him and lead him into the search area, taking him to a table away from where the other Customs officers were standing. He would then open the unlocked case and, of course, see the weed. However, he would shut it again and send our courier on his way.

In the event of another Customs officer wandering over during the search and seeing the weed, the original plan would kick in. The courier would deny that it was his case, the original would be fetched from the carousel and he would be sent on his way. This radically improved our hit rate.

The key to continuing success, though, was always innovation and change. I came up with a way of hollowing out the wood of the pallets and concealing our stuff inside. It was both difficult and time-consuming, but there were lots of pallets in each consignment, and a lot of ganja could be moved in this way. We had several successes until a clumsy driver at the market split the wood of a pallet with the forklift blade and the ganja came tumbling out for everyone to see.

A similar move involved us building false sides in the baggage bins. These were regularly removed from the airport for maintenance at a nearby company. We had a man working in the company.

Some moves, by their very nature, were one-offs. I named one 'The Stiff', and Blacka said that only I could have come up with it. We had one of our men go to the British High Commission in Kingston and request the appropriate permission to ship the body of a deceased friend back to England. The friend had held British citizenship and had been living in England before coming to Jamaica for an extended holiday. He had died whilst on holiday. When the Commission official asked what the cause of death was, our man announced that it was AIDS-related and produced a death certificate from a local Jamaican doctor to prove it. Needless to say, the official didn't ask to see the corpse.

Which was just as well, because there wasn't one. Its place in the coffin had been taken by 100 kilos of Jamaica's finest. Back in England, it was reverently retrieved by our man working in the undertakers!

One problem we did have was that our smuggling routes all ran one way: from Jamaica to England. As a result, we were generating hundreds of thousands of pounds in England. To finance future shipments and pay for living expenses, we wanted this money in Jamaica.

Blacka came up with the solution. A Jamaican friend of his ran a big haulage business with a fleet of dozens of lorries. He was forever buying new vehicles. Our people would buy a new lorry in England and send it by sea to Jamaica. Hidden somewhere inside the bodywork would be hundreds of thousands of pounds of our money.

With everything else in my life running like a dream, the decision to bring Veronica to Jamaica was revealing itself to be a terrible mistake. Veronica was a white girl. This in itself wasn't the cause of the problem, because in the circles I moved in Jamaica was a thoroughly multiracial society. The problem was that she thought like an English girl.

I had a wide circle of Jamaican friends, both male and female. I was particularly close with a small group of young women – the ones, in fact, who had conducted the river ceremony on my previous return to England. Veronica just couldn't get her head around the fact that they were only friends and that I wasn't having multiple affairs behind her back.

This was the last in a long line of last straws. I sent Veronica back to England. Suitably wounded, I moped around for a couple of weeks until a friend advised me that the best way to forget a woman was to find another one.

Amber had been a friend and soulmate from the days of the acid-house parties. Our relationship had always been thoroughly platonic, which was probably the reason it had endured so well. I desperately needed someone to talk to about my recent failed romance. Amber was ideal. I asked her to come to Jamaica to see me. She agreed to come as a friend.

I picked her up from the airport. From the moment she got in the car with me, I felt my mood change as I relaxed in her company. We chatted light-heartedly about mutual friends back in England, but such was the effect of her presence that I found myself sneaking sly glances at her as I drove. Almost as a revelation, it came to me what a beautiful, mystical girl she was. I found myself questioning why I had never really noticed this before. Her West Indian heritage would mean that there would be none of the jealousy about my girlfriends that had so exercised Veronica. But, then, Amber and I were only friends.

With Amber's luggage safely ensconced in the spare bedroom of my apartment, I set about showing her the Kingston social scene. Amber was no prude, but she was no party animal either. I soon got the impression that such things quickly bored her. I had the idea of getting away from it all with her, but where would we go? She had just arrived, so I didn't want to embark on another flight. The solution came to me in a flash. I would take her to Oracabessa in the mountains of northern Jamaica.

With our cases in the back of an open-topped jeep I had rented, I headed north out of Kingston. As we drove, the ever-sensible Amber was giving me sound advice about how to deal with getting over Veronica. I listened carefully but was aware that it was now largely irrelevant. Veronica was far from my thoughts and was rapidly becoming a distant memory.

It hadn't started out as a romantic interlude, but the power and beauty of our surroundings couldn't help but affect us. I caught Amber sneaking looks at me in the same way that I had looked at her earlier. It seemed very natural to reach across and hold her hand.

As we drove ever further north, the mountains towered massively above us. Streams roared and gurgled through rocky gorges as exotic birds swooped and called. The riotous, unrestrained greenery seemed to assault the road on all sides. Occasionally, we had to slow to manoeuvre around a fallen tree or a rockslide. It was all thoroughly primeval. I reflected that this landscape could hardly have changed since prehistoric times. It served to make me and my problems seem quite insignificant. In God's grand scheme of things, we were all merely minor players.

It suddenly occurred to me that Amber hadn't even asked me where we were going. As we neared Oracabessa, I described our destination. Firefly was a tiny hamlet that nestled high in the mountains overlooking the sea. It was famous for its link with Noël Coward, who had had a house there. Sophia Loren and Sean Connery had been regular guests. Ian Fleming had chosen the place to write his James Bond novels.

A darker side to its history was attested to by the several fortified stone houses with built-in gun ports. They had been used by Captain Morgan, the infamous pirate and smuggler, as a lookout point. This was prior to his being appointed as the governor of Jamaica by the British crown. Any romantic analogy to my own situation as a modern-day smuggler was soon dispelled by Amber. She soon made it abundantly clear that she strongly disapproved of smuggling and, more specifically, my involvement in it.

It wasn't enough to rupture the mood, especially as Firefly more than lived up to expectations. We booked into a small inn, Amber specifying a double room with single beds, then roamed the places immortalised by Coward's elite circle.

The majesty of the mountains as they swooped steeply down to the sea, the massive peaks that towered above us partly hidden by clouds, and the indescribable riot of colours as nature's blooms and plants seemed to compete to overwhelm the spectrum was almost too much. At times, the senses strained to take it all in.

Amber and I constantly looked at each other as if to measure whether the place was affecting us both in the same way. And it

Me, aged three,
with my first sports car.

Me, aged 22,
with the real thing.

Food and family played
a big part in my
childhood.

Here I am on the run in Negril in 1992 after someone was killed at one of our acid-house parties.

Erica and I posed for a Jamaican newspaper to show off our son Stefan. (© *Jamaica Herald*)

Me and Amber on holiday in St Lucia in 2001.

Me and Amber in Havana, Cuba, in 2002. It was in Cuba that I arranged for the 'moody' cigars to be smuggled to the UK.

Here I am relaxing in my Merc on the way to the 1998 World Cup in France.

A Genesis warehouse party in Ferry Lane in 1989.

Another of our 1989 parties.

Despite initial scepticism,
I soon found myself getting into the
acid-house scene in a big way.

Me and Wayne setting up for our party
in Leaside Road in 1988.

LEFT: This flyer for the first Genesis party can now be seen in the Museum of London. *RIGHT*: Our joint New Year's Eve party was voted the best event in 1988 by the *NME*.

Big crowds gathered at the Freedom to Party rally in Trafalgar Square in 1990.

Wyclef Jean at the Reggae Sunsplash
concert in Victoria Park in 1999.

Ky-Mani Marley and Marcia
Griffiths on stage at Reggae
Sunsplash.

A crowd of 40,000 turned up to the Sunsplash event.

Glen Scarlet, Saracen from *Gladiators* and Denise Jones, the mayor of Tower Hamlets, presenting the Sunsplash five-a-side football trophy.

The Sunsplash event almost never happened, as I had to fight more than one battle for the right to stage the event. (© GV Media Group)

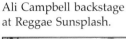

Ali Campbell backstage at Reggae Sunsplash.

Mel B of the Spice Girls helped to calm the Victoria Park crowd after Wyclef Jean had wound them up.

The windscreen of Amber's Merc was smashed when the
Customs officers arrested me in connection with what
I thought was our consignment of cigars.

A Nissan pick-
up loaded with
contraband.

A copy of a PII (Public
Interest Immunity) form,
many of which were used to
conceal intelligence relating
to my case.

was. A golden glow seemed to surround us. We wandered, hand in hand, like two characters from one of Coward's novels. By the evening of the second day, I was sure that I was in love with this woman. It took a further day for me to ask her to marry me.

Amber pondered the question for what seemed like a long time. Her reply, when it came, was ambiguous. 'Yes, but . . .' she answered, then paused. My heart was in my mouth, and my pulse raced frantically. How would I handle a rebuff from this woman? But I needn't have feared. She would marry me, although there was one condition: I had to give up smuggling!

Amber emphasised that it wasn't that she was a prude, although she did add that all her friends and her family were respectable, hard-working people. Her decision was based on sound practicality: she didn't want to be married to me only to see me carted off to prison. I didn't have to agree to the condition immediately. In fact, she said that it was best that we both think things over. She would return to England at the end of the week. It would take another month for me to settle my affairs in Jamaica. We could both make up our minds when I returned to England.

I explained the situation to Blacka, and he said that he understood completely. He wished me well and gave me his blessing. Over the next few weeks, I collected all my cash together and said goodbye to my many friends. I had already decided that I would have another go at the music business. I was both refreshed and fully cashed up. It would just be a question of selecting the right project.

Eight

Making a Splash

IN MANY ways, the music business hadn't changed a bit since I'd been away. All the usual unreliable people running around with hare-brained projects that had little chance of success were still around. From my own personal experience, I had found the music business to be full of people who couldn't seem to make their minds up whether they were working or playing. Many had fearsome drug or drink habits. They seemed to be forever caught between the two worlds of partying and working. So not only would I be looking for a good project, I would also be looking for a good partner.

I didn't choose wisely. If I had a fault, and I had many, it was that I would stand for someone who wasn't really up to the mark. With my finely developed sense of fair play, I was forever giving someone a chance, and this is what happened now.

Jakey had been around the music scene for years. A small guy who moved with quick, ferret-like movements, he was a couple of years younger than me. Unfortunately, he had been known to go missing for days, especially when it was crucial that he be on message. He rejoiced in the nickname of 'Sadim', an inversion of Midas, of kingly fame. However, whereas everthing the latter touched turned to gold, everything the former touched inevitably turned to shit.

I had been back in England only a few days when I heard that Jakey was looking for me. In laid-back Jamaican mode, I agreed to meet him. At first glance, what he had arranged was quite impressive. I don't know how he had managed it, because he didn't have a penny to his name, but he had got on good terms with someone high up on the Swansea Council and received permission to stage a live musical event at Swansea Airport.

Jakey talked a good gig, even if he could rarely stage one. Soon I was hooked. The venue looked ideal: a giant open space but with security fencing surrounding it. Furthermore, we did seem to have the full support of Swansea Council, even though they weren't willing to put up any money towards staging the event. Because Jakey was forever in a state of poverty, it was left to me to finance the event.

Initially, everything went swimmingly. Jakey put himself about and found us excellent offices in the Old Truman Brewery in Brick Lane, which had recently been converted into a business centre. He hired a crack-head mate of his to decorate the walls. Being occupied with other things, I took this to be a simple case of painting and decorating. In the event, Jakey's mate turned out to be an unbelievably good artist. Jakey had decided to call our new business the Eleventh Commandment, quite an inspired name for someone who wasn't in the least literary.

In keeping with our new name, the decorator set out to construct giant murals all over the walls and ceiling of the outer office. Each had a biblical tone, and a couple had a distinctly Renaissance theme. Over the next week or so, as I bustled in and out of the offices, I noticed the work in progress. First, he drew outlines with some kind of pencil until every wall was a spider's web of chaotic lines and drawings. Then he started to fill in the colour. Slowly but surely, it began to take shape.

During this time, I went away for several days on a long weekend to Swansea. On my return, I found myself in the Sistine Chapel, or, rather, our decorator's approximation of it. It was unbelievably good. God, or maybe Zeus, sat with his arm outstretched amongst billowing clouds as cherubim and seraphim swooped around him. The influence of Michelangelo was clear.

As the days passed, all the walls were finished until we had a multicoloured mural that stretched over every surface. The effect was amazing. It had transformed our outer office into something resembling a cross between an enchanted grotto and the National Gallery. You could spend hours staring at it and its multitude of detail. It also had a startling effect on any visitors, often causing them to stand open-mouthed. It served as excellent PR for us. Visitors could only conclude that a business that had created such a work of art must surely be a company of substance. Unfortunately, that turned out to be very much not the case.

By then, Jakey was in the advanced stages of terminal delusions of grandeur. For someone without a dime to his name, he had managed to line up an all-star cast that brought the cost of staging the event to over £1 million. When I asked him if he was confident of raising all the money, he replied that he was sure that he could always blag someone for it. I could only conclude that perhaps he was right, for he had certainly blagged me for over 80 grand by that point.

One day, Jakey came in looking particularly stressed. I was standing with two friends who had both put money into the event. Around us, various office staff we had hired beavered away. Calling the three of us together, he ushered us into the outer office and then into a large broom cupboard that stood in one corner. He closed the door behind us as the receptionist looked on in amazement.

Explaining that we should keep our voices down lest the staff hear what we were talking about, he convened this extraordinary general meeting among the brooms and the mops. The upshot was that many of the agents of the artists, together with some of the contractors who would supply lights, stages, etc., were asking for substantial deposits. Jakey asked us if we would put our name to a loan of £250,000 each, adding that he was perfectly willing to do so himself.

I looked at my two friends and rolled my eyes, then the three of us looked at Jakey. All he owned was what he stood up in; he had nothing to lose. We had flats and decent cars. In the event of a flop, we would be left destitute. Thus ended the Swansea Airport concert and the Eleventh Commandment. I retired to lick my wounds, all the while bemoaning the fact that I had done 80 grand in cold blood.

I had always loved reggae and felt it to be an important part of my cultural heritage. Together with a friend of mine called Ricky, who was also a long-time reggae fan, we began to discuss the possibility of doing a reggae concert. He suggested that we get together with a music lawyer we both knew called Glen. Glen was second-generation Jamaican and also had a passion for reggae. He agreed to meet us for breakfast the next day.

I put it to Glen that we wanted to revive the Reggae Sunsplash concert, at one time one of the most famous musical events in the world. It originally began in Jamaica with the One Love Peace Concert on 22 April 1978, staged at the national stadium. Out of this grew the first Reggae Sunsplash, which was held in Montego Bay in June 1978. The event was organised by a company called Synergy Productions, who believed that reggae was a powerful vehicle that could attract tourists and therefore foreign-exchange earnings to Jamaica. They were quite evangelical in their zeal to promote reggae, and by 1981 Sunsplash had grown into a massive concert that attracted thousands of tourists to Jamaica each year. It was such a successful multicultural event that one music critic referred to it as 'the melting pot of humanity'. Such was its international appeal that in February 1983 the newly formed Channel Four ran a 12-part Reggae Sunsplash television series.

In 1984, Reggae Sunsplash came to England for the first time. It was staged at Crystal Palace football ground as part of the Capital Radio Music Festival. A film of the concert was made, called *Splashing the Palace*. By 1985, the event was being staged in the United States, Jamaica, Japan and across Europe.

In 1987, a massive open-air free concert was held at Clapham

Common. It was staged as a tribute to Marcus Garvey, one of Jamaica's national heroes. The event attracted over 250,000 people. With such a large group of people in one place, the police became concerned. They insisted that the next event be held indoors so that the crowd could be better controlled. This went directly against the spirit of Sunsplash as an open-air event. The organisers called it sacrilege and refused. That was the end of Sunsplash.

Now, 12 years later, I wanted to revive it. But not just for the money. And not for my love of the music. I had strong ideological reasons. My intention was to stage a multicultural event that would help smooth race relations in England.

Glen's first question concerned who held the rights to the Sunsplash name. Ricky suggested that he thought they were owned by a cousin of mine back in Jamaica. Junior wasn't a blood relative, but, according to Jamaican custom, we had grown so close that I always referred to him as my cousin. With Ricky in tow, I flew to Jamaica and stayed at the luxurious Wyndham Hotel. Appearances were everything. If people didn't think you had money, they wouldn't take your proposals seriously.

Junior had long since retired. However, I convinced him to come to a meeting with me at the Wyndham. By coincidence, the English cricket team was also staying there at the time. Junior was duly impressed as he breakfasted just yards from England's finest.

Junior still had a passion for the music, but he said that the situation was complicated. Several of the partners who had rights to Sunsplash had fallen out and were no longer speaking to each other. One had died, and it wasn't known if his heirs had inherited his rights. Junior said that the situation would be difficult to untangle, but, if the money was right, not impossible. He said that he would try to sort it out. Following that, he would come to England to meet with the other interested parties.

Back in England, I was under no illusion about the difficulty of what I was about to try. Since I had been out of the music business, the staging of major musical events had been largely tied up. Harvey Goldsmith and Vince Powell ran most of the major festivals and open-air concerts. They were well organised and well funded. We would be in direct competition with them. For that reason, I would have to surround myself with the very best people.

John Burrows, OBE, certainly qualified as one of those. In his late 50s and originally from Yorkshire, he was a courtly, silver-haired gentleman, who was always immaculately turned out. He had gained his honour for achievements in music. As director of live entertainment for Capital Radio, he had staged over 1,500 live events. He had been involved with bringing Sunsplash to England for the first time. Later, he worked at Classic FM.

I also approached the internationally famous DJ, David Rodigan. As a white guy, David had been well ahead of his time in his love for reggae. Together with John Burrows, we now had a team with thousands of great contacts and loads of credibility. I was confident that I was making a positive start.

The event was now in pressing need of offices. I saw a sign offering premises to let in Old Street and phoned the number on the board. Thus I came to meet Maxine and Kelvin, who were janitors responsible for several premises in the area. They were a couple of characters who wouldn't be put off by some of the more bizarre goings on that usually surrounded my events. They found us suitable offices in Corsham Street, close to Hoxton and Old Street.

Once we had kitted out the offices, we were ready for our first important meeting. Junior had by then arrived in England with the good news that he had managed to secure the agreement of all the Jamaican partners of the Sunsplash name. I sent limousines for John Burrows and David Rodigan. They joined Glen, Ricky and me for our inaugural meeting in our new boardroom.

Both John and David loved the idea of resurrecting Sunsplash and agreed to get involved. However, they strongly stressed the need for us to get everything properly tied up legally. They recommended a firm of lawyers who would prepare all the paperwork necessary for staging such an event.

Now that I had the talent on board, I put my mind to finding a company that could handle the logistics of assembling the infrastructure of the actual concert. Chromatic Productions Ltd came well recommended as a highly experienced team. They would arrange it so that we had the best lighting and staging and everything else we would need. They would also take care of any special requirements of the authorities who controlled the venue.

So, with the team and infrastructure now taking shape, it was time to look for a suitable venue. We did consider Crystal Palace Arena, but because it only had a 16,000 capacity we decided that it was too small. We were looking for a much bigger, open-air space that would lend itself to staging a concert, would accommodate perhaps 50,000 people and was centrally located so that people could get to it easily.

I don't recall who suggested it, but we now considered Victoria Park. It was certainly big enough and centrally located. Further, Tower Hamlets, in which it was situated, was one of the most racially diverse areas of London. If ours was to be a multicultural event aimed at promoting good race relations, we could hardly have found a more suitable location.

Initial approaches to Tower Hamlets council met with an enthusiastic response. We were put in the capable hands of Brian Oakaby, the head of the park authority. He assured us that there was no official resistance to the staging of the event but that it was his job to make sure that everything was done properly. It would be a very big event, attended by many thousands of young people. In the volatile inner-city areas, such things had to be carefully organised. We managed to convince him that we were responsible people and got his full cooperation.

By then, with preparations well advanced, I had put in £200,000 of my own money. If the concert failed, I would be virtually penniless. Furthermore, with my funds completely expended, it was clear that we would need more financial backers. As we went about approaching interested parties, we received some news that hit us like a bombshell.

Someone brought my attention to the latest issue of the *Black Echoes* music paper. It stated that a Reggae Sunsplash concert was to be staged that coming summer at Wembley Arena. It named Jamaican businessman Lawrence Ho-sing as the promoter. I got him on the phone and explained that I had the rights to Sunsplash. Ho-sing replied that when Synergy had gone into liquidation in Jamaica, a company called Reggae Sunsplash International had bought the rights to the concert. He had obtained a licence from them. Junior was adamant that he was wrong and that we had the rights to stage the event in England. Suddenly, we had a major legal battle on our hands.

It was a costly, time-consuming and very public dispute. In the early stages, a headline appeared in the *Weekly Gleaner* that read 'Promoters Battle Over Sunsplash'. The eyes of the music industry, if not the world, were upon us.

Litigation is always a costly affair, and we soon ran out of money. I had to ask an old friend of mine if he wanted to invest in the concert. Ned was second-generation Jamaican and had done well for himself. He was now a successful gold dealer in Hatton Garden. Fortunately for me, he still had a passion for reggae. He agreed to put in £200,000 for a share of the profits.

The case dragged on, but we finally triumphed. The court ruled that we had the Sunsplash rights in England. Financially weakened, we pressed on with the concert.

Even though I was thoroughly straight at that time, I still managed to find it difficult to totally divorce myself from my former criminal associates, and I would often be asked for a favour. One of my old friends requested permission to use one of our offices to hold a business meeting at night. All our staff would be off duty, as would the workers in the offices above and below. I couldn't see the harm in it and gave my permission without even asking the nature of the business.

Later that evening, the four participants in the scheduled meeting showed up at the offices. One of them was carrying a large sports bag. I ushered them into a small office at the end of a corridor and returned to my desk to work. About half an hour passed, and I had completely forgotten about them. The empty offices almost hummed with silence, perfectly complemented by the silent streets outside. Suddenly, there was a thunderous explosion that made me jump clean out of my chair. I ran out of the office, into the corridor and stared in the direction from which the noise had come. The door of the office slowly opened and a face cautiously peered out.

'What the fuck's going on?' I shouted. I was beckoned towards the office. As I entered, I saw the other three standing around a table, on top of which lay two pump-action shotguns. 'What happened?' I asked again as the four gathered around, all looking suitably shame-faced. One of them explained that they had been doing a deal to sell the shotguns, and a cartridge had become jammed in the chamber of one of the weapons. They had struggled to free it by jacking the chamber backwards and forwards, and the gun had gone off.

I looked around for evidence of damage, then looked at the four guys. 'Anyone hurt?' I asked. All of them shook their heads, but they still looked uncomfortable. 'Any damage?' Reluctantly, one of them led me behind a desk and pointed at the floor. I stared downwards.

At first, I was confused. The hole in the floor was very dark, but there was depth to the darkness. It was only as I peered more closely that I managed to make out a typewriter on a desk. The shot had blown a hole clean through the ceiling of the office below!

I sent the four guys packing and considered what I should do. I thanked my good fortune that no one had been in the office below at the time. Office work was considered to be relatively safe employment. Around me, though, it seemed that typists could be shot dead at their desks.

I had no way to gain access to the office below, so I had to just hope that the shotgun pellets wouldn't be easily recognisable. Fortunately, the ever-understanding Maxine managed to smooth things over. Without blinking an eye, she accepted my unlikely explanation of accidentally dropping something extremely heavy onto the floor and went below to assure them that I would pay for the damage.

With the sky remarkably clear of clouds for once, I decided it was a good time to try to attract further investment in the concert. A group of businessmen came forward and offered £500,000. We sat down with our lawyers and drew up the relevant contracts. Once again, everything seemed to be running smoothly. It wasn't to last.

Right out of the blue, I got a phone call from a German guy calling himself Hans Becker. The gist of the conversation was that he was saying that we didn't own the trademark rights to the Reggae Sunsplash brand. I immediately told him that we had been down this particular road already and that a court had decided in our favour.

'No, you silly boy,' said Hans in his thick German accent. 'I'm not referring to the rights to staging the concert. I'm talking about the rights to the name "Reggae Sunsplash".'

I ignored his less than respectful 'silly boy' because I was now intrigued and not a little concerned. He seemed to be very confident. 'Well, if we don't own the rights to the trademark, then who does?' I asked.

'I do, of course, you silly boy,' he replied, chuckling to himself.

Still holding my temper in check, I said, 'And how did that come about, then?'

'Because I made it my business that it was so. Anyway, you will have to talk to me sooner or later. I trust my number has come up on your mobile? Give me a call when you are ready.' And with that he rang off.

I sat back to contemplate this latest nightmare. It seemed that no sooner had we got over one hurdle than another presented itself. I called Robert Lee, one of the original members of Sunsplash, and discussed it with him. He confessed that he didn't know the answer but said that he would come with me to meet this Hans Becker.

I called the German and made arrangements to meet him at his offices the following day. In the meantime, I called everyone who was anyone in the music business, trying to find out something about my adversary. The picture that emerged was not a pretty one.

Hans Becker was a very wealthy German businessman who had made his fortune in the music industry. He owned the rights to an extensive catalogue of music. However, his particular speciality, one that he had become notorious for throughout the industry, was to secretly trademark brands that were nothing to do with him. He would identify a new brand then search to see who owned the trademark to its name. It was amazing just how many people neglected to trademark the name of their brand. Hans would then slip in quietly and register the trademark for himself. As a result, the original company would have to pay him a lot of money just to have the right to trade under what they had thought to be their own brand name. There was a rumour that he had done this to a German singer who had died in poverty. It was thinly disguised extortion, really, and now he was doing it to me.

I was mulling all this over as I journeyed to meet with Hans at his offices in Wandsworth. I was very much in passive mode. I had Robert Lee with me, a quiet middle-aged guy who was singularly unthreatening. At this first meeting, I wanted Hans to be at his ease so that I could weigh him up, as I had already realised that paying him was out of the question. He would hold us to ransom in the way that had already made him very wealthy.

We arrived early and told the receptionist that we had a meeting with Mr Becker. She picked up the intercom and passed this information on to him. He kept us waiting for over half an hour. Eventually, she ushered us into his office and directed us towards two chairs that stood in front of an immense desk, behind which lounged Hans with his feet up and a large cigar in one hand.

I sat down and tried to suss him out. He was seriously overweight, with thick folds of fat that hung down around his chin. The suit he was wearing was very expensive, and everything else about him spoke of money. He was sitting down, so it was hard to tell exactly, but he seemed to be quite short. I guessed him to be in his late 40s.

He certainly seemed to be very pleased with himself. There was a broad smile on his fat face, which spoke of smugness. He clearly thought that he was fully in charge of the situation. This was not unrelated to the fact that two very large men were sitting in the corner of the office. As I looked across, they stared back at me impassively. Standing by a coat rack, I saw two baseball bats.

It was quite obvious to me that Hans had done this sort of thing many times before and that he was prepared for trouble. I sat back, as unthreateningly as I could, and waited for Hans to begin. 'I assume it was you I spoke to earlier, my dear boy,' he said, pointing at me. I acknowledged that it was. 'Well, I won't waste precious time, so let's get down to business,' he continued. 'You own the rights to stage the Sunsplash concert. I own the rights to the Sunsplash trademark. So, unless you are going to change the name of your event, you will have to come to some arrangement with me.'

I sat forward, trying to make eye contact with him past the barrier of the soles of his shoes. 'We have already done so much work and spent a lot of money,' I said.

'And what has that got to do with me?' replied Hans, avoiding my gaze.

I tried another approach, but knew I was wasting my time. 'As a second-generation Jamaican, I've always thought that

Sunsplash was part of my heritage,' I said.

'Pah! What is this heritage nonsense?' exploded Hans. 'It is purely a matter of business. I own the trademark, and you will have to deal with me. I have no more time to waste. Call me when you are ready for the next meeting.'

As the meeting was clearly at an end, I stood up and walked out of the office with Robert Lee silently following. He hadn't said a word. In the circumstances, I was quite pleased with myself. I had maintained my self-control and learned a lot about Hans Becker in the process. Now I would prepare my next move.

With 200 grand now invested in the project, my Hatton Garden friend, Ned, wasn't at all amused by the antics of Herr Becker. 'Let me get my hands on the German cunt,' he raged, fully intent on going to see him right away.

'Patience, Ned, patience,' I said. 'Let's be very clear about what we are going to do.' I explained my plan.

Arranging the next meeting was a mere formality. Quite clearly, Hans had been expecting it. And equally clearly, he felt that, having met me, he had nothing to fear from me. Which was exactly what I wanted him to think.

I met up with Ned at the office. He had brought an old friend with him. Ned was a powerfully built bear of a man with massively broad shoulders. Billy 'the Stick' stood perhaps two inches taller and was even broader. Both were no strangers whatsoever to violence. I had cautioned them that we mustn't alert Hans' suspicions too soon. Towards this end, both were attired in smart business suits complete with bowler hats. We would need our lawyer to be present, so we picked up Glen on the way. I hadn't told him anything about my plan. As far as he was concerned, we were all going to just another business meeting.

We sat waiting in Hans' reception as the receptionist informed him that we had arrived. He still kept us waiting for over 40 minutes. I was now aware that not only was this part of his strategy, he enjoyed humiliating people to boot.

The secretary finally ushered us into the great man's presence, and from the look on his face it was obvious that Hans knew he had made a mistake. He had clearly expected me to return with someone equally as unthreatening as Robert Lee. Even in their business attire, both Ned and the Stick had an ominous air about them. There was no sign of his two minders, a fact that I guessed Hans was now regretting.

Nevertheless, he made a brave face of it in front of his receptionist. Telling her that that would be all, he waved us towards the chairs. Glen and I sat, whilst Ned and the Stick stood behind us. By that point, Hans was looking seriously worried.

With absolutely no preliminaries, I sat sharply forward and began. 'Look here, you dirty German cunt. Do you think for one minute that I'm going to let a fat, useless fucker like you blackmail me?' The rhetorical question hung in the air. Very white about the gills, Hans failed to answer.

'As I said to you before,' I continued, 'Reggae Sunsplash is my birthright, and I'm not going to let a prick like you take it away from me.'

'But I own the rights to the trademark,' spluttered Hans, who was clearly frightened.

'Let me show you what I think about that, dear boy,' I replied, signalling to Ned.

Ned and the Stick closed in on Hans, who was now reaching for the intercom switch. He didn't make it. Sweeping him up from his chair, they ran him across the room and threw open a large window.

'What are you doing? What are you doing?' cried Hans in a high-pitched squeal.

I was now standing beside him. 'Giving you a bit of fresh air to clear your head, dear boy,' I replied and nodded to Ned. Reaching down, he and the Stick upended Hans and, taking a firm grip on his ankles, hung him out of the window. Eighty feet below, Wandsworth's shoppers went about their business. Hans, though, immediately pissed himself.

'Now, either you sign the rights to Sunsplash over to me, or my colleagues will let you fall,' I threatened him.

'OK, OK,' cried Hans, the urine staining his shirt and running freely under his chin.

Ned and the Stick hauled him back in and set him in his chair. It was only then that I remembered Glen. He was stiff with shock. He hadn't been expecting this. He was just a lawyer, thinking he was going to another business meeting. It took my shout of 'Glen, Glen' to bring him out of his shock. 'What do we need him to do?'

Recovering slowly, as if coming out of a dream, Glen replied sluggishly, 'He has to sign the papers. He will have the relevant papers.'

'Send for them,' I shouted at the still-cowed Hans.

He pressed the intercom switch, and the receptionist, who also doubled as his secretary, came in. Trying hard to hide the urine stains on his shirt with his jacket, Hans told her to bring the papers for the Sunsplash deal.

She turned and was about to leave when suddenly she remembered her good manners. 'Does anyone want tea?' Her question hung in the air.

'Yes, I'll have a nice cup of tea,' I replied, giving a sly wink to Ned, who got it immediately. It was important to keep up appearances for the receptionist. It had to seem like a normal meeting. We didn't want her to call the police.

'Two sugars for me,' said Ned.

'Any biscuits?' enquired the Stick with a polite smile on his face. Glen sat stiffly, incapable of either asking for or drinking anything.

The receptionist left and was quickly back with a pile of papers. As we gathered round his desk, Hans sorted through them. Pulling Glen from his chair, I asked him where they should be signed. He indicated the appropriate places. All that was left was the ritual of the tea.

The receptionist returned again and passed around the cups. We sat, politely sipping our tea, and the Stick nibbled at his biscuits.

It was a thoroughly civilised setting – English businessmen in the final stages of a business deal. We thanked the receptionist warmly as we left.

If I had thought that I had heard the last from Herr Becker, a phone call the following day soon disabused me of that notion. It was from a police inspector from Tower Hamlets – by coincidence, the very same inspector who I had meetings with each week in my bid to organise the concert. With the surprise clear in his voice, he said that he had received a call from Wandsworth Police Station saying that a German businessman had filed a complaint that claimed I had threatened him and coerced him into signing some papers. He asked if I knew anything about the incident. I said that I did, but it was nothing like what the German was describing. I went on to say that it was, in fact, Becker who had been threatening me. He was trying to muscle in on the Sunsplash gig, and when I had gone to his offices to confront him he had pulled a gun out of his desk drawer. I assured the officer that I had two business colleagues and my lawyer who would back up what I was saying.

'I've known you for months now, and I didn't think it could be true,' said the inspector. 'It's amazing what some people will try to do just to get money,' he added. I reflected that the inspector didn't know how right he was.

With the German now out of the picture, I set about finalising the all-star line-up for the concert. My first triumph was in signing up the legendary Dennis Brown, who people in the industry referred to as the 'Crown Prince of Reggae'. He had been performing publicly since the early 1970s, making over 50 albums and over 400 singles. He was one of my heroes from the days when I ran my sound system.

No king should be without a queen, so I signed up Marcia Griffiths, the 'Queen of Reggae'. She had started out in the 1960s and had an international reputation. Her crossover hit 'Young, Gifted and Black' had made it to number five in the charts.

With two legends now in the line-up, I felt we would satisfy the older, more traditional reggae fans. But I had something just as special for the new generation. Wyclef Jean of The Fugees had come to be called the 'Beethoven of Hip Hop'. His original recordings as well as his inspirational remixes of the work of other artists had brought him to superstardom. He would perfectly complement Dennis and Marcia.

I also managed to secure Gregory Isaacs, another legend who had been in the business for 31 years. Ky-Mani Marley and the Asian Dub Foundation were just two more of several supporting acts. *Rolling Stone* magazine waxed lyrical in their praise of the line-up.

DJs playing during changeovers between the live acts would be David Rodigan of Kiss FM, Daddy Ernie of Choice FM and Chris Goldfinger of BBC Radio One. David Rodigan and Richard Blackwood would also be among the several masters of ceremonies. It was a line-up to die for. All these people had been my heroes for many years. Now they would be coming to play at my concert.

To emphasise the community nature of the concert, we organised a five-a-side competition between children's teams from Tower Hamlets. We put up prize money and donated free tickets for the winners. We bought a winners' trophy and arranged for Denise Jones, the mayor, to present it. Saracen from *Gladiators* would present the lesser prizes, the whole competition was officially sponsored by Leyton Orient Football Club and scores of celebrities were scheduled to attend. I had 20 tons of sand delivered to the site and made a tropical beach setting. Free barbecued food would be served by a West Indian chef.

The concert date was finalised as 1 August 1999, Emancipation Day in Jamaica in remembrance of the freeing of slaves. With exactly a month left before the event, I decided to go to Jamaica to ensure that everybody who had said they would appear did so. My overnight flight landed early the next morning, and I took a leisurely drive across the island in my hire car. The sun was shining brightly and all around me lay the riotous beauty of the Jamaican countryside. Despite all the earlier problems, I didn't have a care in the world. All that was missing was the soundtrack from my life. I turned on the radio.

They were playing a Dennis Brown track, and I could only reflect how fitting it was. Then they played another, and another after that. I wasn't about to complain; I loved the man's voice. After a while, though, I did feel like a change and turned to another station. They too were playing Dennis Brown, closely followed by another of his tracks. I turned the dial and every station was playing his music. I knew he was very popular in Jamaica, but surely not that popular. Finally, at a break in the music, the presenter announced that they were playing these songs as a tribute to Dennis Brown, who had died earlier that day.

I couldn't believe my ears. As the implications dawned on me, I couldn't believe my bad luck. This man had enjoyed a career that spanned a quarter of a century, yet fate would have it that he should die just one month before appearing at my concert.

I completed my business very quickly and hurried back to England. I wanted to be close at hand should anything else go wrong. In my own personal version of Sod's law, mishaps always travelled in packs. I wasn't to be disappointed.

Not long after, there was an explosion in Brixton. A parcel left in the street had exploded, seriously wounding many people, some of them from ethnic minorities. Another attack followed in Brick Lane; this time, several Asians were injured. Then, just to demonstrate how broad his prejudice was, the bomber exploded a device in a Soho gay bar, killing one and seriously injuring many others. There was a mad bomber on the loose, targeting minorities. No doubt our multicultural concert would be high on his list.

The police certainly thought so. We met with them daily to discuss various security precautions that could be put in place. But what could you do against a faceless phantom? How could he be prevented from smuggling a bomb into our event? And in the face of a threat like that, wouldn't people just stay away in droves? Suddenly, the success of the whole venture was at stake.

To add insult to injury, a particularly deadly gang war now broke out between Jamaicans in south London. In the space of a few weeks, six Jamaican males were shot dead. The press was full of stories about a Yardie gang war. Once again, the authorities were asking us if we could guarantee that there would be no such trouble at our event.

Officers from Operation Trident, the police squad dedicated to investigating black-on-black shootings, were extremely concerned. They argued that rival Yardies could well turn up at the concert. A gun battle in the midst of such a large crowd could provoke a stampede, in which many people might be crushed to death. What, they asked, were we going to do to prevent it?

I was as baffled as to the solution as they were. Short of banning all black males from the event and strip-searching everyone, how could we stop someone smuggling in a relatively small item like a gun? The park authority was now becoming concerned and was looking for us to put measures in place that would reassure everyone.

All I could think of was to massively beef up the security precautions. To that end, we brought in Show and Event Security, a company with a good reputation. They were employed more as a measure to satisfy the park authority. In reality, they were little more than stewards. What was also needed was a really heavy team that would frighten away most of the potential troublemakers and be loyal to us. I asked Ned to arrange it.

Over the next week, Ned scoured all the low-life bars and clubs. He recruited a crew that included some of the most dangerous nutters in London. Finally, he assembled them for my inspection. I had been around dangerous people all my life, but this crew troubled even me. Broken noses, knife scars and mad stares were very much in evidence. I recalled Wellington reviewing his troops and saying something along the lines of,

'I don't know what they do to the enemy, but they sure as hell frighten the life out of me.' Wellington would have run a mile from this lot.

I called Ned aside and asked if the crew was reliable. He looked thoughtful as he considered my question but failed to answer.

'Are they trustworthy?' I continued.

'Some of them are,' responded Ned.

'But will they be loyal to us?'

'They will while we're paying them.'

'Well, what's the use of having a crew that can't really be trusted?' I demanded.

'You didn't say that you wanted perfect people,' replied Ned. 'You just said that you wanted a really tough crew. Well, these more than qualify. Their real value will lie in the fact that all the troublemakers will stay away when they hear that this lot are doing the security.'

I wasn't convinced, but it was too late to do much about it. Having brought them all together and promised them work, I didn't much fancy being the one who had to tell them that they weren't needed. When Ned said that we would call them the 'Elite Team' to distinguish them from the other security firm, I examined his face closely to see if he was joking.

With what seemed like the forces of the apocalypse gathering around me, we now had a couple of strokes of good fortune. First, the phantom bomber was arrested and consigned to a top-security jail. Then Operation Trident had a breakthrough and several of the Yardies involved in the recent shootings were also arrested. Two of our most serious problems had suddenly disappeared. I wondered out loud about the continuing need for our Elite Team, but Ned chose to ignore me.

Just as insurance, though, we brought on board a friend of mine called Shrugger. He ran a tough security operation called Giants Security, which included ex-US marines in its numbers. I found myself musing that we now had all the ingredients for a full-scale war.

With the other problems now out of the way, it was time to embark on some positive public-relations work. We put out press releases emphasising that Sunsplash was intended to be a family event. We wanted whole families to come along – parents, grandparents and kids. We also decided to dedicate the concert to the memory of Dennis Brown.

In an attempt to reassure people that the event would be safe, we invited as many celebrities as possible. Because their music was inspired by reggae, we asked UB40 to attend. They refused outright, saying that they thought it was too dangerous. Clearly, a bit of gentle arm-twisting was needed. I called their manager and said that we would tell the black press that UB40, a group that played black music, was refusing to attend our multicultural event. It did the trick, and Ali Campbell agreed to come and play a set.

Finally, the day of the concert dawned, and I was a bag of nerves. Disaster could strike in so many ways that I didn't know what to worry about the most. In the event, I just immersed myself in the logistics and forgot about everything else.

I was feeling considerable pride in what I had pulled off. We had the best stage, the best sound system and the best video screens. We had a line-up that read like a reggae hall of fame. Not least, we were staging the largest paying Sunsplash concert ever held in England. We were licensed for 50,000 people.

An early disappointment was that Gregory Isaacs didn't turn up. One of our people had actually taken him to the airport, but he had still managed to miss his plane. However, everything else went like clockwork.

MC Daddy Ernie kicked off proceedings at noon, introducing Blackstones, Timotee K and Peter Hunningale in quick succession. Smoking Joe took over to introduce WCK, then handed on to Richard Blackwood and Lisa Nash, who took us through the sets of Nine Yards, Glamma Kid, Phoebe One and Kloud Nine. At 3 p.m., Curtis Walker and Lisa Nash introduced the Asian Dub Foundation. Miss P was next, followed by Ky-Mani Marley.

Things were running so smoothly that I started to enjoy myself. Reality regularly intruded, though, every time I saw members of our Elite Team crew. All 22 of them were done up in smart black outfits and each carried a walkie-talkie. They strolled about doing that which they did best, namely growling at everybody and generally frightening people. However, there had been no trouble.

Back on stage, Chris Goldfinger introduced Goofy, Buccaneer, Red Rat and Mr Vegas. Then it was the turn of David Rodigan with Morgan Heritage. There was a strong sense of anticipation when Marcia Griffiths was welcomed by Miss P. This nicely segued into a David Rodigan tribute to Dennis Brown. It was left to Richard Blackwood to bring the last act up to the mike: Wyclef Jean.

Even though I was enjoying the music, my main concern at that stage was the money. Not only were there tens of thousands of pounds in gate money, there were also thousands in bar takings. It would be an attractive target for an armed-robbery firm. Then there were the dubious characters who were in our employ. I wouldn't have put it past many of them to help themselves to the takings, given the least opportunity. I walked from till to till to strongroom, making sure that everything was OK.

On my rounds, I discovered a problem. One of Shrugger's crew pulled me aside and said that he thought that some of the Elite Team had been working a scam. They had been collecting surrendered tickets then selling them at a cut rate to customers waiting to come in. This was potentially very dangerous to us and could seriously affect our profits. But the concert was nearly over, and it was too late to do anything about it.

Despite the smoothness of the performance, we were now running behind schedule. We were due to close the concert at 9.30 p.m., but it was that time already, and Wyclef had just started his set. I approached the park authority for an extra half an hour, then asked them for a further 30 minutes. They readily agreed. It was still light, and there had been no trouble. Up until then, that is.

Firmly in the spirit of the occasion, Wyclef lit up a spliff. Calling to the audience, he announced, 'If you like weed, put your hands up.' The crowd responded with a forest of hands. Encouraged, Wyclef called out, 'If you like guns, put your hands up.' Again, the crowd waved frantically. I reflected that he was getting a bit close to the edge.

Suddenly, there was a disturbance at the front of the crowd. Someone shouted out 'gun' and there was a stampede. People were getting crushed. Then all the lights went out for half a minute, although it seemed more like an hour. Pandemonium broke out. Then the lights came back on again.

Mel B of the Spice Girls was one of the invited celebrities. With remarkable coolness, she now appeared on the stage and, together with Wyclef, called for calm. They managed to quieten things down, but the problem was about to be compounded by the park authority. Thinking the concert was over, they opened the main gates to the concert area.

Outside, there was a crowd of about 2,000 who hadn't entered the event. They had remained outside the fence, dancing and singing along to the music. Now they surged into the site. Absolute chaos ensued. Whilst the police and our stewards struggled to restore order, I retreated to the strongroom to safeguard the cash. I supervised as a security van took it away to safety.

However, almost immediately, I had another problem to deal with. It seemed that in all the confusion someone had forgotten to pay our Elite Team. I was instantly surrounded by 22 angry nutters who were in no mood to argue. They rushed about the site, stealing everything of value that they could lay their hands on. What little control we ever had over them was now quite clearly gone.

Although they were potentially violent, I had been around much more dangerous people back in Jamaica. I shrugged off their threats, all the while promising that I would see to it that they were paid. The immediate problem was that I had no money. Pushed for cash before the concert took place, one of the other promoters and I had sold our two Mercs, which had cost ninety grand, for just £50,000. Until I got some of the money back from the bank, I was completely without funds.

I made a call to a friend of mine who was precisely one of the dangerous people I had met in Jamaica. Richie had been a posse leader but had been forced to flee Jamaica to avoid multiple murder charges. He had prospered in England. I told him about my problem and asked if he could lend me seven grand, which would cover the cost of the Elite Team's wage bill. He told me to hold on and that he would be there as soon as he could.

Meanwhile, things were turning nasty between our Elite Team and Shrugger's crew. They stood glaring at each other, seconds away from serious mayhem. It was at that point that Richie arrived. Carrying a large sports bag, he walked past the contending crews as if they weren't there. I led him into the room that served as our office and strongroom and closed the door behind us.

'Got here as soon as I could, Andy,' Richie said, opening the bag in front of me. 'What do you want to give to them?'

Lying right on top of the bag were two lethal-looking Tec-9 sub-machine guns, complete with clips of ammo. Underneath in bundles lay the seven grand. 'It's up to you, my friend,' he added, smiling.

For one mad moment I pictured myself as a cartoon character accepting his offer and mowing down the baddies from our Elite Team. But a calmer inner voice cautioned that this was hardly the spirit of the peaceful multicultural concert that I had tried so hard to promote. 'This time I think I'll give them their money,' I said.

On one level, the concert had been a resounding success. Despite a couple of close calls, there had been no trouble. Apart from criticising Wyclef for his remarks about the weed and the guns, the media were full of plaudits. And in the violent environment that was London in the 1990s, both the police and the park authority could only congratulate us. The general opinion was that everything had gone off very well indeed.

I would have agreed with them except for the fact that financially it had been a disaster. Although we had been licensed for 50,000 people, only about 40,000 came. Of those, only about 20,000 paid. Then there had been the Elite Team scam involving the recycling of already surrendered tickets. I estimated that this had cost us many thousands.

Overall, the cost of staging the concert had amounted to £1.3 million, but the total receipts only came to £700,000. This was a shortfall of £600,000, which included my 200 grand. So quite apart from any pride I could take in bringing Reggae Sunsplash back to England, on a personal level it had reduced me to near poverty.

Over the next few days, I retired to the offices to consider my next move. Unbeknown to me, the police had noted the active criminals who had recently been coming to the offices to discuss business. With the concert now out of the way, they felt it was time to act.

The upshot was that the National Crime Squad raided our premises early one morning to investigate allegations of money laundering. They searched the premises, seized computer hard drives and questioned several people. Nothing was found, and no one was charged, but the owner of the building had been informed and decided he wanted us out. Fortunately, the ever-reliable Maxine managed to find us new offices within a day.

Living in England in straight mode, all I really knew was the music business. Almost half-heartedly, I started to work on smaller projects. Targeting the R & B market, I would bring over artists from the USA every few months or so. I put shows on in the Brixton Academy and the Hammersmith Palais, and I also sold on shows to promoters in venues in Manchester and Birmingham. But after the heady excitement of Sunsplash, it was all very much an anticlimax. I couldn't go on like this. I would have to find a new move.

Nine

Close but No Cigar

ALTHOUGH I tried to put a brave face on it, the Sunsplash debacle had seriously weakened me and not only financially. Most of the money I had accumulated from the Jamaican weed smuggling was now gone, but so also was the positive, upbeat attitude I had returned to England with. It wasn't that I was whipped or beaten, but my normal self-confidence had been severely dented.

The sole saving grace of the situation was my relationship with Amber. She had been a tower of strength through it all and had become the rock on which I depended when things went wrong. She was also very understanding and knew me so well. It was she who suggested that I should get away for a while. Away from my circle of friends and acquaintances, and away from Stoke Newington, perhaps I could clear my head and come back refreshed.

It was only natural that I should go back to Jamaica. It was my spiritual home and had treated me so well in the past. There, surrounded by my friends and extended family, I could lick my wounds and put the recent experience behind me. Amber recommended that I go on my own. There wasn't any friction between us, but after the incestuous closeness of working on top of each other for the concert, it would be healthy for us to have a bit of space for a while.

In the event, I decided to take Dean, my mate from the

fruit market, with me. He hadn't had a holiday in years and had always expressed an interest in seeing Jamaica, no doubt encouraged by all the stories I had told him about the place.

As I stepped off the plane, I felt much of the angst clear from my mind. I found myself taking a deep breath of the fresh air and throwing my shoulders back. I might be wounded, but I was a very long way from being broken. I congratulated myself on deciding to return to Jamaica.

Once again, a relative loaned me the use of an apartment. As soon as Dean and I had moved our bags in, I went in search of my old pal and party companion, Paul. As luck would have it, he was with our friend Sean. They listened sympathetically to the saga of Sunsplash and offered their condolences. Paul confessed that he was stressed out himself, with Sean chiming in, 'Me too.'

And they were on the verge of doing something about it. The following day, they were due to fly to Cuba – Sean to meet up with his Cuban girlfriend, Paul to relax and party. When they asked us to come with them, we readily agreed.

I had always wanted to go to Cuba but had never found the time. I admired Fidel Castro, especially the way he had stood up to the USA. All Western propaganda to the contrary, I was aware that he was revered by the majority of the Cuban people. The latter had a great reputation for hospitality, too.

Paul knew someone in a travel agency, and, at very short notice, Dean and I got seats on the same flight as Sean and Paul. Despite obvious signs of poverty, Havana still hadn't lost its old-world charm. The fabric of the buildings might have been decaying and the roads riddled with potholes, but the people seemed full of spirit and good humour. There was also an underlying air of excitement, especially as night fell. Cuba was well known for its nightlife.

We soon found that although Paul's influence extended to flights, it didn't necessarily stretch to hotel accommodation. The taxi dropped them off at the luxury apartment they had rented, then continued on with us to the boarding house that Paul had found at the very last minute. From the state of some of the dire neighbourhoods we were now passing through, perhaps we should have been prepared for the place, but such was its condition that it still came as a shock.

The barrio was by far the worst we had so far encountered. Many of the decaying tenements were derelict, and those that were inhabited were only slightly better. Our boarding house stood in a row of similarly decrepit buildings. If the taxi driver hadn't known the place, we would never have found it on our own. The sign that announced the name of the street hung lopsidedly from its supporting chains, and the boarding house's number was virtually indecipherable.

We paid off the driver and climbed the discoloured, broken steps towards the entrance. As we neared the top, an aged crone appeared in the doorway. Neither Dean nor I spoke any Spanish, but even if we had been fluent I'm sure it wouldn't have helped us. In a guttural, rasping voice, liberally interspersed with hacking coughs, mine host welcomed us to her establishment. At least, that was my interpretation of it. Her arms were extended, and her wizened, time-eroded face, mouth half agape, was cracked into an approximation of a smile. The overall effect was horrible. No doubt, somewhere in the welcome she had mentioned her name. We missed it along with all the rest. Subdued, we followed her submissively into the building.

Perhaps we should have realised that the state of the receptionist was a harbinger of what was to come. But, in reality, nothing could have prepared us for that. The place was dark, no doubt deliberately so, in a vain attempt to disguise the squalor. A sole light bulb hung high up in a vaulted ceiling. By its dim glow, we climbed the stairs with our luggage. Carefully placing our feet so as to avoid the many holes in the faded carpet, we negotiated the narrow confines of the staircase. We were amazed to see misty clouds rising from beneath our feet and could only conclude that the stair carpet was thick with dust. To the accompaniment of a chorus of creaks and groans from the tortured wood of the ancient stairs, we progressed upwards, past walls bedecked with discoloured wallpaper, much of which hung in strips.

All this turned out to be a suitable introduction to our room. It was small and dingy, but even in the half-light its features were plain to see. Two ancient iron beds stood against one wall, a mattress of indiscernible colour on top of each. Two piles of dusty sheets were placed in the centre. The floorboards were bare, with no carpet. An old wardrobe stood against another wall with two rickety chairs on either side of it.

We followed as the crone waved us inside. She was pointing into a small room that adjoined the main one. It was obviously the bathroom, except that there was no bath. A chipped and dirty toilet, without a seat, jockeyed for space next to a similarly chipped porcelain shower base, over which hung a shower head.

At a sound from the crone, we turned and watched as she rummaged in the voluminous pocket of the garment that passed for her housecoat. With a grunt of satisfaction, she pulled something from the pocket, almost like a magician pulling a rabbit from a hat, but without the '*Voilà!*' She held the something out towards us.

We stepped closer. In the poor light, it was difficult to make out fine detail. Reluctantly, I held out a hand. Beside me, Dean did likewise. Into each of our palms the crone put a single sheet of grey paper. Then she turned and pointed at the toilet. The effort was unnecessary, as I had already worked it out for myself. The crone had just given us our daily issue of toilet paper!

She had to be joking. I peered more closely into the wrinkled face but could only conclude that any variations of expression would be beyond my interpretation. However, one thing was crystal clear. There was no way in the world that we could stay. Thrusting a $50 bill into her hand, we rapidly retraced our steps and soon found ourselves out in the street again. Within five minutes, we had managed to hail a taxi. We instructed the driver to take us to a good hotel.

Our destination was suitably five star and expensive to boot. However, although my funds had been significantly reduced by the Sunsplash fiasco, I wasn't quite skint. And I needed a holiday memorable for its charm, not for its nightmares. A good hotel was a basic necessity.

We lodged our bags in our room and phoned Paul and Sean. They wondered what had taken us so long and were raring to get out on the town. We asked the concierge to call us a taxi and headed for their apartment. The luxury of their place only served to put the squalor of our boarding house into context. Cuba was clearly a land of extremes. Due to my embarrassment, I cautioned Dean not to mention the state of the place. And I had already resolved to play some kind of trick to get back at them.

Sean's Cuban girlfriend Maria was beautiful, with an effervescent personality. Fortunately, she spoke English. With her as a guide, we headed into the night, thoroughly intent on having a good time.

It was dark, but still somewhat humid. Havana's nightlife throbbed to an ever-present salsa beat. We moved from bar to bar and were introduced to Maria's legion of friends. Everybody was friendly and welcomed us to Cuba. I could only reflect on the contrast to the Hackney I had so recently left. By now, similar tourists to my neck of the woods would have been mugged!

We ended up at one of Havana's swankiest nightspots. The doorman welcomed Maria with a kiss and waved us in for free. She was immediately surrounded by a bevy of hostesses and welcomed like one of their own. I began to wonder what Maria did for a living when Sean wasn't with her.

We were ushered to a table close to the dance floor. A salsa band was playing on a raised stage. As an experienced clubber, I knew how to pace myself, but perhaps due to the pressure of recent events I overdid it a bit with the Cuban rum and was soon quite drunk. I still knew what I was doing, though. When the hostesses descended on us, I had the presence of mind to wave them away. They turned their attention to Dean and Paul, who had no such inhibitions.

The ending was all very predictable. We returned en masse to Paul and Sean's apartment. I lounged lopsidedly on a sofa as the rest partied around me. The night progressed with more drinking, erotic dancing and Paul and Dean disappearing from time to time into the bedrooms with various of the Cuban girls. When Paul and Sean lapsed into unconsciousness, I took it as our cue to leave.

There was one final task to be undertaken, though. On one trip to the bathroom, I had noticed several used condoms thrown haphazardly into a sink. Using tissues and a bowl, I now removed them. With Dean looking on in amazement, I then proceeded to drape them around the lounge, on mirrors and picture frames. I knew that the maid arrived early. My guess was that there would be a minor domestic crisis. That would pay them back for the crap boarding house!

The following day, we sat in the hotel bar nursing our hangovers. Just along the bar from us were two guys smoking large cigars. Back in England, I had long given up smoking cigarettes, but very occasionally I liked a cigar. Here in Cuba, the land of the cigar, it was time to try one again.

One of the barmen was a young guy who spoke fluent English. He showed me a selection of cigars, and I bought one of the best. Dean passed on the offer as I lit up my big Cuban cigar. The action brought back a memory, which gave birth to an idea. I cast my mind back to about two weeks previously. I had been in a pub that had come to double as our office for the Sunsplash gig. I had been deep in conversation with several of my fellow organisers when I smelled a familiar smell. Turning, I could see a short fat guy standing at the bar. He had an enormous cigar in his mouth.

He was a local scallywag who was into everything, and I had known him for years. We had nicknamed him 'Cigar Jack' or just 'The Cigar'. I called him over, but he was more than ready for the inevitable piss-take. Puffing vigorously, he advanced on our table and blew a cloud of smoke across it. There was an immediate cacophony of coughs and curses. Before I could open my mouth, he was on me.

'You make me laugh, Andy,' he said. 'You think you know all the moves, but this is one you don't.' Jack held out the cigar. 'See this? It's a Cohiba. Don't mean nothing to you, I know, but it's one of the best cigars you can get. This one would cost you about 30 quid if you bought it straight. This one's a ringer. Just as good as the real thing, but I get them for a fiver. I don't know why people bother to smuggle puff. Seriously. There's more profit to be made bringing these in and much less risk.'

At the time, I had laughed and let the minor tirade wash over me. Now, sitting in a Cuban bar with a large Cuban cigar in my gob, the words of Cigar Jack came back to me.

I leaned across to the barman and, keeping my voice down, asked if it was possible to buy counterfeit Cuban cigars anywhere. He looked at me carefully, no doubt to judge whether I was serious or not, then replied in a similarly low voice that there was a market at Cathedral where you could buy anything. He cautioned me not to tell anyone that he had said so.

The following day, armed with the barman's information, Dean and I took a taxi to Cathedral, or rather to the cathedral, for our destination was a massive and beautiful church. At first, we wandered the aisles, marvelling at the intricate carvings, stained glass and other decoration.

As we exited at the rear, we stumbled on our real destination. There was an untidy clutter of stalls stretching almost as far as the eye could see. On closer inspection, we could see that goods of every description were on sale. We wandered from stall to stall, looking for cigars.

One stall stopped me in my tracks. Amber and I had recently redecorated our flat in Stoke Newington. I had done the rounds of the local antique shops and markets, looking for a suitably eye-catching piece to grace the lounge mantelpiece. Everything I had seen had either been too expensive or not particularly interesting. Suddenly, here on a stall in Cuba was the very thing. It was an old carving of a monk, done in hardwood, perhaps two feet high. The detail was fantastic, the artistry breathtaking. With a combination of hand signals and a few English words, the stall owner managed to tell us that it was from the sixteenth century. That didn't seem to be too unreasonable a claim, because, from what I had seen, much of Havana was from the sixteenth century, too.

The asking price was quite modern, though. Even from my limited knowledge of the rates of exchange, I knew that $120 was a lot of money in Cuba. It was time to negotiate, something which, from my experience of English markets, I was reasonably skilled in. The negotiations raged back and forth between the asking price and the $50 I was offering. As the stall owner's temper rose, I grew cooler and cooler. Finally, he stormed away from me to stand on the other side of the stall. Holding out the $50, I walked away, calling back to the guy '*El ultimo, el ultimo*', which were two of the approximately fifty Spanish words that I knew. I hoped it would translate as my final offer.

At first, I thought I had overdone it. With my back to the stall holder, I continued to walk away, trying to show a nonchalance I didn't really feel. Just as I reached the end of a row and was about to turn right, I heard a voice shout after me.

'*Señor, señor, el Inglés.*' I turned to see the stall holder waving at me and beckoning me back. Slowly and deliberately, I returned to his stall. The owner held out his hand, and I passed him the $50. With ill-disguised bad humour, he passed me the carving in return. As I turned to leave, I had an idea. After much gesticulating, I managed to convey to him that I wanted to buy some counterfeit cigars.

He smiled a knowing smile and reached underneath the stall. The box looked impressive, as did the cigars inside. I didn't bother to argue with his asking price of $20. With the carving under one arm and the box of cigars in my other hand, I walked off, thoroughly pleased with myself.

That night, Dean and I decided to go out on the town on our own. We asked our friendly hotel barman if he knew of any good nightspots. He recommended that we go out with a friend of his who drove a taxi and spoke passable English.

Shortly after 9 p.m., we both exited the hotel and found our new guide waiting for us in the parking area. Raul was about my own age and had been working as a taxi driver since he left school at 15. He told us that he knew Havana like the back of his hand. He was remarkably fluent in English and really funny. He soon had us laughing.

His car was a 1960s Buick, badly battered and dented, but with acres of brightly polished chrome. Back in England, it would have been an enthusiast's car, but here in Cuba the reality was much more mundane. Because of the international trade embargoes placed on the country, new imported cars were very few and far between. Virtually everyone drove these old, clapped-out American models, because it was easy to get the parts for them.

I stretched out in the vast expanse of the back seats and felt a wave of good humour wash over me. Suddenly, I remembered the cigars I had tucked inside my jacket. I removed three, passed one to Dean and offered the third to Raul who, shaking his head, refused. Dean and I lit our cigars. Almost at once, the car was filled with the fumes of cigar smoke.

'*Señors, señors, por favor*,' cried out Raul, quite stricken. 'Gentlemen, what the fuck are you smoking?' He wound down both of the front windows and made exaggerated movements to waft the smoke out of the car. I explained my purchase the day before from the owner of the carvings stall. 'Well, whatever you did,' said Raul, 'you must have really pissed him off. A Cuban dog wouldn't be seen smoking one of those.' He prevailed upon us to throw the cigars out of the car, and reaching inside his glove compartment he produced a large box of cigars and passed us two.

The difference was immediately apparent. It was a far cooler smoke – the taste was sweet and the clouds of noxious smoke were notably absent. 'This is good,' I announced, looking at Dean, who nodded his agreement. 'Can we buy more of these?'

Raul turned in his seat, smiling broadly. 'Always ask Raul,' he said. 'Whatever you want in Havana, Raul will always be able to find it for you.' He went on to tell us that we had been at the right place the day before, but we had been talking to the wrong person. At which stage, he burst out laughing, saying that the stall holder had pulled one of the oldest of Cuban dirty tricks. 'I think he sold you banana leaves,' added Raul, who then burst out laughing all over again. Beside me, Dean was also laughing. I reflected that I might be hot stuff on the streets of my native Stoke Newington, but out here in Cuba I had performed like a right mug. I resolved to listen to our new guide in future.

We went from bar to bar, and from club to club. All were lively and interesting, the clientele stylish and friendly. As he dropped us off at the hotel, Raul arranged to meet us the following morning.

Shortly before noon, we joined Raul in the parking lot. Once again, we drove to Cathedral, but this time we didn't go into the market. In a corner of a nearby square, there was a bar. As we entered, someone waved to us from a corner table.

The guy stood as we approached. He was quite fat, with an enormous gut that hung over his trousers, but he was immaculately dressed. A well-pressed white linen jacket hung over similarly well-pressed white trousers. His white shirt was clearly silk, and his black leather shoes were expensive and highly polished. From both wrists dangled chunky gold bracelets and around his neck dangled what looked like a diamond on a thick gold chain. As he held out his hand, I noticed an expensive Rolex on his wrist. He could have passed as one of the drug dealers from *Scarface*.

Suddenly, a beaming smile split his florid face, and he introduced himself as Lazarus in flawless English. He shook both my and Dean's hands and waved us to seats at his table. I was eager to start discussing business, but, quite clearly, there were certain customs to be observed first. In quick succession, he asked us where we were staying, what we had already seen and what we thought of Cuba. He leaned forward conspiratorially, I thought to begin discussing the business at hand, but there was one final question. 'And what do you think of Cuban women?' he asked.

'Impressed' was the word that immediately sprang to mind. We had been told that Cuban women were amongst the most beautiful in the world, but I hadn't come to Cuba looking for women. And Amber would have certainly had something to say about it if I had. However, satisfied with my responses, Lazarus decided that it was now time to talk about business.

When I told him I wanted to buy counterfeit Cuban cigars, he immediately asked how many. My reply of 'about a container-full' shocked him momentarily. He sat back, thinking furiously. 'I am one of the major dealers in counterfeit Cuban cigars,' he said, 'but I may have problems supplying you in those quantities.' He paused to reach behind him and produced a cigar box. 'The cigars aren't a problem,' he continued. 'It's the boxes. Cigar production is carefully controlled in Cuba. Wood for the boxes is in short supply, some of it specially imported. I don't know if I can find enough boxes for a container full.'

He passed me the box, and I examined it and its contents. The cigars looked perfect and were indistinguishable from the real thing. But the box didn't pass the test. The wood was old and poorly polished. Expensive cigars just wouldn't come in a box like this. Saying that he needed some time to think about the problem, he suggested that he meet us in the bar of our hotel that night.

Back at our hotel, I was giving further thought to the logistics of the move, leaving Lazarus to worry about the quality control. The cigars would have to be part of a bigger load. Therein lay another problem. Dean had worked at Spitalfields fruit-and-veg market for years, but for the life of him he couldn't think of any produce that came from Cuba. It seemed that sanctions and embargoes severely restricted trade with Cuba.

It was a serious problem for us and threatened the viability of the whole move. Such was my concern that I took the risk of phoning Gavin in England. I had met him through the rave scene. His parents had run one of the largest fruit-importing firms in Spitalfields for donkey's years. Starting straight from school at the age of 15, Gavin had been working for them for over 17 years. He knew the market like the back of his hand.

On the debit side, he was a small, intense individual who liked to party and was therefore unreliable on a regular basis. An only child, his parents doted on him and spoiled him from an early age. Apart from his unreliability, he had a severe drugs problem. He was currently in thrall to the crack monster and had repeatedly been in therapy. He had been an inpatient in the Priory several times. As a criminal CV, this left a lot to be desired, especially when going up against elite teams of police and Customs officers. However, Gavin reassured me that it would be no problem to receive a container of fruit and veg from virtually anywhere in the world, providing that the contraband was carefully hidden or disguised.

His knowledge of the market was encyclopaedic. If anyone knew what came from Cuba, he would. In very general terms, I asked about Cuban–English trade, and Gavin replied that he had never seen anything from Cuba in the market.

I was now convinced that the move was off, but Dean and I still showed up for the evening meeting with Lazarus out of courtesy. As he bemoaned his problem in finding the wood for the cigar boxes, we admitted that it was all academic, as we couldn't find anything that we could legally import from Cuba anyway. This set Lazarus to thinking. Several minutes of silence passed. 'Guyana,' Lazarus suddenly announced, sitting forward sharply in his seat.

'What?' I replied. What had Guyana to do with anything? As Lazarus explained it, Guyana was the answer to all our problems. First, there was a flourishing industry in producing counterfeit Cuban cigars in Guyana. Cuban tobacco plants were imported, and the resultant tobacco was indistinguishable from the Cuban-grown original. Second, wood for the boxes was in abundant supply, so we would have a first-class product. Finally, Guyanese fruit and vegetables were exported all over the world. At that point, Dean chimed in with the information that they regularly received Guyanese coconuts at the market. It seemed that we had found a solution to our problems.

That night in our hotel room, Dean and I worked out the financial aspects of the deal. The best Cohiba cigars, non-counterfeit ones that is, cost $384 per box. Back in England, once the tax and import duties had been paid, the cost rose to £661 per box, or about £28 per cigar. Quite clearly, once we had paid all our overheads, there would still be plenty of room for a hefty profit margin.

Lazarus would immediately go to Guyana to source the cigars and arrange for them to be put in a container bound for Spitalfields. Dean and I would return to England and make arrangements with Gavin for his friend's firm to receive them. Then it would be just a matter of waiting for the shipment to arrive.

Time always being of the essence, we cut short our holiday, lingering only long enough for Lazarus to fly to Guyana and back. On his return, he presented us with a sample box of Guyanese Cuban cigars. I put them in my luggage so that I could show them to prospective buyers in England.

At the airport, I searched the newsagent's for something to read on the flight. I selected some glossy magazines and grabbed a recent copy of the Jamaican Gleaner almost as an afterthought. I liked to keep up with current affairs in Jamaica.

As I settled back in my seat, I picked up the Gleaner, and the headline jumped out at me. Willie Haggart, notorious don of the Black Roses Crew, had been murdered, along with three others. As I scanned over the names of the deceased, my eyes were fixated on just one – Blackadouch, aka Albert Bonner.

When we landed, I immediately made a call and got a first-hand account from someone who was there. Blacka had turned up for the meeting with Solgy, who was a close friend of his. Blacka had been talking to Willie, reasoning with him, trying to work out a truce between the Black Roses Crew and the other posse. This meeting was of paramount importance, as a street battle between the two sides would be like a small-scale civil war and so was to be avoided at all costs.

Blacka, in his usual laid-back fashion, was sitting kerbside, on the corner of Arnett Gardens, drinking a Dragon Stout as the talks continued. At some stage, the mobile phone of one of the Black Roses Crew rang. He said that he had to go somewhere, rushed to his van and drove off rapidly down the potholed and speed-bumped road. The dust had hardly settled when a white car approached slowly and pulled up at the kerb, close to Blacka. Three men, dressed similarly to Kingston's plain-clothes detectives, got out of the car carrying AK47s. Seeing this, Blacka stood up and slowly took out a 9mm pistol from his waistband, saying that he was a licensed firearm carrier.

The three men immediately opened fire and began shooting everything and everyone in sight. Solgy, wounded only in the arm, desperately dived under the car. Blacka was breathing his last breath on the pavement, one eye hanging out and one leg almost torn off by the fusillade. Haggart was in the process of trying to run as he was cut down.

Over all the chaos, the driver of the car was heard to call out, 'Mek sure dem dead!' Taking this as his cue, Solgy launched himself from under the car, dived under a fence and ran for his life. He escaped, but the others weren't so lucky. The gunmen went to each body and pumped in the last fatal shots. According to Solgy, they definitely intended to kill Blacka too.

Willie Haggart's subsequent funeral was a monumental affair. In the intense heat of Jamaica, funerals are held within days. Nevertheless, more than 5,000 mourners attended the service, which was held in Jamaica's National Arena. Prominent among the mourners were Dr Omar Davies, Dr Peter Phillips and Dr Karl

Blythe, who were respectively ministers for finance, transport and housing in the ruling PNP. In his funeral oration, Dr Davies said, 'I am here to pay my respects to a man who has assisted me in achieving some of my objectives in this community.'

Until I could come to terms with Blacka's murder, I knew I had to stay away from Jamaica. Being emotional, the ramifications of going back with an irrational mindset could lead to bad decisions or, worse, the loss of my own life, so I resolved to stay away until things cooled down.

Back in Stoke Newington, I set about finalising details of the move. I did feel guilty around Amber. I had promised her that I would give up smuggling, but not only was I nearly skint, smuggling cigars didn't feel like real smuggling at all. Jamaican weed was clearly a narcotic, as it was a class B drug. It was illegal even to possess it in England. Cigars, though, were quite legal, if equally harmful to one's health. How could it be right, I rationalised, for governments to take a commodity that had cost very little to produce then slap a massive duty on it? In many ways, I was on the side of the consumer by bringing them a cheaper product. However, I was sure that the Customs people wouldn't see it like that at all.

For this reason, I gave much thought to how to conceal the contraband. The boxes of cigars could be put into sacks identical to the ones that held the coconuts, but even a cursory inspection would prove disastrous for us. Coconuts are round; boxes of cigars are indisputably oblong. The difference in shape, even partially hidden by the sacking, would give the game away.

Suddenly, I came up with an idea, one that I had toyed with whilst smuggling weed from Jamaica. The containers that transported the coconuts were refrigerated. At the back of each container was a large refrigeration unit. I had taken several to pieces. Inside the main unit was a large metal drum. I was sure that I could pack a large amount of contraband in it. It would seriously affect the working of the unit, but that would only result in a few rotten coconuts at the other end. Our cigars, safe in their boxes, wouldn't be harmed at all.

Gavin was ecstatic. Not only was it a lucrative move, it was also one where his role was relatively safe. He and his workers would just have to unload a bona fide shipment of coconuts. The empty container would then be sent to an outside company for its refrigeration unit to be serviced. I, of course, had someone working in the outside company. I could gain access to their premises at night and retrieve the contraband cigars.

Overall, it seemed like a plan that could not only work, but work over and over again. To the best of my knowledge, the Customs teams didn't have sniffer dogs trained to detect cigars. So, unless some particularly keen Customs officer wanted to get his hands dirty disassembling a greasy refrigeration unit, our cigars would remain safe from discovery.

My next step was to do some research to check out the marketability of our new product. The obvious move was to run it by Cigar Jack. I found him in our usual pub and gave him a couple of Lazarus's samples. Within an hour, he was on the phone to me wanting to speak.

Back at the pub, he waxed lyrical about the quality of the cigars and asked me where they came from. 'Cuba,' I replied. There was a strong element of truth in this. The plant had started out in Cuba, albeit as a seedling, before its peripatetic journey through Guyana and on to England. But for security reasons, I wasn't about to tell Jack this. All that really mattered was that they looked, smelled and tasted exactly the same as genuine Cuban cigars.

My second visit to the pub that day had some unintended consequences. Gavin had been telling me that someone called Little Tony had been looking for me. Now, Little Tony had been hanging around the fringes of both the drugs and music businesses for several years. It was widely known that he was similarly inept in both. The seat of his problem was undoubtedly a fearsome drugs habit. He had started out as a speed freak. In that incarnation, he had been reasonably reliable, but, of course, everything was done at a hundred miles an hour. Needless to say, mistakes were made and parcels of drugs lost. Irate partners would then want to do him some serious bodily harm. Someone was always after him, and he was permanently on the run. A standing joke among our crowd was, 'Anyone seen Little Tony?'

A dalliance with the crack monster was his complete undoing. A severe beating was closely followed by a three-year prison sentence. Little Tony's name was now synonymous with disaster, and people avoided him like the plague. But he was nothing if not insistent and thick-skinned to boot. It went without saying that I was in no hurry to find out what he wanted to speak to me about.

Suddenly, I saw him hovering just along the bar from where I was talking with Jack. He had known better than to barge in on our conversation, but from the way he was staring in my direction and impatiently moving his feet I guessed that he was intent on speaking to me. The conversation went something like this.

'I need to talk to you urgently,' Little Tony said as I walked away from Jack and made to leave the bar.

'Fuck right off out of it,' was my immediate reply.

'But this is really important and something you'll really want to hear,' he continued.

'What part of "Fuck off" don't you understand, you prick,' I responded. 'Now fuck off before I chin you.'

His response surprised me. Planting himself right in my path, he held out his chin. 'Well, if I've got to take a punch to get your attention, then so be it,' he said with grim determination, '''cause if I don't tell you and you find out about it later, you'll chin me for not telling you in the first place.'

I had to give it to him for his nerve, as he was only a little guy and no fighter. Beckoning him to a table in the corner of the bar, I motioned for him to sit down.

'My brother-in-law's just come out of the SAS,' he began with no preliminaries whatsoever. 'He's got a brother who works in Customs. He's a member of one of the elite FAST teams

[Flexible Anti-smuggling Teams]. He works at Tilbury on the X-ray machine. The team want to do business. They'll pass any container through unopened, for a price.'

Now this was very interesting information indeed. It was every smuggler's dream to have a bit of help from a Customs officer. But to have a whole team was an absolute gift – if it was true. Among his other failings, Little Tony was known for telling a few whoppers. But not only did it all have a ring of truth to it, he had known of the existence of the FAST teams. Would someone as low down in the criminal pecking order as Little Tony have known of their existence?

He could see that I was interested and was pondering his words. 'You can meet my brother-in-law and ask him yourself,' he volunteered. I specified a large, busy pub in Stoke Newington High Street and told him to meet me there with the guy the following night at seven. 'And if you're as much as five minutes late, I'll never fucking speak to you again,' I added for good measure.

With Dean at my side, I walked into the busy pub at five to seven the next night. I was relieved to see Little Tony sitting at a table with someone whom I took to be his brother-in-law. We sat down next to them, and I handed Little Tony a tenner and sent him to the bar to get some drinks. Then I turned my full attention on the guy. This bit would be very important. It could all be a trap, and this guy could be working with the police. What he said over the next few minutes would be crucial.

I looked him over, carefully weighing him up. He was in his mid-30s and had the fit, capable look that many ex-servicemen have. Since we had some Special Forces guys do security for us in the acid-house days, I had some idea of what to look for. It was no use asking about his unit or whose command he had been under. These ex-military boys all still feel bound by the Official Secrets Act when they leave the forces. This doesn't stop some of them from engaging in quite serious criminal activity, though.

He introduced himself as Bob and sat there, quietly confident, not at all intimidated at being in the presence of serious smugglers.

'Been in the SAS, then?' I began.

'Yes,' he replied quite simply. Clearly, he was a proud guy who was used to being taken at his word. He wasn't about to try and prove himself. Nor did he bother with interesting war stories. They wouldn't have proved anything anyway. Already, I was quite impressed by both his demeanour and his economy with words. In our game, a chatterbox can be a deadly liability.

Suddenly, he leaned forward. Lowering his voice, he virtually whispered, 'Look, my brother works in Customs at Tilbury. His team X-ray and search suspect containers. For a price, and we're not talking a couple of grand here, they're willing to pass any container through unopened. Whatever the load. Are you interested in doing business?'

That was straightforward enough. I liked what he was saying and the way he was saying it. I immediately decided that he was genuine. 'Explain the full details. How will it work?' I asked.

His explanation was succinct and matter of fact: 'You know that every container in transit has a registration number?' His question was rhetorical. 'Once your container is on its way, you give me the registration number and its approximate time of arrival in England, although the latter is not essential – we can find that out ourselves. I will then pass that information on to my brother. His team will place a "hold" order on that particular container. No other Customs team will be allowed to touch it, and when it arrives it will come straight to them. There's only one team on duty at a time at Tilbury. Only his team will be in the warehouse when they put the container through the X-ray machine. But they won't bother to switch the machine on. Whatever's in it, they will pass it as passed and issue it with a clearance certificate. It will continue on to its destination unopened.'

This was all exceptionally good news and almost too good to be true. But such was the guy's calm manner and seeming sincerity that I believed him. There was only one fly in the ointment, and that was supping its pint next to his brother-in-law.

'What about him?' I asked, pointing at Little Tony.

'Don't worry about him,' said the guy. 'I've got him right under control.' Tony looked at his brother-in-law, then down into his pint. I could only conclude that that much was true as well. I took Bob's number and said that I would definitely be in touch very soon.

This put us very much on an action footing, but there were still several details to finalise. Dean and I met with Gavin and explained the plan. Gavin said that, despite the fact that the Customs wouldn't open the container, the boxes of cigars would still have to be hidden, and there would still have to be coconuts. Otherwise, when they unloaded the container at Spitalfields, people not in on the move would see cigar boxes being unloaded. It was agreed that part of the load would still be coconuts and that the boxes of cigars would be put in sacks identical to those that held the coconuts.

An attractive female courier who was unlikely to invite suspicion was despatched to Guyana to meet with Lazarus. She carried £15,000 to pay for the cost of the coconuts, the cigars and some expenses. She also carried specific instructions regarding sending me the registration number of the container once it was on its way, as well as details of how the container was to be packed.

Now that I had a clear idea of everything involved, I could work out what the move would cost and what profit would be left for us. I met again with Bob and told him that the load would be counterfeit cigars and coconuts. He said that it didn't matter what it was – the price would still be 50 grand sterling. Bearing in mind that it would be shared between himself and the several members of the Customs team, I reflected that, in the circumstances, it was very reasonable indeed.

At the other end, the sourcing of the coconuts, cigars and boxes and the bribing of a Guyanese official to pass the container through the docks, together with a decent drink for Lazarus, would come to about 25 grand. The cost of transport and ordinary clearance would be paid for from the profit on the coconuts. This meant that the total cost for importing 1,000 boxes of snide Cuban cigars would be about 75 grand, or £75 per box. From my enquiries in the English market, I reckoned I could get at least £200 per box. This would leave a tidy profit of one hundred and twenty-five grand to split three ways between Dean, Gavin and me. For a first load, that wasn't bad at all, and on subsequent loads we would be bringing in 5,000 boxes at a time.

Unfortunately for all concerned, leopards never change their spots, and neither did Gavin. I suppose I should have known that if anyone was to be instrumental in our collective downfall it would be him.

Even at a later date, no one could ever work out where the information had come from, but it was quite specific: a man called Costas, driving a blue Cherokee jeep, would be in possession of six kilos of cocaine, somewhere in the vicinity of the Holiday Inn at Walthamstow.

David Martin was the senior investigating officer in charge of HM Customs and Excise investigating team Echo One. Their remit was to track down and apprehend those who imported or dealt in class A drugs. Their speciality was cocaine busts. With Jamie Shan, another member of the team, beside him, he settled back in the front seat of their unremarkable car. In the darkness, he fiddled with a tiny state-of-the-art radio he held in his hand. Then, one by one, he communicated with the other members of the team, spaced about the Holiday Inn parking lot.

Martin's thoughts turned to Costas, his intended quarry. They had been after him for a couple of years. He was on the fringes of a Greek firm that regularly brought in large amounts of cocaine. Perhaps tonight would mark a turning point. Maybe they could now roll up the entire gang. That had certainly been the intention at the earlier briefing. As they had left Customs House, Operation Castaway had slipped smoothly into gear.

Gavin, of course, was oblivious to all of this. By complete coincidence, he had earlier booked into a room at Walthamstow's Holiday Inn, together with a small bag of cocaine and two junkie brasses. The attraction for the two brasses was undoubtedly the cocaine. Although they regularly shagged to get the drugs they needed, their sexual companion of choice was each other. In that respect, the weasel Gavin held no interest for them. In truth, this didn't particularly bother him. All he was after was some company while he smoked the crack.

The amount of cocaine in the universe being finite and the demand for it infinite, their supply was soon exhausted. He still had some cash left. It was time for Gavin to call his friendly neighbourhood crack dealer. He didn't have to search for the number in his phone memory because he knew it by heart. Picking up his mobile phone, he called . . . Costas!

Now, no doubt Costas said that he was busy. He might even have mentioned that he had an urgent errand to run. But he must have known how insistent and persuasive crack heads could be. Then there was the fact that Gavin was a regular customer. The upshot was that he agreed to drop some coke off to him at the Holiday Inn.

David Martin hated these waiting periods. There was always the possibility that nothing would happen and then he would feel silly having called the whole team out on false information. He slid ever deeper into his seat, as if by so doing he could hide from his responsibility.

Suddenly, there was the sound of a car entering the parking area. Bright headlights swept the parked cars, partially illuminating Martin in their glare. Ducking even lower, he peeked over the dashboard. In the reflected light, he saw the unmistakable shape of a blue Cherokee jeep. 'Echo One, Echo One, await my orders,' he whispered into his radio.

Quite unaware, Costas parked the jeep, turned off the engine and lights, and jumped out. 'Wait for it, wait for it,' cautioned Martin over the radio. Although it was quite a cold September night, Costas was wearing just a T-shirt. Clearly, he didn't have six kilos of cocaine on him.

Costas locked the jeep and ran towards the reception. He already knew the room number, so he ran straight to the lift. He knocked on the appropriate door, and Gavin opened it. Costas was in a hurry, so there was no time for small talk. However, good manners, as well as sound drug-dealing practice, demanded that the ritual sharing of a line be observed.

With that over, Costas wanted to be on his way, but there was one further obstacle. The money to pay for the coke was downstairs in the glove compartment of Gavin's car. He hadn't wanted it with him just in case the brasses stole it when he was off his face. Taking the car key, Costas ran back down to the parking area. Finding Gavin's car, he rooted through the glove compartment and came up with the cash. Locking the door after him, he ran back into the hotel to return the key to Gavin.

All this had not only been quietly observed by Martin and his team, it had also been videoed on a hand-held recorder. They also got Costas when he returned to his jeep and drove off.

The full extent of Operation Castaway now became apparent. Martin's team had extra help that night. Several members of a sister team were waiting in unmarked cars in the surrounding streets. A helicopter hovered high above. It was a simple matter to follow the jeep, especially as Costas didn't realise that he had company. While he manoeuvred to enter the car park of The Coach and Horses at Woodford, one of the Customs cars actually managed to slip in front of him. Within seconds, the two occupants, a man and a woman, were standing at the bar of the pub.

Costas parked the jeep and got out. Unlocking the boot, he took out a rucksack. It clearly had something in it, because he hefted it across his shoulder. Then, locking the car, he headed for the pub. The Customs team were already in motion.

An avalanche of bodies carried Costas clean into the bar. As he was forced to the floor, one of their number seized the rucksack. It was later found to contain six kilos of 80 per cent pure cocaine.

There were several sequels to this event, not the least of them being that Costas was subsequently sentenced to six years in prison. More importantly for us, they were now on to Gavin. He was made a target for surveillance and issued with a Zulu number for identification. Customs were watching him when he came out of the hotel the next morning. They had already run a check on his car, which Costas had so thoughtfully identified for them. When he switched on his phone and made a call from it, they electronically snatched the signal, thus enabling them to listen to all his calls and identify the numbers he was dialling. They listened in to this first call.

Fortunately for us, Gavin was in something of a panic. He had been missing for over a day, and he knew that I had specifically warned him to stay in touch and would be irate. He needed to get out of the way for a while, so he called the clinic.

The clinic was understanding. They knew all about crack heads and their crises. Arrangements were immediately made for Gavin to be admitted as an inpatient. As he was signed in, they took away his phone. Mobiles were not allowed in the clinic, so Gavin would be making no calls for several days.

Meanwhile, our first shipment was only one day away from arriving. Logistically, everything was running very smoothly. Lazarus had given me the container registration number when it had left Guyana. We had passed it on to Bob, who assured us that he had given it to his Customs-officer brother. Apparently, if we were to believe Bob, the latter's team had identified the ship carrying the container and had an accurate estimated time and date of arrival. They put a hold order on the container, ensuring that it would come to them and them only. The rest was purely routine.

The container was unloaded from the boat and taken to a secure area. It was then moved into the Customs shed, the domain of the FAST team. The routine, so Bob told us, was that our friendly FAST team operated the X-ray machine. The machine was passed over our container but with the scanner switched off. It was then passed for inspection and an official clearance certificate was issued.

The next bit was the most fraught for us. If the Customs were on to us, they would swoop once we had unloaded the container and were in possession of the contraband. We had carefully planned our procedure. Gavin had arranged for the container to be delivered late at night, when there were comparatively few other workers in the market. It was delivered to a company adjacent to his friend's company and a forklift driver and two van drivers began to offload it.

First off were the pallets of coconuts. These were stacked in Gavin's friend's store to be sold according to normal practice. Next off were the pallets containing the cigars. Even wrapped in the coconut sacks, they stood out as unusual. Instead of the round bulges of the coconuts, the sharp corners of the boxes were obvious through the sacking. Wasting no time at all, these sacks were thrown into the backs of the two waiting vans, and the drivers immediately left to rendezvous with me in a lay-by close to the market. Then, with me following close behind, we drove the couple of miles to the safe house and unloaded the sacks. We were home and dry!

It took just over a week for me and Dean to sell all the cigars. We arranged to meet with Bob and were relieved when he showed up without Little Tony. We handed over the 50 grand and said that we were arranging another shipment right away. We then called Lazarus and, using a specially agreed code, told him that everything was OK, his money was waiting for him and that he should embark on sending the next load.

I needed a holiday. I was stressed out due to the pressures of the recent move. I was flush with money, and I needed to relax before going through all that stress again with the next load. Then there was Amber. I had told her nothing about my new smuggling activities, for obvious reasons. It was a clear violation of my promise to her. However, she knew me too well not to miss the obvious signs. The phone calls at strange times, the comings and goings, and my generally stressed state pointed to the fact that I was up to something. She never pried, but I could tell that she was worried. We both needed a holiday to find ourselves again.

Tobago was absolute bliss. We lay on the beaches, frolicked in the sea and enjoyed long romantic meals in candle-lit restaurants. Amber laid down one proviso, and I readily accepted it. I had to switch off my phone for the duration of the holiday.

Back in England, it immediately became a case of 'when the cat's away'. Bob called Dean and insisted on a meeting. In the meantime, Lazarus had called him and said that he was coming over personally to pick up his money and arrange the details for the next shipment. To add insult to injury, when Dean mentioned this to Bob, the latter insisted that Dean bring Lazarus to the meeting.

Needless to say, I would have allowed none of this to happen. Dean was a nice guy but not particularly strong. He no doubt felt intimidated by an ex-SAS figure.

Lazarus duly arrived in England. He was paid the money he was owed along with the money for the next shipment. Dean then took him to meet with Bob. Outwardly, everything seemed fine. Bob explained to Lazarus specific details about packing the next container. There was only one cause for concern. Returning from a toilet break, Dean noticed them both deep in conversation. Bob was entering something into his phone, and it looked like phone numbers had been exchanged. However, when they looked up, they carried on as usual, and Dean didn't feel obliged to question what was going on. The meeting broke up amicably.

Gavin duly came out of the clinic intent on a new start. But unbeknown to him, he was now a prime target for one of Her Majesty's elite Customs teams. He switched on his phone and called, in quick succession, Dean, Bob and Lazarus. He also tried to call me. Now they were well and truly on to all of them. Everyone was a target and all were assigned Zulu numbers. All that really remained was for me to be fully initiated into the club. This would happen when I next answered my phone to one of the guys involved in the move.

We were nearing the end of the first week of what was intended to be a two-week holiday. I was tanned and relaxed, and Amber and I had re-established our rapport. Once again, we were deeply and unreservedly in love with each other. But you can't be successful in the smuggling game for any length of time without developing a sixth sense. Now mine came fully into play.

At first, I thought it was down to anxiety at having to bring the bliss that was Tobago to an end in seven days' time and returning to England and the pressure of the next move. But there was an incessant niggling at the back of my mind that told me that something was wrong. I spoke about it to Amber, but she told me not to turn my phone on. She wanted to delay the inevitable as long as possible.

By Sunday morning, the niggling had turned into something approaching an obsession. I just knew that something was wrong. Around noon, I switched my phone on and called Dean. I didn't know it then, but I had just become a target, complete with my very own Zulu number!

Dean's news confirmed all my worst fears. He told me about the meeting with Bob and Lazarus. When pressed, he admitted that he had seen them exchanging numbers. A couple of days later, Bob had then called him to another meeting. Dean was told that Bob had found a customer for the whole of the next shipment of cigars, and, what was more, he could get us another 50 quid a box. Bob said that he could handle all the arrangements for receiving the next shipment and that we should just sit back and wait for him to pay us the money.

Despite Dean trying to put a positive spin on it regarding the extra 50 quid, it was very bad news for a whole raft of reasons, not least of which was the fact that we had now lost control of the move. No doubt Bob would have problems convincing Gavin to go along with his plans, but with Lazarus in his pocket it would just be a matter of time before he could receive the container straight from Customs and unload it himself.

Amber wasn't at all pleased when I told her to pack up her things. We drove to the airport, looking for the next available flight to the UK. The first thing on the agenda was an urgent meeting with Bob. I phoned to set it up.

Dean looked thoroughly crestfallen when we met up. All through the journey to the meeting, I roundly berated him. 'How could you have been so fucking stupid?' I shouted. Dean sat there in silence.

The meeting went well enough. Now he realised that I was on to him, Bob backed up at an amazing rate of knots. It was the first time I had seen him flustered. Quite clearly, he wasn't set up yet to receive the container on his own. It was firmly established that the next shipment would proceed exactly as the first one had. Gavin would unload the container, the drivers would rendezvous with me and I would take possession of the cigars and sell them. Then I would pay everybody, just as before. With as much good grace as he could muster, Bob acquiesced.

This time we had given Lazarus the money to pay for a shipment of 5,000 boxes of cigars. This would still leave room for some pallets of coconuts, but they would be just the first two rows. The coconuts were more for appearances while unloading in the fruit market. As we were told by Bob that our Customs guys were going to pass the container through whatever its contents, there was no need to disguise anything.

David Martin must have been feeling very pleased with himself. Not only had he brought Operation Castaway to a successful conclusion, it had led smoothly into Operation Cyprus – targeting us. Now that he was able to monitor all the conspirators' phones, he knew about the next shipment. Surveillance was stepped up on me and all the targets. But he didn't know the registration number of the next container, nor did he know its exact time of arrival. He would just have to sit back and wait.

We carried on in blissful ignorance of the gathering storm.

Lazarus duly despatched the next shipment from Guyana on 23 October 2004. We received the registration number by a secure method – public phone box to public phone box and in code. I passed it on to Bob personally. The container was unloaded in Jamaica and sat on the quay for a whole month before continuing on its way to us. It arrived at Tilbury on 2 December.

Just as before, our friendly FAST team swung into action. In a handwritten note, they specified that our container be put on hold for their special inspection. At 12 noon on 3 December, our container was X-rayed and released, at which point Gavin was phoned and advised to pick up his shipment. Martin must have been seriously concerned at this point. Could there be corruption in Customs? There were two possibilities: the first was that our FAST team and Bob were double agents, working for Customs. The thought had crossed my mind. It would explain some things, specifically during the trial, but not others. For example, why did Martin need to get the container out of hold? Surely he should have removed it when it was first X-rayed. The second explanation was that Martin was bemused by the X-ray certificate and was concerned at the present lack of information. He knew all the players. He even knew that the next shipment had been despatched. But scores of ships left Guyana bound for the UK every week. And between them they carried thousands of containers. How was he to know which one should be the target of Operation Cyprus?

The broker's phone call to Gavin immediately supplied the missing piece of the puzzle. It was then a simple matter to identify the container cleared to be delivered to the fruit company. Martin closely examined the handwritten note ordering that the container be held for inspection by the FAST team. It seemed genuine, so he would have passed it on to his superiors. His utmost priority was to examine the contents of the container.

Using only members of his own team, he had the container moved to a secure warehouse at the other side of the docks.

Doors were locked and sentries posted. They wanted to be neither seen nor disturbed. He broke the seal and opened the container door personally. The first row of pallets was removed by one of his men driving a forklift. Eager hands snatched at the bulging sacks with 'Produce of Guyana' stamped clearly on them. Sharp knives cut into the twine securing the tops of the sacks, and the contents tumbled out onto the floor.

Coconuts. Hundreds and hundreds of coconuts. They rolled about the floor, clearly discernible in the bright glare of the warehouse lights. But Martin knew most of the tricks of the cocaine smuggling trade. These wouldn't be the first smugglers to put the cocaine inside the coconuts.

One after the other, he threw several coconuts forcefully to the floor. They spilt to reveal their white interiors, as coconut milk welled out. He turned and gave orders for the next row of pallets to be off-loaded.

Once again, coconuts rolled on the floor and, once again, some were split open. But Martin had just lost interest in the coconuts. He was staring intently at the next row of pallets. The sacks were the same, but, if the evidence of his senses was to be believed, these sacks contained square coconuts. For instead of the round lumps of the first sacks, these lumps had sharp corners.

Sharp knives again cut at the securing twine. This time it was blocks that tumbled out onto the floor. And through their clear wrapping, he could see that they were off-white in colour. Martin had seen enough kilo blocks of cocaine in his time. A small cry escaped his lips as he realised that he had hit the jackpot.

Now it was a matter of collating all the evidence, for that was what the shipment had just become. Everything would be carefully examined and fingerprinted. The goal was to wrap up the entire operation. Merely to arrest one branch would leave the rest to regroup and reorganise. Then there would be other shipments.

Over the next couple of hours, Martin and his team emptied the container and carefully opened all the sacks. The blocks of cocaine were fingerprinted, weighed, their dimensions measured, then stacked against the wall. Martin was ready for the next part of his plan.

Within the hour, the blocks of wood had arrived. They were the same size as the blocks of cocaine. Gloved hands carefully placed them back in the sacks, and they were sewn up again. The coconuts were then put back, with replacements for those that had been broken. Martin was taking great pains to attend to the smallest detail. He didn't want anything to alert the smugglers.

The container was locked and fitted with a new seal. Then it was sent on its way to Spitalfields as a controlled delivery. A massive surveillance operation had now swung into gear. The container would be watched every step of the way. So would all of the targets. Everything they said or did over the next few days would be very closely monitored. Operation Cyprus was in its final stages.

However, Customs were still unsure as to how many people working in the market were involved. In the event, they decided not to warn Spitalfields security department. Instead, they mounted cameras at strategic vantage points. They also infiltrated members of their team into the market posing as workers. Then, in an advanced state of alert, they waited.

Ten

Armageddon Now

THIS, THEN, was the elaborate trap that I walked into on the evening of 6 December 2004. Christmas might have come early for Martin and his team, but I could well have done without the present that I got. I did give Customs one uneasy moment, though. My U-turn in the road outside the market caught them completely unawares, especially when I had pulled up right behind one of their cars with two officers in it. And seeing them trying to hide their fluorescent jackets had given me advance warning. I had then tried to phone Gavin, but, as the observation cameras were to reveal later, he had been busy cutting into the sacks, trying to steal something for himself.

As I lay in my cell, I tried to assess my situation. Smuggling cigars was only VAT fraud. The crash, bang, wallop arrest had really been a bit over the top for a few moody cigars. Which brought me back to the senior officer saying something about 500 or so kilos of cocaine. What had that to do with me? Surely some other firm's load hadn't got mixed up with ours? No doubt all would be revealed in the morning. Both physically and emotionally drained, I turned my face to the wall and fell soundly asleep.

I was woken by my breakfast being delivered. Normally, a tray was brought to me in bed by Amber, but the bench I had slept on was hardly a bed, and the strapping Customs officer carrying the tray was most definitely not Amber. It all went to confirm that it had not been a bad dream and I really was nicked. The scrambled egg had the consistency of rubber and the tea was without sugar. I was so hungry, though, that I wolfed it all down.

I then tried to mentally prepare myself for what I knew was to come. The problem was the cocaine, a hefty 500-plus kilos of it. Where had it come from? If it had just been the cigars, seeing as how I was caught 'bang to rights', as they say, I would have seriously considered putting my hands up. But how could I put my hands up to 500 kilos of coke, especially as it wasn't mine?

I tried to work out what had happened. I dismissed the idea that the Customs officer had been trying to frighten me. I couldn't see what he had to gain by that. So they must have found the coke in our container. I tracked backwards through events to try to figure out where it had come from. I was sure that Dean hadn't been part of the switch; he didn't have it in him. As a confirmed crack head, Gavin had to come into the frame, but very few people have the contacts to sell 500 kilos of coke. I knew that Gavin didn't. Further, although I had learned that he could be a bit slippery at times, I was sure he wasn't capable of the major treachery that the switch had involved. I ruled him out.

Suddenly, it came to me. It was all so very obvious. It could hardly have been put in the container at sea, so it must have happened at source in Guyana. That meant that Lazarus was definitely involved. However, he would have known that my crew had unloaded the last container themselves.

Which brought me to Bob. He had tried to take over the handling of the shipment. He had told Dean that he would sell it and that he would return us an extra 50 quid per box just to make the idea seem attractive. Maybe he had been talking to members of our friendly FAST team. Perhaps they had argued that it was as well to be hung for a sheep as a lamb. They were used to finding shipments of cocaine, and it didn't matter what the shipment was, as they wouldn't compromise it with the X-ray machine. It all made sense. Who knew what contacts Bob had as a former SAS man? Maybe he could sell it all himself. Yes,

Bob was definitely the prime mover, and Lazarus was no doubt an enthusiastic accomplice. Well, we would all be appearing in court together soon enough. I was looking forward to seeing their faces.

Thinking about Bob and Lazarus's situation inevitably brought me back to thinking about my own. It would be absolutely no consolation for me if they got a savage sentence and I got one too. And I couldn't really expect them to admit that it was they who had made the switch. If found guilty, I could expect something over 30 years.

As the realisation hit me, I doubled over, my head in my hands. I was nearing 40. By the time I got out, I would be an old man. There would be no having a family with Amber. And, in reality, there would be no Amber, either. I would have to do the decent thing and tell her to go and start a new life without me. She was still a young woman. Looking at the implications of my situation, I realised that my life would be over.

Perhaps it was the bending over with my head in my hands that did it, but I suddenly realised that a Customs officer could walk in and see me. I straightened up and looked at the spyhole in the door. The pinprick of light told me that no one was looking through. At the end of the day, whatever else I was, I was a proud man. I always stood up to a situation and dealt with it as best I could. There would be no more feeling sorry for myself. I would stand and fight the charge with my head held high. If I failed, then so be it. But at least I would go down like a man.

The door opened again, and it was the Customs guy for the tray. As he left, he said that my solicitor had arrived and that my first interview with the arresting officers would take place shortly. I tried to tidy myself up. My pride demanded that I make a good appearance. I washed my face and upper body in the small sink, drying myself with a towel that hung nearby. However, I had to put the shirt that I had been sleeping in back on. It was a rather crumpled urban smuggler who walked into the interview room.

My regular solicitor was David Turner, of Keenan and Co., but he hadn't been available at such short notice. It was their duty solicitor, a young guy called Alan, who awaited me in the interview room along with two Customs officers. One of the latter said that I could have a few minutes alone with my brief before the interview proper began.

As the door closed behind them, Alan waved me to sit down at a large table next to one wall. Although he might have been young, he wasn't stupid. Pointing up at the ceiling, he whispered that the room was probably bugged. Still keeping his voice low, he asked, 'Do you know what they're saying?'

I was bursting to answer, 'Yes, and it's a right lot of bollocks,' but I was experienced at playing this game, too. Instead, I just nodded and said, 'What do you think of Millwall this season?' Keenan's was a south London solicitors, and I guessed that young Alan was a south London boy. Sure enough, a smile split his face, and he sat back in his chair. We were soon deep in discussion about the merits of the various players.

The two Customs officers returned and made quite a meal of setting their papers out on the table and putting a new tape into the tape machine. They did the 'Testing, testing, one, two, three' bit and played it back, but everybody in the room knew they were wasting their time.

I sat quietly through the caution, then confirmed that I was Andrew Pritchard and that I lived at Barretts Grove. However, when they asked if I knew a Gavin Hunt, I pointed to Alan and said in a loud, clear voice, 'On my solicitor's advice, I won't be answering any questions at this stage.'

The two Customs guys still had to go through with the charade, though. One after another, they put perhaps 20 questions to me. I answered 'No comment' to them all. Eventually, they both stood up and announced that the interview was over.

There was a brief reprise of the interview later that evening at about 9 p.m., but the presence of my solicitor and the continuous stream of 'no comments' finally convinced them that they were wasting their time. They told me to get ready, because they would be taking me to Peckham Police Station very shortly.

Still in the custody of Customs staff, I was handcuffed, put in a car and driven across London. We drove into the yard at the rear of Peckham nick. There were some papers to be signed before the Customs handed me over to the police. This done, it was the latter who led me into the charge room.

It was a large room, and a lot was going on. People were being fingerprinted and photographed as part of the reception process. Even though they had their backs to me, a couple of them seemed familiar. As I looked more closely, they both turned, and I saw that it was Gavin and Dean. Gavin made as if to speak, but Dean quickly pulled at his arm and led him away. At that stage, until we knew exactly what they had on us, it was best to not even acknowledge that we knew each other.

I was put through all the various procedures, and it was finally time for us to be charged. I was lined up in front of a long desk next to Gavin and Dean. Three other guys I had seen about the fruit market stood next to them. A dozen police officers gathered round and several Customs officers chatted at the margins. One particular female Customs officer stared directly at me. Her face brought back a memory. About two months previously, she had stopped me in the street and asked me for directions. Clearly, I had been under close observation for some time.

A senior police officer suddenly appeared behind the desk, and the whole room fell silent. My pulse quickened as an air of expectation spread through the gathering. Although important to all, the proceedings meant different things to different people. I felt a surge of excitement, underpinned by the stirrings of fear.

In a clear, measured tone, the desk officer read through the suspects' names and addresses. Quite deliberately, he emphasised that we were being charged with the importation of 572 kilos of cocaine. Any doubts I had ever had about the Customs playing a trick on me were immediately dispelled. Now I had it officially: I was in deep, deep shit!

Once we were charged, a sense of anticlimax spread through the room. We were told that we would be appearing at Horseferry Road Magistrates' Court. Then we were all put into individual cells.

In the privacy of my cell, I walked up and down, my mind racing furiously. I now had a much better idea of what I was facing. The three guys lined up with us to be charged were the three who had helped Gavin to unload the container, so there was no mystery there. But my confusion stemmed not from who had been nicked with me. It came from the realisation of who had not.

Both Lazarus and Bob were missing. If the Customs had been on to all of our crew, they must certainly have known about them. To the best of my knowledge, Lazarus had stayed in Cuba, so there was an explanation for his absence. Bob was a different story, though. Through their surveillance, the Customs must have known about Bob. This meant that they must also have known about his Customs-officer brother and the involvement of the FAST team. Yet none of them had been nicked. They could always show up as co-defendants at a later date, of course, but at the moment it was beginning to look like a cover-up or that Bob was double-crossing us and was really working with Customs. The cover-up alternative didn't look good.

I was well aware that the system always looked after its own. There would be great reluctance on the part of the authorities to acknowledge that serving Customs officers were part of such a serious conspiracy. Not only would it undermine the good standing of HM Customs, but it could compromise the convictions of all the cases that members of our friendly FAST team had previously been involved in. If they had been party to the passing through of half a ton of cocaine, quite clearly their evidence could not be trusted. Perhaps scores of guilty men would have to be freed.

However, Bob was a different story. Perhaps who his brother was had kept him off the charge sheet. Or perhaps, as a former SAS man, it was to be expected that he would get special treatment. Who knows what secrets he knew? Who knew what black ops he had been involved in?

My disappointment at the absence of these crucial people wasn't borne of spite. Just because I had been nicked, it wasn't the case that I wanted others nicked too. I wanted them in court for a very good reason. I was sure that Gavin, Dean and the three fruit porters hadn't been involved in substituting the cocaine for the cigars. It had to be down to Bob and Lazarus.

When I was unlocked in the morning, I was handed some clean clothes that had been dropped off for me at the station. I reasoned that Amber must have brought them, which set me to thinking about her. How was she taking it all? Would she ever forgive me for breaking my word to her about never getting involved in smuggling again? Amongst all the other pain and worry I now had, I also had to face the possibility that I might never see her again. It brought to mind the ironic saying that the chaps often used: 'It's at times like these that you wish you hadn't done it.'

I put the clean clothes on and immediately felt a bit better. Hardly had I sat down to wait when the door opened again. In reception, I was handcuffed to a policeman. He led me out into an enclosed yard where a big bus waited. There was little resemblance to a normal bus, because this was the secure transport they used to take prisoners to and from court. The chaps called it the 'sweatbox', and it was a good nickname. You entered from the back and a narrow corridor ran the length of the bus. There were very small holding cells on either side. Each cell had a tiny barred window of opaque glass set high up on the outside wall. It was difficult to see out, and it only let in a small amount of fresh air. In summer, you would literally sweat in this cell. However, even in cold weather, the waiting and the worrying on the way to court could cause you to sweat anyway.

The sweatbox duly pulled into the backyard of Horseferry Road Magistrates' Court, and I was led into the building and put in a cell on my own. I settled back against the wall trying to accustom my mind to the fact that for the immediate future at least my life would be one of waiting.

Some time later, the door was opened by a prison warder. 'Lawyer's visit,' he called out, as if he were announcing it to the whole building. Around him stepped a big man, wearing a wig and gown. He hurried into the cell, shook my hand vigorously and introduced himself as Graham Wilson. Almost as an afterthought, he added that he was the barrister sent by Keenan and Co. to represent me. Any satisfaction I might have taken from the fact that I had a barrister at the magistrates' court was immediately outweighed by the implication that the charges against me were so serious that they merited such senior representation so early.

'Not much happening today, Mr Pritchard,' he said in a plummy voice. 'Just a formal remand in custody. As you might have guessed, with the seriousness of the offence, it isn't worth asking for bail.' In a couple of short sentences, he had answered all my most pressing questions. I had indeed guessed that bail was out of the question. Even so, his confirming it still depressed me.

I was led into the dock first, with Gavin, Dean and the three fruit porters following behind. I sat at the extreme right of the dock, closest to where the jury would sit when there was one. Quite obviously, mine was the first name on the indictment. Equally obviously, they were making me out to be the ringleader.

As my barrister had warned, it was very much a formality. The charges were read out, and we were each asked if we had anything to say. Gavin, Dean and the three fruit porters all asked for bail. It didn't do them any good, and we were all remanded in custody. I did take some satisfaction from that. Not out of spite, but because I wanted to keep a close eye on Dean and Gavin. On such a serious charge, the prosecution was bound to try to do a deal with one of the lesser defendants. They would try to get someone to turn Queen's evidence and give testimony against all the others in return for a reduced sentence.

I wasn't worried about the three fruit porters. They knew

nothing about the arranging of the shipment, so there wasn't much they could say. And I was quite confident about Dean. We had been mates for a long time, and he came from a long line of market workers. Even though they were all straight, they still honoured the code that you never grassed on anyone.

However, Gavin was very much an unknown quantity. He had never been inside before, and he was weak. It wasn't that he would be under pressure because he couldn't get the drugs he needed. Most prisons were awash with drugs, and I would make sure that he was well supplied. But in the face of a very long sentence, as well as his parents urging him to make a clean breast of it, he could well fold. I wasn't concerned about him confessing, just as long as he confessed truly, but I was worried that the prosecution could get him to confess falsely that we had indeed been expecting the cocaine.

As I stood up to leave the dock, I glimpsed Amber at the back of the court. She waved and gave me a weak smile. Next to her sat her friend Georgie. Gavin's parents sat behind them and stared grimly ahead. Then I was taken down the stairs and back to my cell.

I guessed that they wouldn't lay on a coach just to take us five to prison. Sure enough, we had to wait until the court finished later that afternoon. Then we were loaded back into the sweatbox, along with a dozen other prisoners. I managed to ask one of them where we were going. 'Wandsworth,' he replied.

I didn't shudder, but inwardly it did give me pause. Wandsworth Prison, or 'Wanno' to the initiated, had a fearsome reputation. In the old days – and not so long ago at that – a heavy mob of prison-officer bullies had enjoyed a reign of terror. Prisoners were regularly beaten severely in the punishment block, and there had been a couple of deaths. The inquests had always ruled that they were accidents or suicides, but the effect was to force the Home Office to clean the place up. The heavy mob of bullies was dispersed, but Wanno still had a reputation as a place where the screws ruled.

It was dark by the time we arrived. The gates swung open, and we drove inside. Impatient screws barked orders as we were hustled out of the sweatbox. We were quickly processed through reception and given our prison kit; as remand prisoners, we could wear our own clothes. Then, following a cold meal, we were led on to the wings.

All the other prisoners had long since been locked away. As we entered E wing, I took in the towering, vaulted ceiling high above and the metalwork landings that ran along the walls. I counted four landings, one above the other. Metalwork staircases ran between each. In the half-light, it resembled a scene from Victorian times. It occurred to me that Wanno had been a prison even then.

Suddenly, I was aware of an extreme chill. It wasn't that the wing was cold – if anything, it was stifling hot – and the chilliness wasn't a physical thing, either. It seemed to be in my mind. All at once, I shuddered. I had always been a spiritual person and recalled my mother once saying in similar circumstances, 'Someone has just walked over my grave.' Something terrible had happened at the spot I was now passing. Shaking my head to free me from the sensation, I hurried on. Later, I found out that I had been passing the cell where condemned men had been hanged.

Like a lot of the old Victorian prisons, Wanno had several wings that radiated outwards from a circular 'centre', resembling spokes around a wheel. Wanno's centre was about 30 feet in diameter. It was very brightly lit, courtesy of dozens of lights hung from the landings that towered overhead. Right in the middle was an extraordinary construction. It was another circular area, a giant grating really, about 15 feet in diameter, made entirely out of steel. The design was quite intricate, and it was very highly polished.

As the first of the night's new arrivals made to walk across the centre, there was a loud shout: 'Oi! Don't you walk on the metal bit. That's for prison officers only. You walk on the tiled part round the sides and only in a clockwise direction, OK? Otherwise you're nicked. Remember that, all of you.'

There was a small, wooden office to the side of the centre, something like a garden shed. From behind it walked a portly, elderly screw, displaying the insignia of a chief officer. Clearly, he had been doing the shouting.

Like ducklings behind the mother duck, we followed the lead reception around the centre in a clockwise direction. We were headed for C wing, so the obvious, shortest route was across D wing in an anticlockwise direction. The clockwise route we were taking was across both A and B wings, and therefore longer. There was no sense to it. I reasoned it was just the screws' way of telling us that they made all the rules in here.

We were each assigned a cell number, and we climbed the metal stairs to the landings. As I stopped outside the cell assigned to me, other receptions walked past. I was relieved when Gavin stopped beside me. He had been assigned to the same cell. Just before the door closed on us for the night, we managed to shout a subdued goodnight to Dean as he passed, his face a picture of despair. I took comfort from the fact that my proposed strategy was working out quite well. With Gavin as my cellmate, I would be able to keep a very close eye on him.

Even though we were locked in a cell, I still allowed my paranoia to get the better of me. We had been deliberately put in that particular cell. It wouldn't have been too difficult for the authorities to have bugged it. Putting my finger to my mouth, I signalled that we shouldn't talk about anything serious. 'We'll talk tomorrow on the yard,' I whispered. With that, the night screw turned out the light, and we both climbed into bed.

Waking up in Wanno in the morning was a bit like waking up in a breaker's yard. There were the sharp crashes of heavy metal gates being slammed and the thunder of heavy boots running up the metal stairs. Loud voices, distorted by the closed cell door, shouted incomprehensible orders. Suddenly, it would all go quiet. Then a bell would ring and there would be a shout of 'Unlock'.

The sound of doors being unlocked came ever closer until our door was swung back on its hinges. We had been located on the topmost 'Fours' landing. 'Fours down for breakfast,' came the shout from the invisible screw, and we followed all the others on our landing as they descended the stairs to collect their breakfast.

There was a hotplate and several tables set up on the Ones or ground-floor landing. I was given a slice of bacon, some beans, a ladleful of porridge and four slices of bread with a blob of marge. I filled my plastic mug from a tea urn. Then we climbed the stairs again to our cell. A screw came past and slammed the door shut.

'This is it, mate,' I said to a somewhat crestfallen Gavin. 'It will be "Down for breakfast", "Down for dinner" and "Down for tea", day in, day out. A couple of times a day, it will be "Down for exercise". Then there will be legal and social visits. Other than that, that's life in Wanno.' Gavin didn't look impressed, but it was better that he knew exactly what he was up against.

Perhaps an hour passed, and a screw came round opening all the doors again. At the shout of 'Down for exercise', Gavin and I followed all the rest down to the Ones and out a side door into a large yard. It was about the size of two football pitches and was enclosed on three sides by the wings. The fourth, outer side was cut off by a high mesh fence, beyond which stood the prison wall. There was a circular area of grass in the middle, and an oval-shaped brick pathway ran around it. The prisoners in front of us started to walk around the ovoid in an anticlockwise direction. Gavin and I followed in their footsteps.

Even out on the yard, I was careful. The cameras mounted on the wings, fences and walls could easily pick up facial expressions. Perhaps an expert could watch the footage and make out our lip movements and therefore decipher what we were saying. I cautioned Gavin to cover his mouth with his hand when he spoke.

It was no use talking until all the others were present. We stood to the side of the path looking for Dean and the three fruit porters. Just as a screw shouted at us to move on, Dean and the three others came out of the wing. They joined up with us, and we began to walk round the yard. The three fruit porters were still in a state of shock. They had been promised a few quid for helping to unload some moody cigars. Now here they were in a top security jail, facing an endless sentence for half a ton of cocaine.

I cautioned all of them about covering their mouths when talking and asked them what they had said to Customs. After a few initial questions, the Customs officers had given up with the three fruit porters, realising that they knew nothing beyond that they had been asked to help unload some cigars. Dean, though, had been questioned at length and threatened with 30 years in jail, but he had been strong enough to keep his mouth shut.

I now wanted to discuss our collective strategy for the coming trial, but that didn't include the three fruit porters. There were things I had to say that weren't for their ears, as they could pass my words on to Customs – you never knew. Saying we would see them later, I took Dean by the arm and led him away with Gavin.

On our own now, I emphasised that it was essential that the three of us stick together and present a united front. I stated that all we had to do was tell the truth, namely that we were expecting cigars. I asked them both who they thought had substituted the cocaine. They both said Bob.

But knowing that Bob had made the switch didn't help us at all, really. He wasn't in custody, and he wasn't likely to come forward at our trial and admit what he had done. Furthermore, he was certainly long gone and would be impossible to find. It was a similar situation with Lazarus. You could bet your life he had gone to ground in Cuba. And I doubted that the UK had an extradition treaty with the Cubans, anyway.

So, we were on our own. We would somehow have to convince a jury that someone else had made the switch and not us. Gavin did suggest that we should try to round up some of the cigars from the first shipment. Apart from the fact that they were probably all sold long ago, what would that prove? The shipment had come through unopened and unchecked. There would be no record of them anywhere. And if we said that cigars had come in on the first shipment, all the Customs would say was that the first shipment had either been a dummy run or had been cocaine as well.

That afternoon, I had a social visit with Amber. I approached this with as much trepidation as the trial itself. Being away from her, I realised just how much I loved her. To lose her now would be a crushing blow. I thought about how we all take certain things for granted. 'You don't miss your water till your well runs dry', a line from an old soul song, ran through my head.

The visiting area was a large room with chairs and tables arranged in rows. Each table had a raised board across the middle, much like the net on a table-tennis table. I guessed that this was to make it more difficult for people to pass things to each other. I was given a thorough search by the screw at the door, cautioned that no touching was allowed and sent to sit at table number 15.

Amber smiled bravely as she approached my table, but I could tell that she was actually very upset. I waved her into a chair opposite me and told her that we weren't allowed to touch. She sat and leaned forward, extending her hand. I reached out and our fingers touched fleetingly. I then asked her how she was, and she admitted that she wasn't good, but she was putting a brave face on it. She asked me how I was, and I assured her that I was OK. There was no condemnation, and I realised that she would be a rock through the coming ordeal. Good, solid, dependable Amber. How I wished we were a thousand miles away in Tobago again.

She told me that the Customs officers had searched our flat from top to bottom. They had taken away the fax, a computer and some pens. They had also asked her if she had known what I had been up to. Over and over she had replied that I never spoke to her about my business activities. It smacked of harassment. Having got nothing out of me, it would probably continue. I told her that it would be best if she went to stay with her family in Tobago for a while. 'But what about you?' she cried.

'I'll be OK,' I replied. 'With you still in England, it will only put more pressure on me. Come back just before the trial.' Amber admitted that she could see the sense in that and agreed to go within the next couple of days. She added that she would arrange for her friend Georgie to come up and bring me anything I might need.

With the visit out of the way, I felt considerably relieved. I wouldn't have to worry about Amber and could fully concentrate on my defence. The following day, David Turner, my solicitor, came up on a legal visit. Long experienced in the wiles of the police, we whispered in each other's ears, even though we were alone in a small room. I told him about the involvement of the Customs staff in our smuggling plot, specifically the assistance of the FAST team. He shook his head in amazement and said that what I'd told him was dynamite. However, he cautioned that the Customs would undoubtedly close ranks, and it might be very difficult to prove.

Day now followed boring day as we waited for the trial date. We all made a couple of further appearances at the Crown court. It was merely a formality, and each time we were all remanded in custody again. To pass the time, as well as to help in my defence, I began to read law books I had borrowed from the prison library. I wasn't the greatest of readers and had problems with some of the legal terms, but slowly and surely I did come to understand something of how the law works.

With Amber in Tobago, Georgie now visited me twice a week. She brought me up clean clothing and other stuff I needed, and she proved to be a very good friend indeed.

Although I didn't have to do a job because I was only on remand, everybody was expected to work in one of the prison workshops at Wanno. It was all thoroughly boring, repetitive work, the type usually done in factories in Third World countries. Not only did I feel it to be demeaning, I thought I could spend my time better reading law books in my cell.

The screws didn't see it that way, of course, which brought me to the attention of Prison Officer Watkins. I had noticed him about the landing, mainly opening doors and shouting at the top of his voice. He was an obese individual with folds of fat hanging from his florid face. His small beady eyes spoke of a limited intelligence, his enormous backside of a sedentary lifestyle. From day one, we didn't get along.

I first noticed it in his brusque manner whenever I had to ask for anything in the landing office. Then he was always chivvying me along the landing, hurrying to get me back in my cell. I was wise enough in the ways of prison to know that if I didn't make a stand he would make my life a misery.

We had already had a couple of quite fierce verbal rows. During one of these, he had suddenly said that I thought I was something special because I was a big-time drug dealer. That's when it had all fallen into place. That was why he was digging me out. When I'd refused to go into one of the workshops, he had taken it very personally. But as I was studying my case, it wasn't something I could be put on report for. All he could do was fume about it privately.

The two half-hour exercise periods soon came to be the high points of my day. Out in the yard, I realised that I knew some of the other prisoners, many of them from my native north London. They had hung back on the first day, realising that I would want to talk with my co-defendants in private. Now they came forward en masse.

The half a ton of cocaine had made me something of a criminal celebrity. The majority of them hadn't seen so much as a kilo of the stuff. Perhaps they thought that I could give them some kind of a connection. Maybe they thought I was fabulously wealthy. I left them in their ignorance, never once mentioning that I was just a cigar smuggler. This was a very important strategy, and

I emphasised as much to Dean and Gavin. I didn't doubt that there were many untrustworthy prisoners in Wanno. If it became known that we were denying the cocaine and saying that it was just cigars, one of them, in order to get a reduced sentence, could possibly have gone to the police and said that one of us had admitted to him that we were expecting the cocaine.

Among those prisoners on the yard who knew me was a Moroccan guy called Ahmed. He was something of a local character around north London and could be regularly seen working in the street markets. He was intrigued by the fact that our smuggling operation had been done through Spitalfields, a market he knew well. However, even though I did trust him, I still didn't discuss our case with him.

I liked his company because he was a very funny guy and life was a continuous lark for him. He was even able to laugh about his present predicament, being on remand charged with several armed robberies. But, as he told it, his story was very funny.

Ahmed had extremely poor eyesight. In fact, he was as blind as the proverbial bat without the thick-lensed glasses he constantly wore. This led to his street nickname of 'The Bat'. He even referred to himself as such. Together with his team of three others, The Bat had taken to robbing jewellery shops. There was little organisation, and the actual raids were pure chaos. Waving imitation guns, they ran into the shops screaming at the top of their voices.

During the robberies, The Bat had a particular problem. The stocking mask he pulled over his face would invariably snag on his much-needed glasses. Fed up with forever straightening them up during the robbery, he decided that he would do his latest bit of work without them.

The target was a jeweller's located next to an underground station. It had two entrances, one in the street and the other in the arcade of shops that led to the station. The Bat and his crew decided to enter through the door in the street. With one of the crew leading the charge, they burst into the shop, screaming loudly. Such was the effect on one customer that he panicked and ran across the shop. The Bat, mistaking him for one of his crew, ran after him. When the customer ran out the other door and into the arcade, The Bat followed him.

The arcade was crowded with people heading for or leaving the station. Suddenly, there was a guy among them wearing a stocking mask and waving a gun about wildly. Unfortunately for The Bat, one of those people leaving the station was a policeman. Taking out his stick, the policeman crept up behind the disorientated robber and, with one mighty blow, knocked him unconscious. The Bat woke up in the cells.

It was a funny story and even funnier the way The Bat told it. For the first time in days, I found myself laughing heartily, as were Gavin and Dean, both of whom knew him too. I was determined to have The Bat in my company every day from then on. If he could keep me laughing like that, it would be good therapy and take some of the pressure off.

About a month after we had been arrested, we made one of our usual appearances at the Crown court. On this occasion, though, the prosecution made their first disclosures. To my amazement, I found out that Gavin had made a statement 157 pages long. On careful reading, I concluded that it didn't do either Dean or myself any harm. However, in trying to deny bringing in what he thought was cigars, his evidence had been inconsistent. This would damage his credibility at the coming trial.

I did glean one other piece of worrying information at the court that day. I had it on very good authority that the Customs officers had offered both Dean and Gavin a deal. They had promised the pair a reduced sentence if they turned Queen's evidence against the rest of us. The reduced sentence would be 17 years' imprisonment!

Needless to say, this wasn't much of an incentive, and they had both refused the offer. Any satisfaction I might have taken from that was soon dispelled by the thought that if the prosecution was going to offer a sentence of 17 years for turning Queen's evidence, what on earth were they going to give me if I was convicted? It served to focus my mind wonderfully, and I read the law books with renewed vigour.

Apart from being a very funny guy, The Bat was a consummate ducker and diver. Whatever scams there were going on in the prison, you could bet that he knew of them. One day, he asked me if I wanted a mobile phone. This was a very attractive proposition indeed. Not only could I make long and intimate phone calls to Amber, I could also speak secretly with people who were trying to help me with my defence.

I gave him £200, and the next day he handed me a mobile phone when we were on exercise. He also told me how I could bind several batteries, which could be bought in the prison canteen, together to make a charger. That night, I gave Amber, freshly returned from Tobago, a romantic midnight call.

Over the following days, I called everyone who I thought might be able to help me. Everyone was willing. However, the burning question I had to answer was, 'How am I going to convince a jury that we only conspired to import cigars and not cocaine?' A couple of my potential helpers did suggest that maybe I should be thinking about escaping. I did consider it, but instead decided to stay and fight the case.

It might have been sheer coincidence, but the following morning our door was opened very early. Gavin and I, together with all our belongings, were put in a van and, with an escort of two police cars, their sirens blaring, taken across London to Belmarsh Prison. Here, in this top-security prison, we were placed on Category A, the highest security category, and lodged on one of the wings. All requests for an explanation were met with stony silence, so I sent for my solicitor. I don't know who he spoke to, but the following week we were both moved back to Wanno.

Watkins wasn't pleased to see me. Muttering under his breath about my not sharing with Gavin any more, he put me in an unoccupied cell and slammed the door with an awesome crash.

He had done me a favour. Gavin was now as fully briefed as he was ever likely to be, so I didn't need to mother him. Further, I would enjoy the solitude. I didn't know it at the time, but Watkins was yet to have the last laugh.

When I went out onto the yard for exercise, The Bat came running up, clearly disturbed about something. 'I must talk to you on your own,' he mumbled into his hand. Asking Dean and Gavin to excuse me, I walked off with The Bat.

'We've been friends for a while, eh Andy?' I had never seen him so serious and on the defensive.

'Yes, Ahmed. What's the problem?' I asked.

'This is nothing to do with me,' he assured me, 'but someone has come to me and told me something, and now I must tell you.'

My curiosity was now well and truly aroused. 'Ahmed, just tell me what you've got to say,' I said firmly.

'There's someone who's got something to tell you,' he continued warily. 'I know him only slightly, but I can see no reason for him to lie.'

'Well, where is he, Ahmed?' My impatience was getting the better of me.

The Bat stopped and waved to a guy who was walking several feet behind us. He came hurrying up to join us. He was a tall, black guy with dreadlocked hair who I was sure I had never seen before. He too looked very wary. 'Look, man,' he said to me. 'This has got nothing to do with me. It's just something I heard.'

By now, all the caution was getting to me. I was seriously concerned and wanted to hear what this was all about. 'Well, go on then,' I said. 'Tell me what it is.'

'Do you know a guy called "Jekyll", a fat Jewish guy who comes out of Chingford?' he continued.

I cast my mind back over everyone I knew from that manor and came up with a face to go with the name. I had known Jekyll on and off for years. He was one of the legion of crack heads who ducked and dived to try to support their habits. I had never done any business with him, but I had helped him out. I had lent him money on several occasions. A couple of times, he hadn't been able to repay me, but I had let it go. I had also intervened in disputes and saved him from being beaten up. He had even been to my house in Stoke Newington. He was a long way from being a friend, but I had certainly behaved like one to him. I acknowledged that I did know him.

'About a month ago, I was doing some business with this Jekyll,' he continued. 'It was then that he asked me if I would be interested in doing a bit of work with him. I asked him what it was, and he said that he knew of a big drug dealer who had recently been nicked for a lot of coke. He said that it was a wealthy guy who had a lot of money stashed away. He said that the guy lived in Barretts Grove, Stoke Newington. He added that the guy's girlfriend still lived there and that if we kidnapped her, then the guy would come up with some money.'

A sheet of white-hot rage passed in front of my eyes, and I clenched my hands involuntarily. I had constantly helped this scumbag out, yet this was how he repaid me. The guy with the dreadlocks took a pace backwards. 'Look, mate,' I said. 'I want to thank you very much for telling me.' I stepped forward and shook his hand. 'If there's anything I can do for you, then just ask. But can you help me out and find where this Jekyll is now? Otherwise my girlfriend is still at risk.' The guy said that he was pleased to be able to help and would do what he could, but he didn't know where Jekyll lived.

Suddenly, my defence was no longer at the centre of my attention. I became totally focused on the search for Jekyll. I sent messages out to everyone I knew, telling them that they should pull out all the stops and try to find the guy. In the meantime, I sent Amber to stay with relatives.

Being a typical crack head, Jekyll was very difficult to track down. Although my friends stressed that there was a big reward for information, lots of people seemed to know where he was yesterday, but no one knew where he was currently. One guy, though, did know that Jekyll had an on–off relationship with a girl out of Canning Town. She was a crack head like himself and just as difficult to track down. However, there were rumours that she sometimes went to Kings Cross to do a bit of brassing and also to buy the drugs she needed. Teams of my friends began patrolling the Cross, handing out rocks to the assorted junkies and brasses and asking after the girl. The rocks convinced people that they weren't the police, and the girl was pointed out to them.

Charlene was a sad case. She had been on heroin since the age of fifteen, and ten years of abuse had wrecked her health. She said that she had fallen out with Jekyll after he ripped her off for some pills. She didn't know where he was right then, but she did know of a doctor's surgery where he regularly went to get his prescriptions filled. Charlene was taken for a meal, given some money and reassured that she would be given a lot more if she helped to locate Jekyll. She readily agreed.

Fortunately for us, the doctor's surgery was only open in the mornings. For two days, my friends sat in their car along with Charlene, looking out for Jekyll. Just before noon on the second day, they saw him. As he entered the surgery, they passed Charlene some money and let her out of the car. Then they settled back to wait.

Jekyll came out of the surgery looking pleased with himself. The prescription he carried in his hand would ensure that he would have the pills that he needed for several days. He gripped it tightly.

The blow to the side of the head knocked him against the wall and that to his stomach knocked all the wind out of him. As he fell, he clutched the prescription all the tighter. He must have thought that someone was trying to steal it. Strong hands gripped him, and he was carried to the car and thrown inside. He was held in a headlock, then wrapped in a blanket as the car was driven off. At some stage, he must have passed out.

It was obvious that he was confused when he awoke. He was

hanging upside down from a rope suspended from the ceiling, and his hands were tied behind his back. A piece of surgical tape across his lips prevented him from calling out. As his inverted gaze swept the dusty floor of the derelict basement, he could only have concluded that he was in serious trouble. He began to cry.

Ignoring him, my friends busied themselves with their preparations. They stacked a pile of firelighters beneath his head and lay balls of crumpled newspaper on top. Then, getting down on his knees so as to talk more easily to the upturned face, one of my friends pulled out a lighter and removed the strip of surgical tape.

'What have I done? What have I done?' cried Jekyll.

'It's not what you've done, but what you intended to do,' said my friend, holding up the lighter.

'No, no,' screamed Jekyll. 'I swear I won't do anything.'

'I know you won't,' said my friend, gently patting Jekyll's face, which was wet with tears. He then explained the rumour that we had heard. At first, Jekyll denied it all. However, when my friend actually lit the lighter, his confession poured out. Yes, he had thought about doing it, but he had decided against it, and there was no one else involved.

'This time we'll let you off with a caution,' warned my friend. 'Any more from you, and the next time we'll invite you to a barbecue. You can guess who'll be on the menu.' Then Jekyll was untied and let go. It seemed to have done the trick, because I never heard from him again.

Time passed, ever more slowly, and we were finally committed to Blackfriars Crown Court. I continued to read law books, and the more I read the more despondent I became about winning the case. To pass the time, as well as to expend some excess energy, I had begun to go to the gym for an hour each day. As I returned one day, I saw Watkins outside my cell, a smug grin on his face. I ignored him as he opened my cell door then closed it behind me.

I was so intent on what Watkins was looking so pleased about that I nearly collided with the guy who had stood up from one of the beds to meet me. I no longer had a cell all to myself. This wasn't the only reason for Watkins' glee, however. I didn't know it at the time, but my new cellmate was a very unsavoury character indeed.

The guy introduced himself, and his posh accent perfectly complemented his double-barrelled name. He was about my own age, with sleeked-back black hair, greying at the temples. He stuck out his hand.

There were several things about his performance that aroused my suspicion. He wasn't your typical working-class criminal. Coupled with Watkins' ill-concealed glee, it instantly put me on the defensive. 'I hope you're not a fucking sex case,' I said aggressively, ignoring his outstretched hand.

'No, no,' said the guy, backing away rapidly. 'I've just got a life sentence for fraud,' he added quickly.

'A life sentence for fraud?' I said, the disbelief clear in my voice. 'That must have been some big fucking fraud, mate.'

'Well, actually, I'm a conman. I tricked a lot of important people out of their money,' he confessed.

As he told me his story, it was so incredible that I actually believed it. He had regularly posed as an MI5 agent. Over the years, he had convinced scores of people to take part in various operations he had devised. All the time they thought they were working for MI5. Some parted with all their money, others were left broken and one woman had had two children by him. In short, he had tortured, tormented and exploited people, ruining many lives in the process. I could only conclude that he wasn't a sex case, but, as the saying goes, 'He'll do until one comes along.'

The bottom line was that I was stuck with him. Watkins would refuse my request to move him out or to give me another cell. Short of bashing him up and finding myself on further charges, he would be my cellmate for the foreseeable future.

In the event, it wasn't too much of an imposition at all. He was scrupulously clean and was forever tidying the cell. Furthermore, he was highly intelligent, and I could have a decent conversation with him. I was careful never to discuss my case with him, though. I tolerated but never trusted him.

A couple of weeks after his appearance, I returned from the gym one day to find him holding a large brown envelope. As I put my gym kit on my bed, he handed it to me, saying, 'I think this is yours.' I thought that it would be legal papers from my solicitor and sat on the bed to read them.

There were about 150 sheets of A4-sized paper, all with closely spaced typing on them. As I flicked through, I saw my name mentioned several times and references to my co-defendants. But the thing that really caught my eye was that at the top of each sheet in bold lettering were the headings 'SECRET', 'RESTRICTED' and 'SENSITIVE'. It seemed that I was reading classified documents.

With a roar, I came up off the bed and grabbed him by the throat, pushing him to the floor. 'What the fuck are you up to?' I raged. 'Trying to con me, are you?'

As he struggled to free himself, he cried out, 'For God's sake. I don't know what you're talking about. The envelope was pushed under the door. I didn't even open it.'

I let him go and thrust the documents into his face. 'What's this, then?' I demanded, pointing to the page headings.

He peered closer, then, now interested, peered closer still. 'They look like classified documents,' he finally said.

'And you'd know a classified document if you saw one?'

'Of course I would,' he said with some irritation. 'With my background, don't you think I've forged some in my time?'

'So, how do I know that you haven't forged these?'

He took some of the documents from my hand. He examined them for several minutes. 'Well, for a start, there's a lot of confidential details in here that I couldn't possibly know,' he said. 'The home addresses of your co-defendants, for example.'

It was enough to give me pause. The more I read the papers, the more intimate detail was revealed. There was information from the Jamaican authorities, information from various special Customs operations, data from covert human-intelligence sources, including details of informers, and finally some stuff from the DEA in Washington. Even to my untrained eye, if what I had was genuine, it was dynamite.

I spent the next couple of hours reading the documents carefully, while he sat in the corner of the cell sulking. I came to several conclusions simultaneously. These papers were definitely a gift from providence. The second gift from providence was sitting in the corner of the cell. If someone was to receive papers like these, then he was definitely the ideal person to interpret them.

'Look,' I began, 'I didn't mean to have a go at you.' As he lifted his face to look at me, I was conscious of the red welts around his neck where I had grabbed him. 'What do you think these are?' I held out the bunch of papers towards him.

He came off the bed so fast it startled me. I concluded that the thing that had really miffed him was not being able to examine the documents. He snatched them eagerly from my hand. For the next half-hour, he was lost to the world.

Suddenly, he cleared his throat as if he was about to make an important announcement. 'From my long experience in intelligence matters,' he said, 'it is quite clear that these are highly confidential, official documents, originating from HM Customs. Your possession of them is a clear breach of the Official Secrets Act, and, in view of the fact that they contain details from both Jamaica and Washington, this breach has international ramifications.'

'So, it's serious?' I interjected.

'Very serious indeed,' he replied. 'They seriously damage the prosecution's case, but the only problem is that some of the details they contain seem to be harmful to your own case. I take it you are pleading not guilty?'

'Of course I am,' I said. 'So how can I use them to my advantage?'

He sat silent for several minutes. When he spoke, his tone was low and measured. 'Well, you definitely can't show them to your legal team,' he said. 'They would have to excuse themselves from the case. And the prosecution would never allow them to be introduced as evidence. They would claim PII.'

'They would claim what?' The impatience in my voice was clear.

'PII,' he continued, 'is short for Public Interest Immunity. It means that if the Crown determines that something breaches the Official Secrets Act, they can apply for PII to stop it being made public.'

'Which brings me back to my original question. How can I use this to my advantage?' I pressed.

Suddenly, he smiled a broad smile as if he had just done something very clever. 'I've got it,' he shouted, then immediately lowered his voice self-consciously. 'Read the papers out to the jury. The judge will stop you, but the seed will have been planted in the jurors' minds. They will probably ask to see the papers. That won't be possible, because they're covered by the Official Secrets Act. It will seem like the prosecution is being devious and has something to hide.'

Now it was my turn to smile broadly. With his help, I would prepare my strategy. With a little bit of luck, I would have a nice surprise up my sleeve when I next saw Martin and his mates.

I mentioned the documents to both Dean and Gavin, but not before I had had copies made. I made them swear not to tell a soul. Strangely, it was Gavin who asked the question that I should have been asking myself. Who had put them under my cell door?

Now I put my mind to the problem, it was a very strange occurrence indeed. If they had merely been Home Office documents, then their theft would not have been surprising, what with the level of corruption amongst prison staff. But these secret documents had come from inside Customs House, the headquarters of HM Customs and Excise. This meant that they had been stolen by a serving Customs officer. Not only that, he had somehow managed to persuade a prison officer to put them under my door.

My cellmate was of the opinion that the whole thing smacked of a 'black operation'. He went on to say that maybe someone high up in Customs wasn't at all pleased that the involvement of one of their FAST teams in a smuggling operation had been covered up. Perhaps this was their way of trying to bring it all out in the open. Whatever the reason, I was deeply grateful to my unknown benefactor and wasn't about to question the motivation behind my good fortune.

Eleven

Trials and Tribulations

OUR TRIAL started on 13 October 2005, a date that troubled me more than Amber. She was a deeply spiritual person and had become even more so since my arrest. Her days were filled with prayers and rituals, which she referred to as white magic. I wasn't concerned by this, as spirituality is an integral part of West Indian culture, and I was quite spiritual myself. I took it to be Amber's way of dealing with the pressure.

Like actors in a play, all the leading characters soon introduced themselves: Judge Byers would be presiding over proceedings; Tom Cark would be prosecuting; Mike Broadman, QC, would be leading my defence; and Colin Nichols, QC, would be appearing for Gavin.

The jury were duly sworn in, and I scanned their faces looking for some kind of clue to their individual attitudes. It was a pointless task, really, because I knew from long experience that you could tell very little about a person's value system from their appearance. In sum, they were a totally average group of people. They were mostly white, except for one elderly black lady. The rest were middle-aged men and women, apart from one young woman, who looked at me and smiled sweetly. These, then, were the people I had to convince of my innocence. These were the people who could consign me to jail for the rest of my life, who held my and Amber's future in their hands.

The prosecutor opened his case, and the massive size of the

surveillance operation against us soon became apparent. A total of 86 Customs officers had been involved, and there were statements from most of them. All of my and my co-defendants' phones had been tapped, linking us all together, and there were pages and pages of transcripts of conversations, many of which were incriminating. There were reams of pages detailing forensic evidence and an absolute rogue's gallery of photographs showing all the defendants in various settings. I stared at the myriad photos of myself and mused ruefully that they had been well and truly on me for several months. If mine had been a not-guilty plea to any criminal activity whatsoever, on the face of the evidence against me it would have been a non-starter. Fortunately, my case was that I had been trying to import moody cigars.

The prosecutor made much of the fact that at 572 kilos the cocaine bust had been the largest in British criminal history. He followed on to say that those involved were at the pinnacle of crime in the UK.

First up for cross-examination was Gavin. As he stood in the witness box, he bit at his bottom lip to try to stop it quivering with fear. I could only reflect that he had reason to be fearful. The 157-page statement he had made had given the prosecutor plenty of ammunition, especially as Gavin had contradicted himself several times.

Not unexpectedly, the prosecutor made mincemeat of him. Time after time, he caught him out on inaccuracies and distortions. Gavin tried to make the point that at the time he made the statement he was intent on denying any wrongdoing, including the illegal importation of cigars. The prosecutor made the more telling point that if he had been lying then, how could the court believe what he was saying now?

The only positive point in the whole examination came when Gavin talked of his coke addiction and the various periods spent in clinics such as the Priory. I could see several of the jurors leaning forward, paying close attention. This evidence made Gavin seem quite sad and vulnerable. It hardly squared with the image that the prosecutor was trying to portray, that of a top-level international drugs smuggler.

When it was my turn to enter the witness box, the pace of the trial noticeably quickened, and a buzz ran around the court. It took a couple of raps from the judge's gavel to quieten things down.

The prosecutor took full advantage of the situation, drawing himself up dramatically and opening his case against me with an 'Ah, Mr Pritchard', then letting the expectation hang in the air. But I was ready for him. I had been living this moment for many months and had clearly thought out my strategy. I wasn't at all concerned by the evidence, especially that provided by the surveillance. After all, I was admitting that I was a cigar smuggler. The surveillance just confirmed me going about my business to that end.

The prosecutor made much of the fact that I had been in possession of six mobile phones and that there were transcripts of my making calls on all of them. 'Why would any normal person have six mobile phones?' he asked. 'In my experience, the only people who have that number of phones are drug dealers or other criminals.'

I spent the next ten minutes explaining my background in promoting musical events. I took the court through the line-up for the Reggae Sunsplash concert and other occasions when top performers had been brought in from overseas. I explained that among the things these visiting stars wanted as part of their package was an English mobile phone. Sometimes, multiple artists arrived, and that was why I had six phones. After they left the country again and gave me the phones back, there would often be credit left on them. I would then use the phones to take advantage of this unused credit. It was a perfectly reasonable explanation, one that stopped the prosecutor in his tracks. He stared at me for a while, his look saying that he thought me a clever so-and-so, but there were no more questions about mobile phones.

Over and over again, he laboured the point that I had, in fact, been expecting cocaine to arrive and that it was only now, after I had been arrested, that I had changed my story to one in which I had been expecting cigars. He asked me what evidence I could show the court to prove this. This was obviously a very strong point for his case, one to which I had no good answer. So, this was the stage at which I decided to introduce the next part of my defence.

Specifically looking at the jury, I told the court about Bob, the former SAS man and his brother who worked on the Customs FAST team at Tilbury. I explained about the first shipment of cigars and how the FAST team had been complicit in first putting a hold order on the container so that it came directly to them and then passing it through the X-ray machine while it was turned off. I said that this was exactly what had happened with the latest shipment.

Firmly in my stride now, I asked why no one from this FAST team had been arrested and stated that if the court was looking for an explanation of how cocaine had been switched for cigars, then the natural suspects would be Bob and the crooked FAST team.

The prosecutor was having none of it. He accused me of making it all up and asked me who would believe that Her Majesty's Customs could ever be involved in such a thing? It was precisely the question that I had been waiting for. With a flourish, I pulled out the sheaf of papers that I had concealed inside my jacket and waved them at the court. Singling out individual sheets, I held them out to the jury and deliberately pointed at the 'SECRET', 'RESTRICTED', 'CLASSIFIED' and 'SENSITIVE' headings.

'These,' I announced, 'are classified documents from Customs House, the headquarters of Her Majesty's Customs and Excise. I'm not willing to say how they came to be in my possession, but they contain evidence about this case and give details of major corruption in Customs and Excise.' I began to read from the documents.

There was instantaneous pandemonium. Everybody seemed to be shouting at once. The judge was shouting at the jury that this was inadmissible evidence and that they should ignore it. The prosecutor was shouting 'Inadmissible, inadmissible', and both my and Gavin's QCs were on their feet calling for the judge's attention. Over the hubbub came the stentorian tone of the clerk of the court calling 'order, order'.

In the confusion, I ran from the witness box towards the bench and threw the sheaf of documents in front of the judge. This so startled him that he bolted and ran into his chambers. As I was led from the court, I could see that one of the jurors was in tears.

It took a full 20 minutes for the court to reconvene. I immediately stood up and apologised, making a small bow to the jury, and said that I regretted if I had upset anyone but that the papers were important evidence in support of my case and that I had felt it was essential that the court be aware of them.

For a split second, Judge Byers looked confused, bemused even. Recovering quickly, he addressed the jury: 'Members of the jury, it is my instruction to you that you ignore the documents that Mr Pritchard attempted to introduce into evidence. They are not relevant to this case.'

The prosecutor continued with his interrogation, but I kept referring to the documents at every opportunity. 'If the court would just look at those documents, they would see that I am telling the truth,' I argued. In the circumstances, the prosecutor probably realised that continued questioning was proving to be counterproductive, and he finished his case against me early. I returned to the dock.

There were a few minutes' silence as the prosecutor prepared himself to call the next defendant, and the foreman of the jury took the opportunity to ask the judge if the jury could see a copy of the documents I had presented. Judge Byers looked suitably grim as he addressed the jury once again: 'No, you may not see a copy of the documents. Further, if you even make reference to them or speak to each other about them, I will hold you in contempt of court. Are you quite clear about that?'

The prosecutor continued his case, and Dean was the next defendant up. After the pyrotechnics of my interrogation, though, it was all very much an anticlimax. It was a similar situation when the turn of the three fruit porters came.

As the members of the jury were sent out to consider their verdicts, I could only conclude that it had all gone quite well for me. Our QCs might not have made many important points in our defence, but then they were quite in the dark about the existence of the classified documents. The real damage had been done when I had brought them to the attention of the jury. At least there would be some doubt in their minds now. For the present, it was just a question of waiting.

At first, it seemed that we wouldn't have to wait long. Within forty-five minutes, the jury returned, and they acquitted the three fruit porters. Then they retired for further deliberation. It took another two days for them to return again. This time they acquitted Dean but admitted that they couldn't come to a verdict regarding the charges against me or Gavin. The judge remanded us both in custody for a retrial. It was a week before Christmas.

Festive occasions are always grim in prison, but the holiday period was especially trying for me and Amber. We tried to look on the positive side. The four acquittals proved that the prosecution's case wasn't as strong as they had thought it was. But was that any consolation to me? Perhaps it could be brought to the next jury's attention.

Early in February 2006, there was a strange development in what was turning out to be a thoroughly unusual trial. Amber told me that a letter had been delivered by hand to our door. It was from a company called Dare Films. It stated that they were the production company that made the *MacIntyre's Underworld* programmes and that they were very interested in making a programme about my case.

I was aware of the programmes and had, in fact, seen a couple of them in the past. They usually involved Donal MacIntyre going undercover and interviewing criminals talking about criminal activity. For a moment, I questioned whether I wanted to be involved with him. However, I was keen to publicise the case and plead my innocence, especially my suspicions about Customs involvement. Perhaps I could use them as a hedge against my being found guilty and launching an appeal. I told Amber to go ahead and cooperate.

It wasn't possible to film or otherwise interview me, but we could have an informal, unrecorded chat during a visit to the prison. Donal MacIntyre had been banned from visiting Wandsworth due to an earlier programme, so he sent up Michael Simkin, Dare Films' series producer, and Tom Cordell, their associate producer. Both men were consummate professionals. They explained that the programme couldn't be aired until after my next trial had finished, but they assured me that they would be conscientious and deal with the subject matter sympathetically. I told them about the case, going into great detail about the corrupt FAST team. They seemed especially interested in the latter and went away saying that it would all make for a great documentary.

For the next few months, they followed Amber about, filming her on virtually a daily basis in various locations. They also filmed her talking to me on my illegal mobile phone. I doubt there was a connection, but a few days afterwards PO Watkins burst into my cell late at night and caught me using it, for which I spent a few days in the punishment block. The Bat provided me with a new phone the same day that I returned to the wing.

The second trial started the third week in February, and Gavin and I were again brought to Blackfriars. This time there were just two of us in the dock. I mused on the old saying about there being strength in numbers. I certainly felt more exposed sitting there with just Gavin for company.

There were other obvious differences from the first trial. Now, I was being searched every time I came into court, so there would be no reading from classified documents this time. The other noticeable difference was that the court was packed with journalists. Quite clearly, the news about the classified documents had got out and was now a major story.

Someone had scanned the documents and placed them on a website. Gavin and I were told about it, and we memorised the address by heart, as I had expected that I would be prevented from bringing the classified documents into court.

As before, Gavin was first into the witness box. He gave his evidence in chief, then refused to answer any questions, saying that the experience of doing so in the first trial had seriously upset him. Addressing the jury, he launched into an explanation of the classified documents and their relevance to our case. Before the judge could stop him, he called out the address of the website, saying that this was where evidence of all the corrupt Customs officers could be found.

Once again, there was uproar in the court. Judge Byers solemnly warned the jury that if they so much as looked at the website it would be a serious case of contempt of court. He then asked Gavin if I had put him up to his recent outburst. My QC was instantly on his feet, strenuously objecting. The judge withdrew his comment and asked the jury to ignore it, but he repeated his warning about their not looking at the website.

I had guessed that with a breach of the Official Secrets Act imminent, the authorities would try to close down the website. It originated in Turkey but was routed through a US server and took over a thousand hits in the first hour it was posted. The help of the FBI was enlisted, and they closed the site down, but it was up on another server within the hour. This happened four times. As fast as they closed down one server, the documents were put up on another one.

Phase two of the operation then kicked in. A very popular east London pirate radio station began broadcasting the website address every hour and even read excerpts from it live on air. Apart from informing the general public, I knew that the journalists must be getting all of this. It would add to the importance of their story. If the Crown were going to railroad me into jail, then I was giving them advance notice that I wouldn't be taking it lying down.

Throughout the two trials, Amber had sat quietly in court, taking no part whatsoever in the proceedings. However, seeing me sitting in the dock, seemingly being gagged by the judge, it all suddenly became too much for her. She jumped to her feet. Clearly distraught, she began railing at the judge that a cover-up was taking place and that it was a disgrace that I wasn't being given a fair trial. She was removed from the court and banned from entering again, but it had an effect on the jury. Some of the jurors could be seen talking to each other.

With both the prosecution and defence cases now completed, the judge began his summing up, but a very strange thing happened. As part of Amber's prayers and white-magic rituals, she had asked that the judge should have problems in speaking. Up until that point, Judge Byers' performance had been faultlessly efficient. All of a sudden, he lost his place in the summing up and stopped to refer to his notes. For a while, he looked almost bemused. Collecting himself, he proceeded to the end, but it hadn't been a convincing performance. I could only hope that if the trial judge seemed unsure about the case, as demonstrated by his summing up, then the jury would have some serious doubts, too. They were sent out to consider their verdicts.

The following day, the case was all over the media. The treatment was very circumspect, though, as the case was now *sub judice* with the jury out. It was a case of once again patiently waiting for the jury to return. As Gavin and I paced our cell in the bowels of the courthouse, I could picture Amber doing likewise outside the court. The pressure was now intolerable. So very much depended on the outcome. I found myself wishing that it was all over.

Neither of the two trials had run smoothly, and the bizarre had regularly managed to intrude. This second trial wasn't to be without one last irregularity. We were all called back into the courtroom. Looking singularly ill at ease, Judge Byers announced that there had been a violent altercation in the jury room and that he was sending everyone home for the weekend to cool off. As I pondered the implications for me and Gavin, the prosecutor stood up, apologised and said that due to other commitments he wouldn't be able to attend on Monday or take any further part in the proceedings. I fervently hoped that the prosecution case was now a sinking ship and that the prosecutor was one of the departing rodents.

With a rising sense of anticipation, we returned to court on the Monday morning. An initial favourable sign was that all the jury were now sitting in the jury box wearing their coats and jackets. To my mind, it certainly undermined the permanence of their continued participation.

Judge Byers asked the foreman if the jury had reached a verdict. The foreman replied that they had not, nor were they likely to do so. With two hung juries in succession, the judge's actions were now a formality. He ordered me and Gavin to stand, found us not guilty and told us that we were free to go. The nightmare was over.

Twelve

Life Begins at Forty

AFTER BEING found not guilty, Gavin and I were taken back downstairs to the holding cells for our paperwork to be processed before we could be released. Once again, I was in the cell where I had spent so many hours waiting. About 20 minutes passed and a screw came for Gavin. Now I was left on my own. I lay down on the hard bench to gather my thoughts. For a man who had just escaped a life sentence, I wasn't in too happy a frame of mind. The problem was that over the past 17 months I had conditioned myself to switch off my feelings. This was basic self-preservation, just in case it all went wrong for me.

The day I had been arrested, I told myself that my life was maybe over. I would have to become a robot, a machine, just functioning from day to day rather than living and feeling. I had lived in this emotionless state for so long that I now found it very difficult to switch my feelings back on again. I felt empty and without enthusiasm, a strange state of mind for a man who had just had such incredible good fortune.

The door opened again, and it was my turn to leave. I walked through the secure area to find my legal team waiting for me. Lisa, the solicitor's clerk, had spent hundreds of hours inspiring me and keeping my morale up. My old friend and solicitor David Turner had made countless legal visits. My barrister Graham Wilson had risked his reputation by attacking the

Customs and harassing them with probing questions. Last, Michael Broadman, my lead barrister, had stood up to the judge and appealed directly to the jury. They were my legal representatives, but they had become like trusted friends. It was an emotional moment as we shook hands and embraced.

As I entered the foyer to the court, my father and sister were waiting for me. It had all been too much for my mother, and she had remained at home throughout the trial. My father had aged considerably, and my sister had lost weight and looked strained. It brought home to me the fact that it hadn't only been an ordeal for me.

They remained inside to avoid the waiting press as I exited onto the court steps. Amber was waiting, and she rushed into my arms. We clung together for what seemed like an age. We were surrounded by our friends: Ned, Georgie, Rico and Kenny, all of whom had helped me get through the trials and tribulations that I had faced. It did occur to me that in the short walk from the cells I was meeting all the people who I was closest to and who had supported me in my darkest hour.

The press were waiting at the foot of the steps. There were three camera crews and several photographers, but I wasn't in the mood for interviews. With just the MacIntyre TV crew in tow, Amber, my friends and I headed off up the street.

There was a massive church a short distance from the court. Quite spontaneously, Amber pulled at my arm, and we went inside. Taking their cue to give us some privacy, my friends left, and a short time afterwards so did the MacIntyre crew. Side by side, Amber and I knelt in the pews. Heads bowed, we thanked God for delivering me from a fate worse than death. Both of us had prayed so hard for this moment. In some ways, it was a vindication of our spirituality.

There was little triumphant about my return to Barretts Grove. I walked about my childhood home almost greeting the rooms like long-lost friends. It was still just getting through to me that I was actually free again. I realised that it would take a long time for me to clear my mind of the memories of Wandsworth.

A complete break was now a priority. I booked first-class tickets to Mexico for an all-inclusive holiday. Not that there was any distance between us, but I was aware that Amber and I would have to get to know each other again. It was plain that she still carried a lot of pain. Together, in idyllic surroundings, we could heal each other.

On our return, the MacIntyre team were waiting for us with the finished programme. Very unusually, they were going to allow us to have a preview before it went out on TV. As Amber, Georgie and myself settled into our seats, *Cocaine and Coconuts* began to play on the screen.

For all of us, it was an emotional roller-coaster ride as we relived the 17-month ordeal. Focusing as it did on Amber, it brought home to me just how much she had suffered. By the end of the programme, the girls were both in tears, and I was too overcome to speak.

The holiday had given me plenty of time to think about the future. One thing that was very clear to me was that my days as an urban smuggler were over. No doubt Customs were smarting from the recent stinging defeat. They wouldn't forget me in a hurry, and if I so much as thought about another smuggling coup, they would be all over me from the start. In fact, there had been a nasty moment as I passed through Mexican Customs. As my passport was processed, the expression on the guy's face had changed. Then, as I'd collected our baggage, I'd seen two other guys closely watching me. This would be the shape of things to come.

The MacIntyre documentary had given me an idea. From my vantage point of the lead actor in the role of my life it did occur to me that I had lived an interesting life. I began to think about making it the subject of a film. I broached the idea with Amber.

She reacted angrily, saying that she wanted to put it all behind us and that if I went through with it she would leave me, as she just couldn't stand any more. I had no choice but to put the idea on the back burner. The only thing left was for me to go back into the music business.

I rented my old offices in Corsham Street and, together with Carl and Sheldon who had worked with me previously, started to promote musical events. We brought the American rapper T-Pain over for a gig in Luton, but we actually lost money. We hired the Brixton Academy and brought over the American R & B singer Joe. The concert was a sell-out, but we just broke even.

Promoting concerts was a time-consuming business. Sometimes it took months to promote just one gig. Some of them showed a small profit, others showed a loss. It was becoming apparent to me that I wouldn't grow rich in the music business the way I was going. By that point, Amber had fallen pregnant, which further brought home to me that as I approached my 40th birthday I should really be laying the foundation for a successful future.

One evening, Amber and I were sitting at home watching TV. A programme came on about racial demographics in Britain. The main point made was that mixed-raced people would become the country's largest ethnic minority within the next 25 years. As Amber and I were both of mixed race, we watched with interest. We realised that our child's offspring would be part of this majority. It made it all very personal.

On Tuesday, 22 May 2007, not long after my 40th birthday, Amber gave birth to our son Hayden. Both were pivotal moments in my life. I feel that I am on the brink of a new beginning. The urban smuggler has come of age. Perhaps life really does begin at 40.

But as they do say, the road to hell is paved with good intentions. I never deliberately lie to people who are close to me; it's more like I seem to get overtaken by events. For me, everything is an opportunity, and I'm always looking for the next deal. Finally, for someone who is permanently fixated on being a success, imminent penury tends to focus the mind wonderfully. It was for this reason that I decided to embark on my next project.

I was aware that I had promised I wouldn't. I fully realised that I was taking a terrible chance. I knew I would have to mix with people more ruthless than the Mafia and more deceitful than a back-street crack dealer. In short, I was entering a world populated by the dregs of society. Yes, you guessed it. I was entering the film industry!

To be continued . . .

Epilogue

I AM now coming to the end of my story, and I wanted to finish on a bright and positive note. However, there has recently been a major change in me, and I have had a crisis of conscience. Perhaps it was the onset of my 40th birthday, more likely the birth of my son, but there is something that I must say.

I did indeed manage to bribe a Customs FAST team to pass our container through unchecked and unopened. Should you require documentary proof of this, there is the secret document showing the photocopy of the handwritten note putting a hold on our container by the FAST team. Then there is the document certifying that the container had been passed through the X-ray machine. Finally, there is the indisputable fact that a second Customs team searched the container that had supposedly already been checked and found half a ton of cocaine!

There is certainly evidence to suggest that a corrupt FAST team was involved in my case, so why were they and Bob not put on trial with me? Could it be that Customs chose to close ranks and hide the corruption? Of course, I can't be sure that Bob was acting for a corrupt element of Customs, but if he was not, why was I charged with cocaine smuggling in the first place? If Bob and the FAST team had been legitimate, I would have just been done for cigar smuggling. As it was, they wanted me to take the fall when their importation of cocaine was discovered by Martin and his team.

Today, we live in a world of international terrorism, so this isn't just about cocaine or counterfeit cigars any more. It is a matter of national security. All the international law enforcement agencies are well aware of the close links between international drug smugglers and international terrorists. So, if my friendly FAST team is still in business, perhaps the next consignment they pass through unchecked and unopened could be half a ton of high explosives, or half a ton of dirty-bomb material, or a fully equipped al-Qaeda team!

It is for this reason that I have come forward and done my part. My conscience is clear. I would never have been able to forgive myself if I had remained silent and at some future date there was a major terrorist incident involving material being brought into the country via the corrupt FAST team. There needs to be a government inquiry. And if that did now come about, the urban smuggler really would end on a high note.

Acknowledgements

THROUGHOUT MY life, I have met many amazing people, without whose help and support this book would not have been possible. Some of these people deserve special acknowledgement.

First, thanks to my parents, sisters and nephew, who have never given up on me, no matter what I may or may not have done. Without your support, I would be lost. I love you all dearly.

Thanks to Amber for always believing in me and sharing my dreams, but most of all for bringing my beautiful son Hayden into the world. And thanks to Marilyn, my mother-in-law, for all the support you have given us both.

Thanks to Georgina Hill and her beautiful children, Georgia and Ciara; I will never forget the visits you made to see me in Wandsworth Prison through rain, snow and flood. You gave me strength at my weakest moment. And thanks to Jamielyn for your endless enthusiasm and dedication.

Thanks to my legal team: David Turner, Graham Wilson, Michael Broadman and, by no means least, Lisa. You won me back my freedom. God bless you all.

Thanks to Michael, Donal, Kirsty, Lizzy, Tom, Sally and everyone at Dare Films and those people who worked on or took part in the television documentary Cocaine and Coconuts. Thank you for allowing my story to be told to the world.

Mishka and Erica, thank you for having two wonderful sons

for me. Thanks to Eddie Reardon and family for being true friends to me over the years. Thanks to Ona, little Edd and my goddaughter Hollie.

Norman Parker, who performed a miracle and turned this book around in less than four weeks, thanks for chronicling my life, with a little artistic licence, and showing me Valencia.

Thanks to my extended family, James and Laura, Carl and Jo, and to my cousin Mathew and his wife Melanie for all your hard work.

Thanks to Wayne, whose Class of 88 was a source for this work. As the lyrics in the song say: 'Don't ever give up. Just keep on reaching!'

Mash, my friend for as long as I can remember, I feel blessed to have you in my life. Thanks to Maxine and Dawn for getting me back the old offices that I've been in and out of more times than a fiddler's elbow. And to the whistleblower at HM Customs and Excise, whoever you are – thanks for letting your conscience be your guide.

Looking back over this memoir, I realise much of my life has been documented. However, there is still so much more to tell and only one way to do it. Therefore, look out for my new book Behind Every Empire Lies a Crime.

If you're in a dark tunnel and have travelled too far to turn back, the only way out is to head for the light.